THE
50 Greatest Jewish Movies

THE
50 Greatest

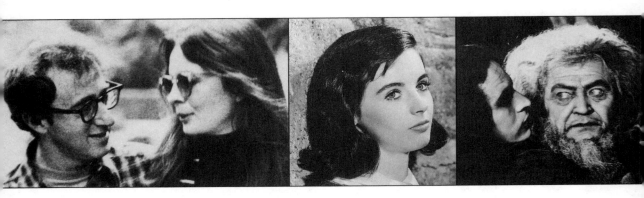

A BIRCH LANE PRESS BOOK

Jewish Movies

A CRITIC'S RANKING OF THE VERY BEST

Kathryn Bernheimer

PUBLISHED BY CAROL PUBLISHING GROUP

To my mother, Louise Bernheimer,
who gave me not only life but the good sense to enjoy it

A Birch Lane Press Book
Published by Carol Publishing Group
Birch Lane Press is a registered trademark of Carol Communications, Inc.

Editorial, sales and distribution, rights and permissions inquiries should be
addressed to Carol Publishing Group, 120 Enterprise Avenue, Secaucus, N.J. 07094

In Canada: Canadian Manda Group, One Atlantic Avenue, Suite 105, Toronto,
Ontario M6K 3E7

Carol Publishing books may be purchased in bulk at special discounts for sales
promotion, fundraising, or educational purposes. Special editions can be created
to specifications. For details, contact Special Sales Department, 120 Enterprise
Avenue, Secaucus, N.J. 07094.

Manufactured in the United States of America
10 9 8 7 6 5 4 3 2 1

Library of Congress Cataloging-in-Publication Data

Bernheimer, Kathryn.
    The 50 greatest Jewish movies : a critic's ranking of the very best / by
    Kathryn Bernheimer.
        p.   cm.
    "A Birch Lane Press book."
    Includes index.
    ISBN 1–55972–457–9
    1. Jews in motion pictures. 2. Motion pictures—United States—Catalogs.
    3. Motion pictures—United States—Reviews. I. Title.
PN1995.9.J46B47   1998
791.43'65203924—dc21   97–47098
                                                                CIP

Contents

Acknowledgments   vii
Introduction   ix

1. *The Chosen*   3
2. *Fiddler on the Roof*   7
3. *Schindler's List*   12
4. *Shoah*   17
5. *The Jazz Singer*   21
6. *Annie Hall*   28
7. *Funny Girl*   33
8. *Gentleman's Agreement*   37
9. *Exodus*   42
10. *Ben-Hur/The Ten Commandments*   46
11. *Crossing Delancey*   52
12. *The Golem*   55
13. *Au Revoir, Les Enfants*   59
14. *Almonds and Raisins: A History of the Yiddish Cinema*   62
15. *Enemies, a Love Story*   65
16. *The Great Dictator*   68
17. *The Apprenticeship of Duddy Kravitz*   72
18. *Blazing Saddles*   76
19. *Chariots of Fire*   80
20. *Body and Soul*   83
21. *The Pawnbroker*   87
22. *Goodbye Columbus*   90

23. *Bugsy*   94

24. *Cabaret*   98

25. *Crimes and Misdemeanors*   102

26. *The Last Angry Man*   105

27. *The Outside Chance of Maximilian Glick*   108

28. *The Revolt of Job*   111

29. *Homicide*   114

30. *Madame Rosa*   118

31. *Driving Miss Daisy*   121

32. *Reversal of Fortune*   125

33. *Europa Europa*   129

34. *The Big Fix*   132

35. *Broadway Danny Rose*   135

36. *Julia*   139

37. *Marathon Man*   143

38. *A Majority of One*   146

39. *Oliver!*   149

40. *Down and Out in Beverly Hills*   152

41. *Holocaust*   156

42. *Dirty Dancing*   160

43. *The Front*   163

44. *Biloxi Blues*   167

45. *The Diary of Anne Frank*   170

46. *Shine*   174

47. *Daniel*   178

48. *Yentl*   183

49. *The Young Lions*   187

50. *Marjorie Morningstar*   190

Afterword   195

Bibliography   199

Index   205

Acknowledgments

My longstanding desire to write a book about Jewish film would have remained just that had it not been for my husband, Dan Weingast, whose support on so many levels allowed the desire to become a reality. I owe my entire family a debt of gratitude for their faith in me as I left the security of a career in newspaper journalism to strike out in the unknown territory of book publishing. In that endeavor, I also drew inspiration from the example of my father, Paul Bernheimer, from whom I learned the value of making a living doing something you love.

The encouragement of Rabbi Joseph Telushkin also helped me to make the leap of faith this book represents. In undertaking this adventure, I have also drawn encouragement from the many audiences whose enthusiastic reaction to my frequent speaking engagements convinced me that the subject of Jewish film was of great interest.

I am also greatly indebted to the work of Patricia Erens and Lester D. Friedman, whose extensive writing about American Jewish film offered an invaluable grounding in the subject. I have also been inspired by Robert Sklar's high quality coverage of Jewish film in the *Forward*. The work of several other distinguished Jewish film critics has also paved my way, J. Hoberman chief among them.

Working with my agent, Lynn Seligman, has been a great pleasure. I applaud her commitment, integrity, and good humor. I would also like to thank my editor, Jim Ellison, for his enthusiasm and persistence of vision. Publisher Steven Schragis was also instrumental in reshaping my original work into its current form.

This book would not have been possible without the help of Scott Woodland, owner of the Video Station in Boulder, which stocks not only all of the fifty titles listed here but more than 200 other Jewish films I viewed before making my final selections. For help in acquiring photographs, I would like to thank *Boulder Daily Camera* librarian and friend Charlotte Smokler; my Boulder Public Library film programming pal Chuck Lomis; Cinema Collectors; Jerry Ohlinger's; former International Film Series director Steve Wingate; and Sharon Revo at the National Center for Jewish Film.

A blessing on their heads, *Mazel Tov, Mazel Tov.*

Introduction

What is a Jewish movie? For the purposes of this book, I define it as a film that examines an aspect of the Jewish experience and features at least one clearly defined Jewish central character. Ah, but what makes a Jewish film great? That's a more difficult question, one that it has been my pleasure to agonize over. As you read these essays, you will find that in many cases "great" is synonymous with "best." In others, it means "most important." Only rarely does it mean "my favorite." (Okay, so the number one-ranked *The Chosen* is my all-time personal favorite.) Sometimes it means "most popular." In a few rare cases, it means all of these things. What it doesn't mean, however, is "perfect."

Although I greatly admire all of the films included in this book, not one is completely above reproach, and I have tried to point out the virtues and failings of each one. Some are too simplistic and superficial—most movies are. Some can be accused of glorifying their subjects, while others can be deemed too harshly critical. Some are artful but not terribly substantive, and vice versa. Still, every one of my choices has something remarkable and valuable to offer the viewer. The movies that made it onto my list have been chosen either for their artistic excellence, for the fascinating information they impart, or for their vital contribution to the evolution of the Jewish image on the screen. Many are socially significant, marking drastic shifts in our cultural perceptions. I deliberately picked a few films because they are representative of an important trend in the portrayal of Jews or because they are the best example of a popular Jewish film genre.

Some are modest films that delight because they far surpass our expectations; others we can't help but respect even though they fail to live up to their lofty ambitions. Many are provocative, some are comforting, a few are disturbing, and a handful are truly inspiring.

In making my selections, I tried to include representative works by important Jewish directors, including Sidney Lumet, Martin Ritt, Robert Rossen,

Woody Allen, Paul Mazursky, Mel Brooks, Joan Micklin Silver, David Mamet, Bob Fosse, John Schlesinger, Barbra Streisand, Fred Zinneman, Mervyn LeRoy, Barry Levinson, William Wyler, Otto Preminger, Steven Spielberg, and Mike Nichols. There are a fair number of essential offerings directed by non-Jews as well, including Norman Jewison's *Fiddler on the Roof,* Hugh Hudson's *Chariots of Fire,* and Edward Dmytryk's *The Young Lions.*

Similarly, I made sure to include films featuring great Jewish stars such as Paul Muni, John Garfield, Richard Dreyfuss, Dustin Hoffman, Ron Silver, and Barbra Streisand. But because of a long-standing and widespread practice of casting non-Jews in Jewish roles, a large number of films on my list feature non-Jewish actors, including Rod Steiger's bravura turns in both *The Chosen* and *The Pawnbroker.*

Personal taste, of course, played an inestimable role in my choices. There's a saying that "Jews are like everyone else—only more so," which is especially true of the wide diversity of opinion that exists in any population. (Hence another saying: "Two Jews, three opinions.") The last thing I expect, therefore, is complete agreement with my selections. After all, the farting-around-the-campfire scene in *Blazing Saddles* causes some people to laugh uproariously while others find this sort of thing juvenile and vulgar. You will find my taste reflected in the relatively large representation of films by Woody Allen and Paul Mazursky, and the smaller sampling of Neil Simon and Mel Brooks films. Sometimes my subjective taste was tempered with my objective reasoning. For example, while Barbra Streisand's films generally leave me cold, I applaud her intentions and recognize her work's enormous positive impact. I could not in good conscience overlook so profound a Jewish film as *Yentl* even though I find it flawed.

Differences of taste and opinion become more extreme as the gravity of the subject increases. All films that deal with the Holocaust are invariably criticized by authorities on the subject and thus are by definition controversial. There are those who argue that art is intrinsically inadequate to express the ineffable horror of the Holocaust and that any film that attempts to capture the catastrophic tragedy is bound to fail. Others argue that films play an important role in forcing viewers to confront this umimaginable history and that there are lessons to be learned from the Holocaust that films can teach us. Elie Wiesel summed up the dilemma best when he wrote, "How can we talk about it? How can we not talk about it?"

Each film in this book is one piece of a puzzle that, when assembled, only begins to depict the wide range of Jewish experience. My chosen films cover such topics as the Holocaust, post-Holocaust trauma, assimilation, the immigrant experience, growing up Jewish, anti-Semitism, Israel, and Jewish ethics, values, and identity. There is a whole category of films I have dubbed

"Jews to the Rescue"—represented by *Reversal of Fortune*—in which a Jewish character physically or spiritually saves a gentile and serves as the story's moral exemplar.

Among the genres included in this collection are foreign films, biographies, comedies, romances, documentaries, biblical films, made-for-TV movies, and Yiddish films. There are films from every decade, from the 1920 silent classic *The Golem,* to the 1996 Australian sensation *Shine.*

Although movies about men are much more common than movies about women, I have made sure to include a healthy representation of films focusing on the female experience, including *Funny Girl, Dirty Dancing, Julia, Madame Rosa, Crossing Delancey, Yentl, A Majority of One,* and *Marjorie Morningstar.*

I freely admit tearing my hair out as I pared down a list of more than 250 films with Jewish characters and subjects available on video. To compensate for the omissions inevitable in a list of fifty drawn from five times that number, many reviews contain references to other films on similiar subjects or other works by the film artists concerned. The review of *Bugsy,* for example, will lead you to a half-dozen notable films about Jewish gangsters and to a famously de-Semitized Jewish film by director Barry Levinson. *A Majority of One* makes reference to more than a dozen movies projecting positive and negative images of the Jewish mother.

I hope some of my choices will surprise you. As a film critic, I like to think of myself as a *schadchen*—a matchmaker. My job is fixing viewers up with compatible movies. The challenge is getting the right audience together with the right films. I hope this book will introduce you to some new cinematic soul mates and reestablish your connection to old flames.

THE
50 Greatest Jewish Movies

1

The Chosen

20th Century–Fox (1981)
CAST: Rod Steiger, Robby Benson, Barry Miller, Maximilian Schell
DIRECTED BY: Jeremy Paul Kagan
108 minutes [PG]

In Chaim Potok's remarkable first novel, two teenage boys build a narrow bridge of understanding between their seemingly incompatible Jewish traditions and meet somewhere in the middle of the improbable structure. In undertaking this difficult crossing, Reuven and Danny fulfill a Talmudic teaching that a person should do two things in life: acquire a teacher and choose a friend.

Unlike the large number of films in which gentiles come to understand or accept Jewish characters and by extension the Jewish people, *The Chosen* is exclusively concerned with Jews, who, in the course of the drama, reach a deeper appreciation of what it means to be Jewish. One of the most profoundly Jewish films ever made, *The Chosen* explores the still-pressing issue of tension between different branches of Judaism. *The Chosen* is virtually unique in dealing with divisions within the Jewish world rather than with the conflict between Jews and the hostile host culture. *The Quarrel,* which presents the post-Holocaust schism between secular and religious Judaism, is the only other film based on this kind of heated theological debate. While most Jewish films depict Jewish individuals coping with the

A RIGHTEOUS MAN   Rod Steiger plays a charismatic hasidic rabbi who must balance his devotion to his son with his devotion to his faith in *The Chosen,* a stirring film that deals with all the major issues of twentieth-century Jewish life.

demands imposed by the dominant culture, in *The Chosen,* this outside world barely exists. The story is set entirely in a Jewish milieu that features a larger, more secular and assimilated Jewish world, and a tight inner circle of Hasidism.

This insightful and terrifically enjoyable adaptation also encompasses most of the major themes of twentieth-century Jewish life, including assimilation, the founding of Israel, the Holocaust, family bonds, the struggle to create a balance between personal autonomy and cultural connection, the importance of tradition in a changing world, and the transmission of positive Jewish values from one generation to the next. *The Chosen* is also one of the only Jewish films to deal meaningfully with religious and spiritual matters, yet another factor in its number-one ranking.

Potok, the son of an ordained rabbi, grew up in the environment he depicts in his 1967 bestseller. Director Jeremy Paul Kagan, also the son of a rabbi, clearly respects and understands the issues that drive Potok's tale of two boys rapidly approaching adulthood in Brooklyn in the 1940s. Kagan (*The Big Fix*) won first prize at the 1981 Montreal Film Festival for *The Chosen,* which was adapted by screenwriter Edwin Gordon. Kagan and Gordon did an impressive job condensing Potok's complex and informative novel, which includes lengthy sections of Torah study, the history of Hasidism, and much discussion of the founding of Israel. Reuven narrates the story in voice-over with words taken directly from the book, which helps the audience absorb the tale's teachings.

One of the most successful screen adaptations of a novel by a major twentieth-century Jewish author, *The Chosen* is a poignant account of Reuven and Danny's close friendship. In contrast to the large number of movies about the relationship between children and their Jewish mothers, usually negative, *The Chosen* favorably focuses on the boys' relationships with their fathers.

What makes *The Chosen* so deeply Jewish is not just the level of detail with which Orthodox religious customs are portrayed, or the depth with which it delves into the Judaic belief system, or even its insight into the values of the Chosen People. The entire film is built on a distinctly Jewish way of thinking. *The Chosen* honors all sides of the argument it presents, giving equal credence to apparently antithetical points of view, without becoming a disingenuous copout.

Potok has chosen two sets of highly sympathetic characters to argue the debate he stages. On one side we have Reuven Malter (Barry Miller), a gifted, thoughtful, and principled student, and his father (Maximilian Schell), a prominent intellectual Talmudic scholar and Zionist activist. In the other corner we find the even more brilliant student Danny Saunders (Robby Benson) and his equally impressive father, a charismatic hasidic rabbi (Rod Steiger). Although Reuven goes to a yeshiva and is in all respects a devout Jew, he is still light-years removed from his friend Danny, who has been chosen to follow in his revered father's footsteps, an obligation he regards with growing reluctance. Danny lives a carefully circumscribed life that strictly adheres to the letter of Jewish law as it is interpreted by this particular hasidic sect.

The only other major Hollywood movie to depict this fascinating Jewish subculture is Sidney Lumet's *A Stranger Among Us* (1992), featuring a badly miscast Melanie Griffith as a cop who goes undercover in a hasidic community to investigate a homicide. *Vitness* is the title jokingly bestowed on this inferior Jewish variation of *Witness*.

Danny, who has never been to the movies or a museum and has never heard of Benny Goodman, visits the library in secret, devouring books on psychology and reading forbidden authors of secular literature. One of the movie's rich ironies is that for all his greater knowledge of the world, Reuven learns more from Danny than he teaches his innocent but wise friend. Danny, for all his brilliance, represents the heart—shown here to be the essence of Hasidism—while the more secular, intellectual Reuven represents the head. The movie's message is that these two elements must be brought into balance, that knowledge is nothing without the capacity to experience joy and sorrow. As in Potok's book, vision and blindness are key metaphors in the film, with an emphasis on the ability to see through both eyes. (Reuven's injured eye brings the boys together.) Danny and Reuven view the world differently, but together they help each other see more clearly.

Danny eventually follows his passion out into the wider world. His father is able to give his blessings to his son, who is straying from the fold, because he is satisfied that Danny has grown into a *tzaddik* (a righteous man) and will proudly go forth to do good as a compassionate and committed Jew. Reuven, who has often railed against what Reb Saunders represents—a stubborn rejection of modern realities, a narrow view of life, and a zealous, tyrannical fanaticism—decides to become a rabbi. He has, after all, recognized the importance of this *tzaddik's* spiritual leadership.

Most of the story concerns the budding friendship between the boys, who share a love of learning. Their intellectual curiosity extends to each other, and they examine each other almost as specimens of a strange species. They learn the wisdom of Reb Saunders's warning: "It is not an easy thing to be a friend." The central crisis in the boys' friendship occurs after the war, when Reuven's father begins actively campaigning for the formation of a Jewish homeland. Danny's father vehemently believes that only the Messiah can lead the Jews to their homeland. This theological debate is so intense that Danny is forbidden to associate with the "Jewish *goyim*" who want to form a secular Jewish state. Danny must make an agonizing choice between allegiance to his father and his friendship with Reuven.

After the United Nations votes in favor of Israel, Reb Saunders lifts the ban on the boys' association, reasoning that the Jewish homeland is no longer an issue but a fact. The pain caused by their separation is not easily healed, but the friendship is rebonded by Reb Saunders, who includes Reuven in a heartfelt conversation with his son.

Rod Steiger, who gave a critically acclaimed performance as a Jewish Holocaust survivor in *The Pawnbroker,* was originally offered the role of Reuven's father but successfully campaigned for the smaller but showier part of the demanding, commanding, yet searingly soulful Reb Saunders. Steiger, who was raised Lutheran and grew up in a Jewish neighborhood in Newark, attended services to study the famed Rabbi Menachem Schneerson in preparation for his masterful performance—although he admits he picked up the accent eavesdropping in a butcher shop. It takes a great actor to play a great man, and the Academy Award–winning actor is able to project pride and humility, power and compassion, creating a cohesive character from apparent contradictions. In a slow dance performed at a hasidic wedding, Steiger seems to convey the pain and pleasure of the entire Jewish people. His final scene with Reuven and Danny is heartwrenching.

The movie's real revelation is Robby Benson, who has never given such a convincing performance before or after *The Chosen.* Born Robert Segal, Benson combines physical awkwardness with an alert mind and an open spirit, investing Danny with an endearing eagerness. Barry Miller is equally appealing as the sensitive and sensible Reuven.

Maximilian Schell, a Viennese-born actor who fled from Hitler by immigrating first to Switzerland and then to America, is warm and wise as a single father who intuitively understands his son and raises him according to his political and social principles. Schell has appeared in an extraordinarily large number of noteworthy Jewish-themed films, including *The Man in the Glass Booth, Julia, Judgment at Nuremberg, The Odessa File, The Assisi Underground, The Young Lions,* and *Miss Rose White.*

The Chosen ends with an affecting story from the Talmud, which is not Potok's ending, about a son who has gone astray. His father sends for him to come home, but the wayward soul sends back a message that he cannot. His father replies, "Return as far as you can, and I will meet you the rest of the way."

As Reb Saunders concludes, with delicious understatement, upon finding a way to both let his son go and keep him forever in his heart, "So. It is good."

2

Fiddler on the Roof

United Artists (1971)
CAST: Topol, Norma Crane, Molly Picon, Michael Glaser, Louis Zarich,
Neva Small, Michele Marsh, Rosalind Harris
DIRECTED BY: Norman Jewison
184 minutes [G]

Tevye is much more than a Jew: He is the Jewish people. Like the Jews, Tevye has a direct, personal relationship with the Creator. He *kibitzes* and *kvetches*. He offers suggestions and sometimes even curses his Maker, but it is clear the relationship is founded on mutual trust. God will not let Tevye down, and Tevye will not let God down, no matter how much *tsuris* is heaped upon him. Like the Jews, Tevye is severely tested by forces that threaten to destroy him—forces from without and forces from within his own family. Like the Jews, he suffers. And like the Jews, he survives.

The questions Tevye faces strike at the core of Jewish existence: How much can Jewish life be bent before it breaks? How can tradition be preserved in a changing world? Which are stronger, the bonds forged by family love or those that connect us to the Master of the Universe? What is more important, tolerance or autonomy? Where does accommodation end and appeasement begin? Where does the refusal to compromise lead?

In the course of *Fiddler on the Roof,* Tevye grapples with these burning issues. For a simple milkman, he does pretty well. He uses his head and follows his heart.

Tevye is arguably the single most positive, sympathetic, and best-known Jewish character in film history. This larger-than-life, archetypal character who stands for all Jews is one reason *Fiddler on the Roof* remains a high-water mark in the depiction of the Jewish experience on the screen. The sentimental and deeply affecting drama glorifies and dignifies Jewish resilience.

Much of the film's success rests squarely on the broad, capable shoulders of its Israeli star, Chaim Topol, who dropped his first name when the movie was released. Topol, then only thirty-six, had the requisite physicality for the part as well as an equally robust inner spirit. His performance conveys

A RICH MAN   The living embodiment of Jewish resilience and the most beloved figure in Jewish film history, Tevye was robustly portrayed by Topol (right) in *Fiddler on the Roof,* one of the top films of 1971.

endurance, adaptability, vitality, and earthly pleasure—characteristics directly related to Jewish survival.

Writing in the *New Yorker* magazine, Pauline Kael hailed *Fiddler on the Roof* as the most powerful movie musical ever made, calling it a folk opera steeped in Jewish-Americana. Indeed, the musical's considerable power—Brecht by way of Broadway—derives in part from the stark contrast between the characters' richness of spirit and the poverty and persecution they endure. *Fiddler on the Roof* offered a rare glimpse of life in the shtetl—a world wiped out in the Holocaust—which had been the frequent subject of Yiddish writers but had remained unknown to the American public, including many American Jews. The beauty and pain of Jewish life in nineteenth-century Eastern Europe was hardly promising material for a musical. Musicals with expressly Jewish stories were and continue to be a rarity, despite the fact that musical comedy as we know it would not exist without the Jews. (In the first half of the twentieth century, the only major gentile composer was Cole Porter.) There are only three explictly Jewish movie musicals: *Funny Girl, Yentl,* and *Fiddler on the Roof,* although *Oliver!* features a central Jewish character, Fagin, and *Hello, Dolly!* showcases an implicitly Jewish character.

The unlikely genesis of *Fiddler on the Roof* dates back to 1960, when composer Jerry Bock, lyricist Sheldon Harnick, and scenarist Joseph Stein were looking for a new project and considered adapting *Wandering Star,* a novel by Sholem Aleichem, the pen name of rabbi and Yiddish writer Solomon Rabinowitz, who escaped the Russian pogroms of 1915 and immigrated to America. Stein, concerned that the story was too sprawling for the stage, suggested the writer's Tevye stories, which had inspired the 1939 Yiddish film *Tevye,* starring and directed by Maurice Schwartz. The collaborators constructed a single story from four of the Tevye tales and built the passive, simple milkman into a character of greater vibrancy. Stein crafted a diaspora story about the breakdown of community and the dissolution of a culture. The first act ends with a pogrom and the second with the great exodus of Russian Jews to the New World. Not surprisingly, the show was turned down by many producers who felt a musical about poor Russian Jews was not likely to attract a wide audience.

Eventually, Harold Prince was asked to produce *Tevye and his Daughters,* as *Fiddler on the Roof* was then titled, but declined because he felt no affinity for its overt ethnicity. He strongly recommended famed Jewish stage director and choreographer Jerome Robbins, who had scored a triumph with *West Side Story,* but because Robbins was working on *Funny Girl* the project was temporarily shelved. Robbins, when he finally agreed to direct and choreograph, had reservations. He felt that to show the dissolution of a way of life, the musical had to more clearly create a vivid slice of shtetl life. At his insistence, the opening number, "Tradition," was written, establishing exactly what it was that was being threatened with extinction. He also insisted on absolute authenticity. To his credit, Robbins recognized that universality comes not from generalizing a story but from making it as specific and hence as real as possible.

Prince finally agreed to produce with Robbins as director, and the show opened in New York in 1964 with Zero Mostel cast as Tevye. (Tom Bosley, Danny Kaye, Alan King, Howard da Silva, and Danny Thomas were considered.) The reviews were favorable, and Mostel was singled out for special praise. *Fiddler on the Roof* won the Critics' Circle Award for best musical of 1964 and nine Tony Awards. Mostel left the show after his nine-month contract was up, but the show's success continued unabated with Herschel Bernardi, Harry Goz, Jerry Jarrett, Jan Peerce, Paul Lipson, and, later, Theodore Bikel playing Tevye. It ran 3,242 performances on Broadway, becoming the longest-running musical in history when it closed in July of 1971.

Since its opening in 1964, *Fiddler on the Roof* has grossed more than $20 million at the box office worldwide and has been performed in sixteen languages in thirty-two countries. *Fiddler on the Roof* was sold to United Artists for $2 million, and non-Jewish director Norman Jewison was hired. (Jewison, his name notwithstanding, is a Methodist.) Ironically, two years after he created this flattering portrait of Jewish life, Jewison directed *Jesus Christ Superstar*, which drew criticism from Jewish quarters for its inflammatory depiction of Jews as Christ-killers. Jewison, however, did an altogether admirable job producing and directing the lavish, three-hour screen adaptation of *Fiddler on the Roof*, which was made more risky by the absence of Hollywood stars. The enduring movie, filmed on location in Yugoslavia and London for $9 million and released in 1971, was a moderate financial success and earned generally favorable reviews. Nominated for an Academy Award for best picture, *Fiddler on the Roof* won Oscars for cinematography and John Williams's newly orchestrated score.

The movie opens with Isaac Stern's violin playing on the sound track as Tevye explains the symbolism of the title, which was inspired by a painting by Marc Chagall. "Every one of us is a fiddler trying to scratch out a simple little tune without breaking our necks. How do we keep our balance? I can tell you in one word: tradition!" Soon after this cherished way of life is established, we are introduced to the forced eviction of Jews the czar has begun implementing. Although the town's constable (Louis Zarich) has no personal dislike for the Jews and considers the affable Tevye a friend, he is under pressure from above to demonstrate support for the czar's policy.

Tevye, a strapping man who frequently fills in for his lame horse, lives with his stern wife, Golde (Norma Crane), and their five daughters at the edge of town. A volatile but well-liked man, Tevye is a proud patriarch who enjoys his role as the titular head of the household. In some ways, however, Golde rules the roost. The town's matchmaker Yente (played by Molly Picon, who has been called the Yiddish Helen Hayes) arranges a marriage between Tevye's daughter Tzeitel (Rosalind Harris) and the wealthy butcher Lazar Wolfe (Paul Mann). Tevye, who seals the match with Lazar, discovers Tzeitel has already made a pledge to marry Motel the tailor (Leonard Frey). "Unthinkable!" he storms when they ask permission to marry, but he relents when he sees how much his daughter loves Motel. In an amusing dream scene, he tricks his wife Golde into approving the match.

Tevye invites Perchick (Michael Glaser), a student from Kiev, to teach his daughters Torah, apparently subscribing to the young man's radical idea that "girls are people too" and hence deserve a religious education. His daughter Hodel (Michele Marsh) falls in love with Perchick, and when they decide to wed, they strike another blow against patriarchy by asking not for Tevye's permission but only for his blessing. Again Tevye rails against this insulting affront to time-honored tradition and his ordained role in the family. And again, in the end, he gives his blessing—and his unrequested permission.

Tevye recognizes that the world is changing and that young people have the right to choose their destinies. He also knows he will lose his daughters if he stands in the way of their happiness. But when his daughter Chava (Neva Small) secretly falls in love with a Russian (Raymond Lovelock) and announces their desire to wed, Tevye cannot accept this alliance with the enemy. Pushed too far, he disavows Chava and her new husband. In the last moments of the movie, however, there is a suggestion that he is softening his stance. For Tevye, as for many Jews, family comes first. One of the great strengths of the movie is that, no matter how we feel about intermarriage, we understand Tevye's objection and we feel his pain at this mortal blow to Jewish identity. In dramatic terms, it's a great conflict. In sociological terms, it poses a provocative question about assimilation and survival.

Fiddler on the Roof is not a radical film, but it is a profoundly affectionate and proudly Jewish one. It argues passionately on the side of modernity and reason, but is deeply respectful of Jewish ritual, religion, community, and customs. It exalts Jewish values in a way few films have. If that's not love, what is?

3

Schindler's List

Universal Pictures (1993)
CAST: Liam Neeson, Ben Kingsley, Ralph Fiennes
DIRECTED BY: Steven Spielberg
195 minutes [R]

A corrupt industrialist, shameless womanizer, gambler, swindler, schemer, hedonist, war profiteer, bon vivant, black marketeer, and member of the Nazi party, Oskar Schindler bribed and blackmailed his way to a position of power and wealth in the Third Reich—then threw it all away to save 1,100 Jews.

Scoundrels make the best heroes, in part because their noble actions are so unexpected—and inexplicable. Although Steven Spielberg's stunning account of a righteous gentile has been censured for profiling a "good" Nazi, *Schindler's List* is hands down the most widely seen, universally acclaimed, and ambitious feature film on the Holocaust ever made, as well as one of the most artistically accomplished.

The true story of this unlikely savior (played by Liam Neeson) leads to a damning question: If such an impudent rogue was so revolted by the Final Solution that he risked his life and spent every penny of his vast fortune to save "his" Jews, what does that say about the "good people" who did nothing? It also leads to another unanswerable question: What made this German Catholic switch from the lucrative business of manufacturing munitions to the dangerous business of saving souls?

Perhaps Oskar Schindler was simply a weak man with no stomach for suffering. Maybe he enjoyed life so much he couldn't bear to see anyone deprived of the pleasure of living. As a fastidious man of impeccable taste, perhaps his refined sensibilities were offended by the stench of death. An arrogant egotist, he might have resented being told what he could and couldn't do. A crass opportunist, he may have seized the opportunity to distinguish himself with a more lasting accomplishment than the mere acquisition of money. A hopeless romantic in love with the grand gesture, perhaps he couldn't resist this daring escapade. Some survivors have even suggested he was trying to save his own skin after the war's inevitable conclusion. Then again, he may have been motivated by common decency or a latent sense of justice.

MONUMENTAL ACHIEVEMENT   Ben Kingsley, left, plays the silent partner and moral mentor of Oskar Schindler (Liam Neeson), a Nazi who unaccountably engages in the risky business of saving Jews in *Schindler's List,* which won seven Oscars and helped spur a resurgence of interest in the Holocaust.

One of the great triumphs of *Schindler's List* is that it does not attempt to unlock the secret of the man's soul. Indeed, the mystery adds to the richness of this tale of horror, honor, and hope. It is enough that he did what he did. Although the movie's hero is ambiguous, his actions are not. "This is an absolute good," says Schindler's Jewish accountant, confidant, and silent partner Itzhak Stern (Ben Kingsley) of the list of "Schindler Jews." The list contains the names of the slave labor workers in Schindler's enamelware factory in Krakow who, late in the war, are about to be shipped off to Auschwitz and certain death. Unable to abide their fate, Schindler concocts a mad plan to move his factory to his hometown in Czechoslovakia and bribes officials to allow him to take his "skilled workers" with him. Once there, Schindler becomes even more daring by sabotaging his own product, producing faulty ammunition and artillery that will not help the German war effort. When the war ends, the Jewish workers give Schindler a gold ring engraved with words from the Talmud: "Whoever saves a single life saves the world entire."

Schindler later lost the ring, probably in a card game. That hardly matters, however. What matters is this: There are only 4,000 Jews in Poland today. There are currently 6,000 descendents of Schindler's Jews living around the world.

If Schindler's legacy was far greater than he could have predicted, so too has Spielberg's movie had an enormous, positive impact on Jewish life. Not since the 1978 TV miniseries *Holocaust,* which was seen by 120 million people, has such wide public attention been brought to the Jewish suffering during the *Shoah.* Made by the most successful director in motion picture history (Spielberg made four of the ten top-grossing films of all time), *Schindler's List* sent a loud, proudly Jewish message to the masses.

If Schindler was an unlikely hero, so too was Steven Spielberg an improbable candidate to do justice to the Holocaust. Although he had grown up with an oral history of the Holocaust—he learned to count using the numbers tattooed on a relative's arm—and experienced anti-Semitism firsthand while in high school, Spielberg had never made an issue of ethnicity in any of his previous pictures. He had even used Nazis as cardboard villains in *Raiders of the Lost Ark.* But just as Schindler managed to pull off his audacious gamble, Spielberg astonished the world by rising to the challenge. Who had thought the summer blockbuster king capable of creating such a devastating drama? And yet, who better to bring the Holocaust—usually consigned to the commercial ghetto of the art film and the documentary—into the mainstream? Spielberg alone had the clout to make a big-budget, black-and-white, three-hour-plus Holocaust drama with no A-list stars, filmed on location in Eastern Europe. It was a film Spielberg has said he wanted to make for himself, his first film "to tell the truth." Even with his unprecedented track record, he had to invest some of his own money in the $23 million film that defied Hollywood wisdom.

Spielberg acquired the rights to Thomas Keneally's book when it was published in 1982 but determined he was not yet artistically or emotionally mature enough to do justice to the monumentally challenging project, which eventually involved 126 speaking parts, 30,000 extras, 210 crew members, and 148 sets on thirty-five locations. He told Leopold Page, the Schindler Jew who had convinced Keneally to write the book, that it would take ten years before he, and the screenplay, would be ready. Page—the Poldek Pfefferberg of the film—was afraid he wouldn't live long enough to see his story told. Exactly ten years later, the cameras rolled in Poland, with Page serving as the film's consultant.

By that time, Spielberg was forty-five and had rediscovered Judaism. In retrospect, Spielberg was wise to wait for the maturity the project demanded. *Schindler's List* won seven Oscars, including best picture, best director, and best adapted screenplay. Although the critics were initially skeptical about the creator of sentimental childlike fantasies tackling the Holocaust, *Schindler's List* was hailed as a masterpiece. Some Holocaust experts objected to the film's focus on the rare exception of a gentile rescuer, which violates the essential truth for the Jews, who were abandoned by an indifferent world. By focusing on survival rather than death, Spielberg further stands accused of defying the dominant reality of the Holocaust. Other critics complained that he presented the Jews as weak, passive, feminine, and largely nondescript creatures in need of protection from a powerful and virile Christian and that he neglected to portray any acts of active resistance. Additionally, some experts objected to fleeting images that perpetuate negative Jewish stereotypes of cowardice, selfishness, and greed. It must be remembered, however, that films on the Holocaust are subjected to a higher standard than films on almost any other subject and that the film's detractors are in the minority.

Schindler's List, which became a huge international success, reawakened large-scale interest in the Holocaust and opened new dialogue on anti-Semitism. It led to the creation of Steven Spielberg's Survivors of the *Shoah: A Visual History Foundation,* which is dedicated to preserving the stories of the Holocaust. Profits from the film have gone to various Jewish charities and organizations through Spielberg's Righteous Persons foundation. The film and script have been used in classrooms across the country. The film has been hotly debated in numerous forums, including a book of essays arguing the movie's merits and detriments.

Spielberg, known for his stunning use of visual imagery, brought his customary masterful technical skill to the film. The choice of filming in black and white was an especially brilliant stroke, downplaying any tendency toward the lurid and emphasizing the story's starkness. Light and shadow are used to suggest good and evil—Schindler's face is frequently seen in half shadow, for example, especially early in the film. Spielberg entrusted Polish-born cinematographer Janusz Kaminski with achieving the film's harshly realistic look. Spielberg found another valuable ally in screenwriter Steve Zaillian (*Awakenings, The Return of Bobby Fischer*), who brings sensitivity and restraint to the script. The dialogue is succinct yet powerful.

Spielberg's casting of up-and-coming stars proved equally judicious. Neeson cuts a towering figure. Commanding and imposing, his Schindler is an actor who gives great performances, whether it be extemporaneous bluffing, carefully rehearsed bullying, shrewd manipulation, or instinctive charm. Neeson plays Schindler as a sensualist who finds himself "seduced by the power of goodness," to quote *New York Post* critic Michael Medved.

Stern, who serves as Schindler's conscience and the film's moral center, is also the audience's guide. His reactions to Schindler inform our response to the man. Stern gazes at Schindler with a mixture of abject terror and utter incredulity early in the film. Later, confusion gives way to guarded trust and, finally, admiration and gratitude. Kingsley conveys this shift with his facial expressions and the delivery of short lines. Kingsley, who won an Oscar for *Ghandi,* was born to an Indian father and English mother of Russian Jewish descent. This was his third portrayal of a real-life Jew. He previously played the famed death camp survivor turned tireless Nazi hunter in *The Murderers*

Among Us: The Simon Wiesenthal Story and also played the legendary Jewish mastermind of organized crime, Meyer Lansky, in *Bugsy*.

The film makes it clear that Stern was not only the brains behind Schindler's business but also his mentor in the rescue operation. It is Stern who first seizes on Schindler's business offer as a way of saving Jews. He scurries around the Krakow ghetto, selecting a history teacher here, a rabbi there, falsifying papers that endow them with more "vital" skills. Later, when he continues to manage the business from inside the labor camp, he rewards individuals who distinguish themselves by having them sent over to the factory. In one of the film's brilliant (and thoroughly Jewish) scenes, camp commandant Amon Goeth (Ralph Fiennes) has assembled prisoners suspected of hiding a chicken. He asks a man to name the one who's responsible, and when he doesn't reply, shoots him in the head. Trembling and sobbing, a boy of about twelve steps forward. No, he didn't do it, he says, but he knows who did. Triumphant, Goeth asks him to give the man up. Obligingly, the boy points a finger at the man already lying dead on the ground. The quick-witted boy becomes a Schindler Jew, thanks to Stern, whose stoic example of heroism Schindler slowly begins to follow.

If dire circumstances have brought out the best in Schindler, they have brought out the worst in camp commandant Amon Goeth, who, were he not put in a position of absolute power, might have remained a harmless crackpot and petty crook. As it is, his tendency toward cruelty is encouraged, unleashing the sadist in him. The mesmerizing Ralph Fiennes, then largely unknown, plays Goeth as a creepy, unpredictable psychopath, a bloated beast staggered by his own capacity for evil.

Schindler's List is packed with wrenching scenes, such as the liquidation of the Krakow ghetto, yet rarely goes overboard. The scene in which the women, mistakenly routed to Auschwitz, enter the "showers" expecting to be gassed has been accused of crossing the imaginary line between showing too much and too little. The scene also has been criticized for presenting the opposite of the dominant reality for prisoners, who expected showers but were, in fact, gassed.

Spielberg gets sloppily sentimental only once, in Schindler's farewell scene in which he breaks down and blames himself for not saving more Jews. This overwrought scene, which was far shorter in the novel, provides a mantra that also applies to Spielberg and his movie: "I could have done more." While not above reproach, all in all, *Schindler's List* confronts the specter it raises squarely and honestly. Underneath the riveting drama lies a deep respect for the human spirit. "Life is still life," a Jew says, underscoring the sanctity of existence.

Spielberg, who won his first directing Oscar for *Schindler's List,* surprised the world with his story of a man who surprised himself.

4

Shoah

New Yorker Films (1985)
DIRECTED BY: Claude Lanzmann
503 minutes [Not rated]

The criticism leveled at most cinematic examinations of the Holocaust is that they do not give enough focus to the Jewish genocide that is its very essence. *Shoah,* widely regarded as the definitive documentary on the Holocaust, is about nothing else. Its sole subject is the systematic murder of more than 6 million Jews, which it examines in excruciating detail in the course of an agonizing, mesmerizing eight and a half hours.

Narrowing its focus on the Nazi agenda of Jewish annihilation even further, *Shoah* restricts itself to the death camps in Poland whose exclusive function was mass execution. Although some Jews were assigned to gruesome work detail in these camps, because they were witnesses to the atrocities, great care was taken to make sure that they, too, were eventually killed. At Chelmno, for example, 400,000 Jews were gassed. There were only two survivors, one who lived despite having been shot in the head. Amazingly, director Claude Lanzmann found both men and convinced them to tell their stories. Lanzmann focuses so exclusively on the central fact of the Final Solution—death—that his film has ironically been criticized for distorting historical reality by failing to include any information on the Jews who were saved or sheltered.

Lanzmann's answer to this charge—an odd allegation given the disproportionately large number of Holocaust movies that focus on survival—is that *Shoah* does not attempt to document the entire history of the Holocaust. Rather, he says, it is an attempt to incarnate the truth about Hitler's attempt to eradicate the Jews. Lanzmann does not even consider *Shoah* an historical document but a work of art that seeks to transmit to the viewer the horror of the Holocaust. For that reason, Lanzmann does not include any archival footage that would remind the viewer that the events took place in the past, suggesting it is a closed chapter of ancient history. *Shoah* is set entirely in the present, as eyewitnesses relive their memories in front of the camera, often at the very spot where they took place.

There are three major categories of participants. The primary testimonials in this oral history come from the Jewish victims, culled from a tiny fraction of Jews who survived the death camps. (Lanzmann does not deal with the concentration camps whose primary purpose was not the immediate killing of their victims.) Although these heartbreaking interviews form the eloquent core of the film, Lanzmann has also been criticized for insisting that the survivors put themselves through the trauma of reliving the past for our benefit. Although Lanzmann may place the world's need to know above the survivors' desire to forget, he ultimately respects the courage it takes to remember what the Third Reich tried to obliterate and what many today would like to consign to the oblivion of the past.

The second group interviewed consists of bystanders, mostly Polish citizens, who lived close to the camps and saw what went on. Many of these farmers recall working the fields and listening to the screams of the Jews going to their death. These Polish peasants reveal themselves to have been largely indifferent to the suffering that took place on their doorsteps, and quite a few obviously took pleasure in it.

The final category consists of the actual perpetrators. A handful of SS officers who worked in the death camps agreed to be interviewed, and a few were tricked by Lanzmann, who recorded them with a hidden camera. Lanzmann cross-examines these guards and commandants closely, eliciting descriptions but not allowing them to offer any justifications or explanations. Throughout the film, Lanzmann concerns himself only with the "hows" of the Holocaust, never dealing with the "why." This approach allows for no excuses. The strongly implied suggestion is that there can be no reason for the Holocaust, no way to understand or explain it. There is no moralizing or generalizing in *Shoah,* which meticulously and logically establishes the magnitude of the atrocity by breaking it down into its smallest, most specific parts.

The devil is in the details, the saying goes, and Lanzmann indeed finds the evil heart of the Holocaust by painstakingly examining every detail of the decimation. With an obsessive interest in the tiniest minutiae of the Nazi mechanism, Lanzmann wants to know exactly what happened, when, where, and to whom. Lanzmann, who spent eleven years researching, shooting, and editing 350 hours of film, examines every element of the deportations, the transport of victims, the arrival at the camps, the technical methods of death, the dispersal of possessions, the disposal of the bodies. He keeps questioning until he gets the precise information we need to establish a sense of reality. Two survivors of Sobibor, for example, describe being part of a special detail forced to dig up 90,000 bodies of the Jews of Vilna to be burned. That unfathomable experience suddenly becomes more tangible when one of the men adds that they had to open the graves with their bare hands and that they were beaten if they

THE LAST STOP   A conductor who transported Jews to the death camp of Treblinka recalls his participation in the process of genocide for the camera in Claude Lanzmann's exhaustive nine-hour documentary *Shoah*.

wept, even when they uncovered the bodies of loved ones.

Shoah, its title taken from the Hebrew word for annihilation, is an epic drama of a people abandoned by the world to a fate unprecedented in history. The uniqueness of the Holocaust is underscored at every turn and driven home most forcefully in the forty-five-minute interview with former Polish courier Jan Karski, who was charged with the mission of letting the Allies know how close European Jewry was to extinction and what could still be done to save the remaining Jews of Europe. This section is the film's most political, bringing to light the apathy or outright complicity not just of the bystanders but of the world's governments. This subject is examined in depth in another excellent documentary, *Who Shall Live and Who Shall Die?*

Lanzmann employs long periods of silence in *Shoah,* and these wordless segments serve several purposes. They allow the viewer a little relief from the crushing cumulative effect of the film, offering us time to meditate, absorb, and reflect on all we have seen and heard. The silence also reminds us of death, of the eternal silence of the victims. Finally, it suggests the silence that surrounded the slaughter, the failure of the vast majority of witnesses to cry out. Lanzmann, a French Jew who fought in the Resistance and a journalist by profession, is tenacious in his interviewing techniques and exhaustive in his research, occasionally turning to the testimony of noted Holocaust scholar Raul Hilberg to fill in the gaps. Lanzmann emerges as a character in the story, a man of great moral rigor who openly admits not just the difficulty of his endeavor but the ultimate impossibility of fully evoking the unimaginable, inexpressible horror of the Holocaust.

Although *Shoah* is the best known Holocaust documentary, it is only one of several outstanding examinations of the event made by French filmmakers, beginning with Alain Resnais' *Night and Fog.* In 1955, Resnais was commissioned to create a testament to those who died in the Nazi death camps. He enlisted poet, novelist, and survivor Jean Cayrol to collaborate on the har-

rowing half-hour documentary, a swift and brutal film that records the genocide without ever using the word "Jew." When *Night and Fog* was shown in
France in 1956, a five-second shot showing a French gendarme working
inside a camp had to be cut because it suggested the complicity of Vichy
France in the Holocaust. In 1971, Marcel Ophuls rectified the offending omission with a four-hour-plus documentary that focused entirely on the collabo-
ration of Vichy France. *The Sorrow and the Pity,* which shattered the image of
a valiant French Resistance and replaced it with a portrait of cowardice, passivity, and virulent anti-Semitism, was a huge international success.

Ophuls followed his scathing expose of a nation's shameful history with
another long and complex documentary, *The Memory of Justice* (1976), based
on the Nuremberg trials. In 1987, Ophuls won the best documentary Oscar for
Hotel Terminus: The Life and Times of Klaus Barbie, a riveting examination of
the Third Reich that focuses on a single notorious Nazi. In that same year,
Pierre Sauvage released *Weapons of the Spirit,* which told the remarkable story
of a French town of 5,000 that sheltered 5,000 Jews during the Nazi Occupation. (The story of Chambon was also documented in two books by Philip
Hallie.) Sauvage, whose parents took refuge in the village just sixty miles
from the collaborationist capital of Vichy when he was a child, returned to
Chambon to uncover the mystery behind this "conspiracy of goodness."
Although Sauvage concentrates on the miracle of his survival, he also includes
much information on the French national disgrace recorded in *The Sorrow
and the Pity.*

Each of these Holocaust documentaries adds vital knowledge to a history
that no single film could ever convey. At best, films such as *Shoah* succeed in
making the Holocaust as concrete and palpable as possible for those who
were not there and in honoring its victims.

5

The Jazz Singer

Warner Bros. (1927)
CAST: Al Jolson, May McAvoy, Warner Oland, Eugenie Besserer
DIRECTED BY: Alan Crosland
89 minutes [Not rated]

As the first talking picture, *The Jazz Singer* ushered in a new age of the cinema, forever earning this landmark movie a prominent place in film history. At the same time, it immortalized the struggle between first and second generation Jews as they went about adapting to life in the *Goldena Medina,* the land of opportunity. Set on the Lower East Side of New York, which by 1920 had become the largest Jewish city in the world, the story details the clash between an ambitious Americanized singer and his devoutly religious father, depicting a conflict that frequently arose between refugee parents, desperately trying to preserve their culture and traditions, and their children, many of whom were eager to embrace the values and customs of their new home and escape the historic cycle of poverty and persecution. Fulfilling the immigrant dream often meant a loss of Jewish identity. It was a price many second generation Jews were willing to pay, even if it meant breaking their parents' hearts.

This clash between the past and the future is the subject of *The Jazz Singer,* which clearly makes a case for the future. In the movie, jazz itself is a metaphor for the modern spirit "crying out for expression." *The Jazz Singer* sheds a great deal of light on the prevailing attitudes of the times and reflects the experiences of the people who made the movie. The movie's out-with-the-old-in-with-the-new theme proved prophetic as *The Jazz Singer* brought about the demise of silent films. Ironically, if *The Jazz Singer* had not launched the sound era, this sentimental story of a cantor's son torn between duty and desire, tradition and self-fulfillment, might have been forgotten long ago.

Technologically revolutionary yet artistically conventional, *The Jazz Singer* was heralded as a modern marvel by the critics, who declared delight with the advent of sound but were far more reserved in their praise for the maudlin melodrama honored with the distinction of introducing the innovation. It was a surprising honor for a Jewish-themed film, especially in an era when the

Jewish moguls who ran virtually all of the major Hollywood studios avoided drawing attention to themselves as Jews.

A mostly silent film that employed the synchronized sound system called Vitaphone only in the musical numbers and in a few improvised scenes of dialogue, *The Jazz Singer* drew far more attention than any previous film. In so doing, it offered a vision of Jewish life to a wider audience than any of the previous Jewish-themed silent films had reached. *The Jazz Singer* was more than a movie. It was an event. Although it was but one of dozens of films of the 1920s to focus on the Jewish experience, it was one seen around the world. To make sure this story played in Peoria, audiences across the country were given a souvenir program that included a glossary of Yiddish terms such as *kibitzer, shiksa, cantor,* and *Kol Nidre*.

What did rural Americans, many catching their first glimpse of Jews, see in *The Jazz Singer?* On the positive side, they saw a strong bond between a mother and son. They saw a talented young man trying to do the right thing and make his own way in the world. They also saw a number of more negative stereotypes: The tyrannical, closed-minded father; the long-suffering, powerless mother; and the ambitious son trying to distance himself from his quaint, Old World family. Cantor Rabinowitz, played by a grim-faced Warner Oland (a Swedish actor who went on to greater ethnic fame as Charlie Chan), is depicted as the stereotypical stern patriarch. The movie clearly has little sympathy for this man, "his face turned toward the past," who "stubbornly held to the ancient traditions of his race."

When the cantor finds his young son Jakie singing ragtime in a saloon on the eve of Yom Kippur, he whips the unrepentant boy despite the protests of Jakie's adoring but helpless mother, played with much hand-wringing by non-Jewish actress Eugenie Besserer. Shamed and outraged, Jakie runs away, taking with him only a picture of his devoted mother, who accepts that her son does not want to become a cantor. "He has the (religious) songs in his head, but not his heart," she tells her husband, who comes from five generations of cantors and will accept no other future for his son.

Years later and 3,000 miles away, the grown-up and thoroughly acculturated Jakie (now played by Al Jolson) is a struggling singer who goes by the name Jack Robin. Jakie is seen eating eggs and bacon with great relish in a jazz club. Asked to perform for the crowd, Jakie obliges with a rousing rendition of "Dirty Hands, Dirty Face." When the song goes over well, Jakie tells the audience, "Wait a minute, wait a minute I tell ya. You ain't heard nothing yet!"—Jolson's trademark line—and he breaks into "Toot, Toot, Tootsie." This second song, incidentally, was not in the script, and director Alan Crosland feared Jolson had ruined the take by singing it. Only later, watching the dailies, was production supervisor Darryl Zanuck able to convince Crosland

MAMMY   Al Jolson, in blackface, shares a tender moment with his *Yiddische* mama (Eugene Besserer) in *The Jazz Singer,* the story of a modern Jew torn between duty and desire, tradition and secular success.

that this spontaneous snatch of dialogue and the additional number were positive additions.

At the club, Jakie meets Mary (May McAvoy), a successful dancer who takes him under her wing. The pretty showgirl tells him he sings with "a tear in his voice." It is an interesting comment, one that can be taken to mean that although she is a gentile, she recognizes the value of his heritage and musical training as a cantor. Looking even deeper, it suggests that the pain and suffering Jews bring to the arts has made them expressive and hence successful. A romance blossoms between Jakie and Mary, and together they return to New York to star in a new musical revue. Jakie's mother welcomes her son warmly, and they share a tender moment, again improvised, as Jakie serenades her on the piano with "Blue Skies," written for the film by Jewish composer Irving Berlin, and teases her with affectionate ad libbed banter.

Jakie also tries to make amends with his unforgiving father, arguing that it is as honorable to sing in a theater as in a synagogue. The closed-minded cantor angrily turns a deaf ear on his son's attempts to appease him. Just before the final dress rehearsal of his big show, Jakie learns that his father has fallen deathly ill—presumably about to die of a broken heart. His mother comes to his dressing room and begs him to come home and sing the Yom Kippur *Kol Nidre* service in his father's place. She lays on the guilt by telling him, "If you sing, maybe Papa will get well."

Jakie is thus thrown into terrible turmoil. He wants to honor his parents. "The songs of Israel tear his heart," the titles tell us. But this is his big break, after all, the chance to realize his dreams. Torn between his filial obligation and his personal desires, Jakie tells his mother the show must go on. When she hears him sing in the rehearsal, she concedes that his place is in the theater. "He belongs to the world now," she says with a mixture of pride and sorrow.

Although the movie has clearly stacked the deck in Jakie's favor, depicting his plight in the most sympathetic manner, Jakie does go home, forcing the show to be canceled. On his death bed, the cantor tells his son he loves him. Jakie then sings the *Kol Nidre* service, the eternal plea for forgiveness. Jakie does for love what he could not do for mere duty, and his father dies a happy man, listening to his son's voice through the open window. Despite the risk, Jakie has not ended his show business career after all, however, and the movie ends with Jakie singing "Mammy" in blackface in a new show, with his mother beaming proudly in the audience.

This final scene comes without explaining how Jakie has triumphed despite violating the first law of show business: "the show must go on." If the ending seems abitrarily tacked on, it is because it was. The happy conclusion came at the insistence of Crosland and Zanuck, and was not in the original script, which had ended with Jakie taking his father's place in the synagogue. The addition is significant in that it implies that it is possible to have it all, to honor tradition and still make it in the New World. But even without the change, *The Jazz Singer* would still have seemed quite modern in its view of assimilation as the natural direction for second generation Jews to take. The pro-assimilation view expressed in the film, in fact, went unchallenged in the cinema until the 1960s, when a number of films (such as *Funny Girl* and *Exodus*) began to convey the importance of maintaining cultural and religious identity. Only in the Yiddish cinema of the era was this notion challenged, most specifically in *The Cantor's Son* (1937), a direct rebuke of *The Jazz Singer* starring Moishe Oysher, on whose life it was based.

But in *The Jazz Singer* of 1927, Jakie's ambitions are unambivalently accepted. Jakie is not selfish, uncaring, or ruthless. Unlike Jolson, who was by all accounts an insufferably ambitious egotist who could be terribly cruel, the movie's Jakie is simply following his dreams. Despite its unquestioning view of assimilation, the movie still strikes a contemporary chord in its belief in the importance of independence and self-fulfillment. *The Jazz Singer* also takes a liberal religious view, arguing that it is God, after all, who is responsible for our talents and desires, and that it is actually a sin not to pursue them. "If God wanted him in His house, He would have kept him there," Jakie's mother reasons.

The emotional pull of the *The Jazz Singer* is its ultimately old-fashioned sense of filial love. On its simplist terms, this is a sweet story about a man who cannot turn his back on his family, no matter how unreasonable their demands. The answers provided in the movie seem simplistic and dated today, but were surely comforting to the assimilated Jewish audience of the day as well as to non-Jewish audiences who were being assured that the new generation of Jews just wanted to fit in. The central conflict in the movie, after all, depicts the dilemma faced by all immigrants torn between tradition and progress, between roots and success.

The four Warner brothers, whose studio produced *The Jazz Singer,* were products of just that immigrant experience. Technically first generation Jews, the brothers left Poland with their family as children. But like second generation Jews, they believed in the American dream. How could they not? They achieved wealth, power, and fame beyond their wildest expectations. Not surprisingly, therefore, *The Jazz Singer* depicts the victory of the younger generation and expresses dismay at the older generation's rigid way of thinking that manifested itself in a resistance to change, which was perceived as a stumbling block to success in the New World. The movie exhibits a sense of embarrassment with the Old World appearance, dress, and speech. This slight sense of shame reveals itself in the unsophisticated Jewish characters—most notably the *kibitzer* Yuddleson (Otto Lederer)—who are figures of fun or ridicule.

The Jazz Singer was originally written as a short story by New Yorker Samson Raphaelson, who has said he was inspired by seeing Jolson on the stage in *Robinson Crusoe, Jr.* in 1917 and recognizing the emotion of a cantor in the voice of the jazz singer. His story, *The Day of Atonement,* loosely follows the events of Jolson's life. Jolson, the son of a rabbi, was one of the first Jewish performers well known as a Jew and idolized by the American public. Born in Lithuania, Asa Yoelson changed his name, ran away from home to sing on the stage, and eventually married a gentile (Ruby Keeler). Jolson turned his back on Judaism, praying but once a year when he observed his mother's *Yahrzeit.* Throughout his life, Jolson remained devoted to the memory of his mother, who died when he was eight. His father vehemently disapproved of his show business career, even when his son became known as the "World's Greatest Entertainer."

Although inspired by stage star Jolson, Raphaelson adapted *The Day of Atonement* as a nonmusical play for George Jessel, who played the part of Jakie on Broadway in 1925. The popular play, which toured the country with

Jessel in the lead, was a box office hit. Still, it was an unlikely choice for Warner Bros.' highly visible and risky experiment with sound.

Harry Warner, who proudly remained a devout Jew and whose pet theme was racial tolerance, generally did not shy away from Jewish stories like so many of the other Jewish moguls who founded Hollywood. Still, Harry was worried that the story was too Jewish for the wider, less sophisticated audience of film. Concerned about the limited appeal of such a specifically Jewish story, Harry Warner was reluctant to gamble on *The Jazz Singer* for the studio's first experiment with sound, which many nearsighted naysayers predicted would fail miserably. It was Zanuck, always a shrewd predictor of popular taste, who was finally able to convince Harry and Jack Warner that the story of an understanding mother and her loving son, a timeless tale of divided loyalties, had universal appeal. Curiously, Zanuck was the only non-Jewish executive involved in bringing *The Jazz Singer* to the screen.

Jessel, who had made money for the studio playing a Jew who falls in love with a gentile in *Private Izzy Murphy,* had already been signed to reprise the role of Jakie on the screen. But when he learned that he would be required to sing in what was to become the first talkie, he asked for more money. Harry Warner refused to meet his price. The proudly Jewish Jessel was also reportedly upset by changes in the script, which no longer ended with Jakie returning to the synagogue for good, and demanded the original ending be restored. Eddie Cantor, another very popular Jewish performer, was approached but reportedly also had cold feet and did not want to be associated with the experiment should it fail.

Jolson, an exuberant singer and blackface specialist who had acted in a few silent shorts, had long been hoping to star in a musical film version of the play. He had shopped the idea around Hollywood for years. D.W. Griffith reportedly told him the story was "too racial," and other studios rejected it on the same grounds. Jolson now pursued the part and was quickly signed, even though he not only demanded even more money than Jessel but insisted he be paid in cash. *The Jazz Singer* made Jolson, then forty, an international star. Interestingly enough, he never played another Jewish character. *The Jolson Story* (1946) and *Jolson Sings Again* (1949), screen biographies starring Larry Parks as the great entertainer, were highly successful.

The Jazz Singer premiered on the night before Erev Yom Kippur, October 6, 1927. Audiences lined up four deep around the block of the Warner Theatre. *The Jazz Singer* was an instant success, raking in $3 million for Warner Bros. and solidifying the "Poverty Row" studio's reputation. By 1930, virtually every film that came out of Hollywood utilized sound. Sadly, Sam Warner, who had responded warmly to the stage show, died the day before the premiere. The remaining Warner brothers were therefore not in the audience at the historic opening night, when the audience stood and cheered a teary-eyed Jolson after the screening.

The Jazz Singer has been remade twice without much success. Director Michael Curtiz's insipid 1953 remake, starring Lebanese actor Danny Thomas, changed the characters into affluent, assimilated, sophisticated Jews. Refashioned as a vehicle for Jewish pop singer Neil Diamond in 1980, director Richard Fleischer's uninspired version also updated the story, but retained the immigrant aspect by making the cantor (Laurence Olivier) a Holocaust survivor.

To this day, *The Jazz Singer* remains best known as the film that revolutionized motion picture history. But for Jewish audiences, it is perhaps best remembered for giving expression to a crisis common in the Jewish immigrant family, a conflict that continues to exist in various forms today.

6

Annie Hall

United Artists (1977)
CAST: Woody Allen, Diane Keaton, Tony Roberts, Paul Simon
DIRECTED BY: Woody Allen
94 minutes [PG]

Annie Hall was not only Woody Allen's greatest commercial and critical success but also a radical change of direction for the writer, director, and actor, who broke through the narrow confines of comedy to create this heartfelt and humorous love story, the most beloved Jewish romantic comedy of all time as well as one of the screen's most thorough examinations of the inherent differences between Jews and gentiles. Although it does not have the emotional weight of *Shoah* or *Schindler's List,* it is ranked among the very best Jewish films because it so beautifully expresses the idea that seemingly inconsequential cultural differences can complicate romance.

Anhedonia was the original title of what was to become Woody Allen's breakthrough hit. Anhedonia is an obscure clinical term for the inability to enjoy oneself, a condition from which the overtly Jewish filmmaker suffers rather famously. Allen may provide immeasurable enjoyment and pleasure to his audience, but he can't seem to have any fun himself. Allen's dyspeptic disposition is by now legendary. But his *kvetching,* brooding, anxiety, melancholia, and reflexively critical nature were revealed in full for the first time in this confessional comedy about the doomed love affair between a cranky but endearing Jewish comic (Allen) and a flustered but lovable aspiring singer (Diane Keaton).

Annie Hall firmly established Allen's patented persona, a quintessentially Jewish character he has continued to play with only minor variations in virtually all of his films. Allen became a bona fide, if unlikely, movie star playing the film's chronically dissatisfied romantic hero, Alvy Singer. Keaton proved a wonderful foil for Allen, providing ethnic contrast and emotional grounding in this odd-couple romance. *Annie Hall* is essentially a simple, affecting, and affectionate love story, tinged with rueful nostalgia.

The structure of the story, coauthored by Allen's frequent collaborator Marshall Brickman, is playfully jumbled. The script is laced with dead-on humor, but here the jokes—including some old Jewish jokes—are used to illustrate philosophical points Allen is making in the story. Smart, sweet, and uncommonly insightful, *Annie Hall* earned Oscars for best picture, best director, best screenplay, and best actress—rare honors for a comedy. It established the already popular screen comedian as a serious film artist. It also marked an aesthetic shift for Allen, who has become the most prolific and consistently successful director of seriocomic films working today.

Allen's first relationship-oriented, character-driven film, *Annie Hall* is still considered by many to be his best work and is clearly a precursor to such subsequent complex classics as *Hannah and Her Sisters* and *Crimes and Misdemeanors*. With the release of *Annie Hall* in 1977, Allen was hailed as the greatest comic filmmaker since Charlie Chaplin. Indeed, both auteurs manage, at their best, to balance laughs with poignancy and to parody as well as celebrate human nature.

Allen's humor relies on contrasts, including the contradictions within his own personality. The relationship between neurotic *nebbish* Alvy and all-American *shiksa* Annie provided Allen with the perfect opportunity to mine his favorite themes, chief among them the difference between Jews and gentiles. Although religion is never an issue between Alvy and Annie, much of the tension in their romance can be attributed to ethnic conflicts. Some of these differences are superficial. At a New York deli, Annie orders pastrami on white bread with mayonnaise as an aghast Alvy apologetically rolls his eyes at the waiter. But many of the underlying issues run much deeper. Alvy is a typical Jewish, intellectual, neurotic New Yorker. Annie is, in her own way, just as neurotic and eccentric as Alvy, but in all other ways their culturally ingrained qualities are like oil and water. Alvy is caustic, cerebral, and cynical, given to exaggeration, often hostile, and usually contemptuous. Annie is open, naive, intuitive, unsophisticated, and unassertive, unsure of her own intellect, and eager for approval.

Alvy may not be an observant Jew, but he has a heightened awareness of his Jewish identity. He is obsessive and paranoid, suspecting anti-Semitism everywhere, convinced someone deliberately said "Did Jew" instead of "Did you." Then there's his celebrated anhedonia, albeit tempered by a touching sentimentality. "Life is filled with loneliness and misery and suffering and unhappiness," Alvy morosely observes in voice-over, "and it's all over much too quickly." Later he divides life into two categories: the truly horrible and the merely miserable. Alvy traces this morbid view of the world to his childhood, when he became depressed upon learning that the universe is expanding. "What's that your problem?" his mother (Joan Newman) wants to know, insisting that "Brooklyn is not expanding."

Annie has anxieties as well, but they don't inhibit her enjoyment of life and other people. As Alvy fondly looks back on their failed relationship, he remembers how much fun it was just to be with her. Although during the relationship Alvy egotistically takes the role of mentor, molding and cultivating and encouraging "dumb *shiksa*" Annie, in the end she has ironically blossomed and outgrown him. It could also be said that she has a more profound effect on him than he does on her, which is quite a gracious personal admission from Allen. The writer and director went on to cast Keaton as a neurotic woman he rejects for a less complicated one in *Manhattan* (1979), and in his underrated *Stardust Memories* (1980), Allen again chooses a kind, warm, and caring woman over a dark and dangerous one.

Twentieth century literature is filled with images of Jewish men lusting after gentile goddesses. While Allen is content to point out the differences that make Alvy and Annie incompatible, he went so far as to suggest that a Jewish man is better off with a Jewish mate in his *Oedipus Wrecks* segment of *New York Stories*.

CULTURE CLASH COMEDY   Woody Allen and Diane Keaton play lovers who can't quite bridge the cultural chasm in the beloved Academy Award–winning romantic comedy *Annie Hall.*

Allen's depiction of *shiksa* lust as disastrous and self-destructive was not new, however. The theme had, in fact, reached its fullest expression in *The Heartbreak Kid* (1972), a prickly comedy starring Charles Grodin as a newlywed who leaves his Jewish bride (Jeannie Berlin) to pursue the golden girl of his dreams (Cybill Shepherd). Written by Neil Simon (based on a story by Bruce Jay Friedman) and directed by Elaine May, *The Heartbreak Kid* ends with Grodin, having won his symbol of assimilationist success, isolated and alone in the W.A.S.P. heartland, which foreshadows the alienation Alvy experiences when he visits Annie's home.

The difference between Annie's background and Alvy's upbringing is brought into sharp relief in this short but memorable scene juxtaposing a dinner with Annie's family and a meal chez Singer. The split-screen scene illustrates the huge gulf between the two cultures, both of which are ridiculed. Allen's comic condemnation of both exaggerated extremes pits the stifling, superficial Halls, who quietly speak about swap meets as they pick at their skimpy meal and sip cocktails, against the vulgar, emotional Singers, who gobble a vast dinner as they argue loudly. Although Alvy may be embarrassed by his uncouth family, he shows even greater disdain for the cold, repressed, bigoted Hall clan. Annie's brother Duane, played by Christopher Walken, is actually psychotic, and mean-faced Grammy Hall is blithely described by Annie as "a real Jew-hater."

Alvy may be overly sensitive to suffering, analytical and self-absorbed, but he openly scorns those he considers unthinking and unfeeling. On the street, he stops a handsome, happy, and obviously W.A.S.P. couple to ask the secret of their relationship. "I'm shallow, empty, with no ideas and nothing interesting to say," the woman replies. "And I'm the same way," her strapping mate adds cheerfully. It's easy to be happy, Allen seems to be saying, if you're stupid and uncaring. As this funny bit reveals, Allen's absolute sense of superiority is coupled with a profound sense of alienation from mainstream American culture. This distinctly Jewish combination—the arrogant misfit—is a large part of Allen's appeal. He makes fun of himself but he is also proud to be different. He makes fun of others but also makes fun of himself making fun of others.

An intellectual who parodies pseudo-intellectuals, Allen audaciously allows Alvy to emerge as a lustful sensualist. Because of his unprepossessing appearance, Allen's casting of himself as a would-be love god is funny. But it is also touching, defying the movie myth that only perfect-looking people can be sexual beings. Allen may have been brought up to be a good Jewish boy, but he is not about to deny his sexual feelings. Despite his looks, Alvy is actually quite attractive to the opposite sex. Allen's alter ego is a man who is not afraid to express his feelings—in fact, he is unable to be anything less than ruthlessly honest. This rare degree of self-knowledge and vulnerability allows us to laugh at Alvy and genuinely care about him at the same time.

Although Allen is an intensely private person, he has revealed more about himself to the audience than almost any other contemporary film artist. Because he is so thoroughly Jewish, Allen can thus be credited with providing audiences with a detailed profile of a specific Jewish personality. Allen has been criticized for being self-demeaning, but his fans like him precisely because he is so hard on himself. On the whole, Allen engenders a huge amount of sympathy for his screen persona. He is especially unsparing in his depiction of Alvy's hypercritical nature, which, of course, allows the character to unleash a series of seriously funny zingers. But he also affords Alvy a certain amount of grace. Alvy may be *meshuga,* but he's a *mensch.* Alvy is wise enough to know when it's time to let go of Annie. "Relationships are like sharks. They have to move forward or die," he tells Annie. "What we have on our hands is a dead shark."

Annie Hall remains one of Allen's most intimate and ambitious films. But the idiosyncratic director has continued to move forward, gamely swimming into ever deeper waters.

7

Funny Girl

Columbia Pictures (1968)
Cast: **Barbra Streisand, Omar Sharif, Kay Medford,
Walter Pidgeon, Mae Questel**
Directed by: **William Wyler**
155 minutes [G]

Funny Girl is the biography of an ambitious, talented, and unapologetically Jewish performer who realizes her seemingly impossible dream of stardom. An ugly duckling in a world of show business swans, this brash and bold funny girl is determined to use her uniqueness to her advantage. Armed with chutzpah and blessed with a soaring, soulful voice, she proves that "a nose with deviation is no crime against the nation."

Ostensibly the story of famed singer and comedienne Fanny Brice, *Funny Girl* just so happens to be an equally accurate portrait of Barbra Streisand, the unconventional actress who made her screen debut in the hit musical. In fact, Streisand soon became an even more influential multimedia artist than Brice, the star of vaudeville, Broadway musicals, the Ziegfeld Follies, film, and radio who was known as the greatest female entertainer of the day. (Another Jewish performer, Al Jolson, held the male title.) Like Streisand, Brice enjoyed unexpected public acclaim for her broad physical comedy and became an icon of Jewish womanhood.

Brice and Streisand were both born in New York City, in 1891 and 1942 respectively, and displayed talent at an early age. Both aspired to careers on the stage and began auditioning at talent shows as teens. Brice established a following with her comic interpretations of songs, many of which she sang with the acquired Yiddish accent that became her trademark. Streisand, who gained attention with her clowning and singing, became famous for her theatrical renditions of songs. Like Brice, Streisand retained her New York accent. Unlike Brice, however, Streisand refused to surgically alter her prominent, proudly Jewish nose. She was among the first Hollywood stars to gain recognition because of her ethnicity rather than in spite of it. The first modern Jewish superstar, she was soon followed by suddenly "in" Jewish actors such as Dustin Hoffman, Richard Dreyfuss, Woody Allen, Mel Brooks, Elliott Gould, and Bette Midler. Playing a Jewish woman with more raw courage and conviction than had previously been seen on the screen, she also paved the way for the acceptance of strong female characters in starring roles.

Streisand got her first big break in the 1964 Broadway production of *Funny Girl,* which launched her down the same path as the woman she played. The musical was produced by Ray Stark, who was married to Brice's daughter by Nicky Arnstein. This personal affiliation gave Stark the tenacity needed to bring Brice's story to public attention. It also, however, made him overly protective of his mother-in-law's image. Although a movie producer by trade, Stark could not find studio backing for the flattering screenplay written at his behest by Isabel Lennart and so turned to Broadway. Among the established stars considered for the stage production were Mary Martin, Anne Bancroft, Eydie Gorme, Shirley MacLaine, and Carol Burnett (who shrewdly suggested the producers hire a Jewish actress). Jerome Robbins, then slated to direct, first suggested Streisand, who was just beginning to make a name for herself.

Directors came and went—Bob Fosse and Sidney Lumet among them—but when Garson Kanin, who had known Brice, was hired, he hitched the success of the musical to Streisand. When the show finally debuted on Broadway, with Robbins back on board, it was a smash. Weeks after the show opened, Streisand, then just twenty-one, was on the cover of *Time* and *Life* magazines. In 1968, Streisand, who had become the highest paid singer in America, reprised her role in the big-budget screen adaptation of *Funny Girl,* directed by three-time Oscar winner William Wyler, with the musical numbers staged by Herbert Ross.

As she would continue to do throughout her career, Streisand relied heavily on her own aggressive, persistent persona. Luckily, the similarities between Brice and Streisand were striking. Like the character she played, Streisand is demanding, driven, with strong instincts and even stronger opinions. The role, in fact, contained the essential contradiction that became Streisand's trademark. Again and again, Streisand plays strident, emotionally vulnerable extroverts. It was a match made in movie heaven. Streisand won an Oscar, in a tie with Katharine Hepburn, for her performance in the first Jewish movie musical, signifying that audiences were ready to embrace a bumpy-nosed Brooklyn Jewess loaded with personality. By 1968, ethnicity was beginning to be viewed as an asset rather than a liability. Unlike earlier screen biographies that downplayed or erased the Jewish identity of their subjects—such as *Houdini, Lepke, The Eddie Cantor Story,* and *Compulsion—Funny Girl* capitalized on Streisand's obvious Jewish characteristics. The movie, like the play, was a box office smash, although some reviewers criticized it as an overblown, fake Hollywood production. Streisand, however, was universally praised. "She makes tickets something worth buying," gushed Pauline Kael in the *New Yorker* magazine.

Although Streisand was allowed to flaunt her Jewishness in *Funny Girl,* the two men in Brice's life, Florenz Ziegfeld and Nicky Arnstein, had their Jewishness airbrushed, as was the custom in Hollywood. Nothing in the script or the performances indicates that either man is Jewish, and two non-Jewish actors were cast in the roles. Walter Pidgeon plays Fanny's mentor, the legendary showman and creator of the Ziegfeld Follies. Omar Sharif costars as Brice's first husband, Nicky Arnstein. The casting of Sharif as the assimilated Jewish gambler who married Brice, announced just before the Arab-Israeli Six Day War, pro-

BUMPY–NOSED BROOKLYN BEAUTY   Barbra Streisand was catapulted from Broadway to screen stardom playing Fanny Brice in the hit *Funny Girl,* the story of an ugly duckling who becomes a show-biz swan.

voked a storm of controversy. Although Jewish organizations protested the casting of the Egyptian actor, Jewish director Wyler was not dissuaded, and Streisand supported the casting choice. Sharif was officially declared a traitor to his country for his relationship, on and off the screen, with a Jewish woman who had recently given a gala to raise funds for Israel. Streisand quipped, "You think Cairo was upset? You should see the letter I got from my aunt Rose."

Funny Girl begins by detailing Brice's sudden showbiz success. Catapulted to fame by Ziegfeld, who recognizes her talents but doesn't always know what to do with them, Brice takes charge of her career by tailoring material to fit her looks and original style. (Similarly, Brice's songs are anachronistically updated in the film to suit Streisand's unique song stylings.) A klutz in the chorus line, Fanny brings down the house. Asked to sing self-adulatory lyrics, she makes a mockery of the schmaltzy song. She wins the adulation she so craves, but on her own terms.

Funny Girl, which was followed in 1975 by the mediocre sequel *Funny Lady,* is one of the cinema's premier show-biz bios and a brilliant showcase for the most influential female Jewish entertainer of the century, which accounts for its ranking among the top ten Jewish films of all time. The wildly popular, heavily sentimental film charts the predictably rocky romance between Nicky and Fanny. (In another case of life imitating art, Streisand's marriage to Elliott Gould also could not stand the strain of her success, and they divorced shortly after *Funny Girl* opened.) Although Streisand and Sharif generate some odd-couple chemistry, the doomed love story is the least interesting aspect of the movie. Sharif suffers the fate of many of Streisand's handsome, and usually non-Jewish, leading men who appear bland when paired with the charismatic star.

This problem also plagued director Sydney Pollack's *The Way We Were* (1973), a reversal of the *shiksa*-lust story in which Streisand plays a principled Jewish political activist who falls for a W.A.S.P. golden boy (Robert Redford), only to find that their values are radically different. In a departure from romantic formula, she loses her man but retains her integrity and identity. *The Way We Were* features an even more outspoken Streisand than *Funny Girl*, as the actress continued to play proudly Jewish women in *Hello, Dolly!, A Star is Born, The Main Event, Yentl, The Prince of Tides, Nuts,* and *The Mirror Has Two Faces.*

Funny Girl's musical numbers showcasing the talents of Brice via Streisand—or the other way around—are the highlights of this lavish production. One of the best is the re-creation of Brice's famed "Dying Swan" ballet spoof. One of the most famous is set aboard a tugboat chugging past the Statue of Liberty in New York Harbor, a scene that brings to mind Fanny's immigrant roots. One of Fanny's most appealing qualities is that she stays true to her roots. She keeps close ties with her mother Rose (Kay Medford), who owns a saloon in the old neighborhood. Everyone here takes pride in Fanny's success, especially the sweet old neighborhood *noodge,* Mrs. Strakosh, who is played by familiar-sounding Mae Questel, the actress who provided the voice of Betty Boop, and who went on to play Woody Allen's sky-borne mother in the *Oedipus Wrecks* segment of *New York Stories.*

Fanny finds fame and fortune, and pays a high price for her success, but never tries to pass herself off as something she's not. Although she is humorously self-effacing about her homeliness, lack of education, and sophistication, she's never ashamed of who she is and where she came from. With *Funny Girl,* Streisand set a high standard that has continued to serve as a challenge to the traditional screen roles assigned to women *and* Jews.

8

Gentleman's Agreement

20th Century–Fox (1947)
Cast: Gregory Peck, Dorothy McGuire, John Garfield,
Celeste Holm, Anne Revere
Directed by: Elia Kazan
118 minutes [Not rated]

In the years immediately following the murder of more than 6 million Jews, Hollywood ignored the unfathomable horrors of the Holocaust. Although the staggering wholesale slaughter that decimated European Jewry was not deemed a suitable subject for an American film until 1959, the genocide did not go completely unnoticed in the cautious, conservative, and heavily self-censored postwar cinema. In 1947, while social dramas with progressive themes were being scrutinized by the witch-hunting McCarthyites in Washington, the taboo subject of anti-Semitism in America surfaced for the first time in two Hollywood films—*Crossfire* and *Gentleman's Agreement*—released a few months apart, that dared utter the previously unmentionable word "Jew."

Both films were clearly made in response to the Holocaust, outlining the dangers inherent in any society where anti-Semitism is allowed to fester. Ironically, both films were directed and produced by non-Jews and featured only minor Jewish characters. *Crossfire*'s director, Edward Dmytryk, has said the fact that he and his producer, Adrian Scott, were not Jewish was an advantage in that no one could accuse them of self-interest, although he reports there was heavy opposition to the picture. *Crossfire,* an excellent low-budget crime drama, used the subject of anti-Semitism to fuel a gritty little film noir murder mystery. Dmytryk's taut, tough, unpretentious drama exposed the ugly irony of anti-Semitism in the American Army. *Crossfire* starred Robert Mitchum, Robert Ryan, and Robert Young and was a huge critical and commercial success, garnering Oscar nominations for best picture and best director. It lost in both categories to *Gentleman's Agreement*.

Gentleman's Agreement unmasked American anti-Semitism in a first-class, big-budget, all-star prestige picture. Viewed with the benefit of historical hindsight, *Gentleman's Agreement* may seem tame and simplistic, but it was

WHAT'S IN A NAME? Gregory Peck, left, with Dorothy McGuire, John Garfield, and Celeste Holm, plays an upstanding but naive reporter who is shocked by the prejudice he encounters when he poses as a Jew in *Gentleman's Agreement,* one of the first films to deal with American anti-Semitism.

astoundingly courageous for its time and holds up quite well as a condemnation of the insidious bigotry that lurks beneath the deceptively smooth surface of a seemingly liberal, educated society.

Gregory Peck, a sterling symbol of moral decency and ethical integrity, was shrewdly cast in the much ballyhooed screen adaptation of the best-selling novel by Laura Z. Hobson, a Jewish agnostic and the daughter of Yiddish writer and editor of the Jewish daily *Forward* Michael Zametkin. Peck plays an idealistic—and amazingly naive—journalist who poses as a Jew to learn firsthand about anti-Semitism for a magazine article he is writing. Although a rose by any other name would smell as sweet, when Philip Green (Peck) becomes Phil Green*berg,* he gets a good whiff of odious prejudice. Outraged and offended, Phil is even more shocked to discover that his well-bred, sophisticated fiancée Kathy (Dorothy McGuire) unconsciously harbors a suspicious snobbery.

As a Jew, Phil finds he is no longer welcome at a posh resort or at the home of his future sister-in-law. He is subject to slander and discrimination.

He is threatened with eviction. His son is called "a dirty kike" and beaten up. Phil discovers that the privileges he takes for granted are based on his safe, secure standing as a W.A.S.P. These displays of anti-Semitism, which seem almost inconsequential two years after the Holocaust, reveal a deep level of ignorance, hatred, and fear in the host culture. Phil is also distressed to find a pernicious self-hating attitude in his secretary (Jewish actress June Havoc), a closet Jew who says she doesn't want the "kikey ones" to ruin it for accepted, assimilated Jews like her. This internalized prejudice stuns Phil, who turns to his Jewish best friend Dave Goldman (John Garfield) for advice. Oddly, Dave, a soldier, tells him that anti-Semitism is not his battle. Later, however, he opens Kathy's eyes to her own passivity. Kathy learns that by not openly and actively fighting prejudice, she is guilty of perpetuating it.

The daring project originated with powerful producer Darryl F. Zanuck, a Nebraska-born Methodist and registered Republican who was then head of production at 20th Century–Fox. Zanuck had previously raised the subject of anti-Semitism in Europe in his 1934 film *The House of Rothschild* and created a rare proudly pro-Jewish war drama, *The Purple Heart* (1944). Despite the reactionary political climate of the McCarthy era, Zanuck was determined he could get away with making an important social statement—but only if *Gentleman's Agreement* was also artistically successful. To ensure the kind of highbrow quality he desired, he hired Elia Kazan, a non-Jewish Broadway heavy hitter and cofounder of the Actors Studio, to direct. Pulitzer Prize–winning Jewish playwright Moss Hart was engaged to write the screenplay.

Zanuck succeeded in making a breakthrough film that was both popular and respected. *Gentleman's Agreement* earned Oscars for best picture, best director, and best supporting actress (Celeste Holm, who played Peck's enlightened, cosmopolitan colleague). Peck and Garfield were also nominated. The movie was lauded by the critics and became one of the biggest box office hits of the year.

Not surprisingly, raising the subject of anti-Semitism also aroused the suspicions of the House Un-American Activities Committee, which began its Hollywood hearings a month before *Gentleman's Agreement* opened. *Crossfire's* Dmytryk and Scott were among the Hollywood Ten who were jailed and blacklisted for refusing to cooperate. Dmytryk, who was among hundreds of film artists to eventually testify as a friendly witness, was able to resume his career but paid dearly in that damned-if-you-do, damned-if-you-don't era. Elia Kazan also eventually succumbed to pressure and named names. After the H.U.A.C. hearings of 1948 and 1951 that resulted in the blacklisting of left-leaning film artists, no further overtly pro-Jewish films were made for more than a decade. *The Young Lions,* directed by Dmytryk in 1958, again raised the issue of anti-Semitism in the U.S. Army and was among the first films to acknowledge the Holocaust.

In his autobiography, Kazan admits he now finds *Gentleman's Agreement* to be patronizing. He notes that it skated over the surface of an issue that needed a more penetrating treatment. "So much, so horrible, has been recognized about the attack on the Jew since the film was made that it now seems inadequate to the issue," Kazan writes, adding that it lacks the "intimate experience of someone who had been through the bitter and humiliating experience."

Kazan's postmortem may be accurate but is not entirely fair. *Gentleman's Agreement* took a tough stand against the vicious, if often invisible, attitudes that exist even in polite society, where "gentlemen" have a tacit understanding that Jews are to be restricted from entering the hallowed halls of high society. Focusing on the social problems faced by Jews in America, the post-Holocaust book and film suggest that these subtle expressions lead to more virulent and violent forms of anti-Semitism. This point is stated even more clearly in *Crossfire,* which features a vicious bigot who commits a hate crime. Neither film, however, mentions the Holocaust. Zanuck directly confronted those reactionaries who opposed the film by tailoring the screenplay to suggest that anti-Semitism was not only unpatriotic but downright un-American.

It was not just the McCarthyites who sought to block the film, however. In addition to a number of Jewish moguls who wanted the project dropped, some Jewish groups also opposed the making of the film on the basis that it raised the subject of anti-Semitism and hence gave it credence and might even encourage it. Hart incorporated and refuted those objections by creating the character of industrialist Irving Weissman (Robert Warwick) who advises Phil not to stir up trouble by calling attention to anti-Semitism.

Another minor Jewish character is Professor Lieberman (Sam Jaffe), who explains to Phil that although he is not religious (like the novel's author) and, as a scientist, rejects the idea of a Jewish race, he remains a Jew because anti-Semitism defines him as one. While Lieberman represents the proudly Jewish, secular intellectual, Garfield's character is a soldier, a deliberate choice meant to dispel the prejudicial image of cowardly Jews who avoided military service. (*Crossfire* refutes this image even more strongly.) Garfield, who changed his name from Julius Jacob Garfinkle, was a major star at the time but took the supporting role because he felt the film's message was of vital importance. After starring in *Body and Soul* the following year, Garfield was blacklisted and died a broken man, one of the most famous victims of McCarthyism.

Gentleman's Agreement is sometimes faulted for primarily focusing on non-Jewish characters, a once frequent cinematic concession to anti-Semitism based on the assumption that audiences could not be expected to accept or identify with a Jewish central character. While *Gentleman's Agreement* does tell the story of a righteous gentile, because its target audience was the average American who may not have realized how deep anti-Semitism ran, the choice of a gentile hero with whom to identify made sense. Of course, it also led to some obfuscation of the issue. In a famed anecdote—sometimes attributed to screenwriter Ring Lardner Jr.—a stagehand remarked that he had learned a valuable lesson from the movie: From now on he would be nice to Jews because they might turn out to be gentiles.

The plain-talking movie takes pains to point out how prejudice is passed from generation to generation. Phil, a widowed father, tries to explain anti-Semitism to his son (Dean Stockwell), telling him that Jews are Americans who go to different churches, called synagogues. Although this explanation carries the assumption that being Jewish is just a matter of religion and that otherwise Jews are just like everyone else, and Phil does not discuss the causes of anti-Semitism, it is a sincere attempt to make a young boy see why such hatred is wrong.

Phil has clearly inherited his principles from his supportive and sensible mother (Ann Revere), who encourages him to take the assignment when Phil at first resists. "It would be nice not to have to explain it [to our children] someday," she tells Phil. We are still explaining it, of course, more than half a century later. But the film's message is still valid. You can't know the pain of a stranger until you walk in his or her shoes.

9

Exodus

Metro-Goldwyn-Mayer (1960)
CAST: Paul Newman, Eva Marie Saint, Ralph Richardson,
Peter Lawford, David Opatoshu, Lee J. Cobb
DIRECTED BY: Otto Preminger
213 minutes [Not rated]

The most extensive film production to date at its release in 1960, *Exodus* introduced a radically new image of the contemporary Jew to a vast audience. A valiant, virile, and victorious Jew—personified by dashing Paul Newman— was proudly paraded before the American filmgoing public in full Technicolor, Super-Panavision splendor in this epic drama based on the biggest bestseller since *Gone With the Wind.* This Jewish warrior's courage and daring offered a stunning repudiation of the cinema's common depiction of the modern Jew as passive victim, timid intellectual, and awkward, alienated misfit, which had previously been refuted only in biblical epics starring gentiles as ancient Jewish heroes.

Otto Preminger's adaptation of Leon Uris's novel dramatizing and glorifying the events surrounding the foundation of the state of Israel was also instrumental in shaping public opinion; it engendered a great deal of sympathy for Zionism. This big-budget blockbuster was among the first Hollywood films to acknowledge the Holocaust and the first major motion picture to suggest that the Jewish homeland had become a moral imperative following the Holocaust.

Widely seen and respected, *Exodus* was much more than an effective piece of propaganda, however. This story of an Israeli freedom fighter and an American widow who converts to the Israeli cause proved solidly entertaining. *Exodus* offers three and half hours of action, romance, and intrigue, featuring a well-defined political agenda, vivid characters, and stirring speeches, all informed by an abiding humanism.

The project originated with producer Dore Schary, the executive producer of *Crossfire,* the first Hollywood film to tackle anti-Semitism. Schary, a committed Jew, commissioned Jewish novelist Leon Uris to create an epic based on the birth of Israel, and Uris spent two years in Israel researching his

THE PROMISED LAND   Paul Newman, center, plays a sexy Zionist whose daring exploits include masquerading as an English officer in *Exodus,* one of the top five films of 1960, a lavish, groundbreaking epic that celebrated the creation of Israel.

626-page novel. Otto Preminger, a Viennese Jew who came to Hollywood in 1935 as part of an influx of talented refugees who had an enormous impact on the American film scene, purchased the rights to the book. He directed and produced the movie with a $4 million budget. Preminger hired black-listed writer Dalton Trumbo to write the screenplay. Although he was not Jewish, Trumbo, like Preminger, was no stranger to controversy for his liberal leanings. Trumbo had worked under various pseudonyms during his thirteen years on the blacklist, which Preminger and Kirk Douglas simultaneously broke in 1960 by using Trumbo's name on *Exodus* and *Spartacus* respectively. The American Legion picketed both films in protest without diminishing their popularity, bringing to an end an infamous chapter in Hollywood history.

Set in 1947, *Exodus* opens on the Greek island of Cyprus, where Kitty (Eva Marie Saint) has come on holiday, still mourning the death of her photojournalist husband in Palestine a year earlier. Bored and without direction, Kitty volunteers at a detention camp where 30,000 Jews are being held, even though she confesses she feels strange among Jews. A ship chartered by Jews bound for Palestine has just been captured by the British, who are charged with keeping the peace in Palestine and controlling Cyprus as well. The 611 passengers on the ill-fated *Star of David* are sent to the Cyprus dentention camp. Among them is a German–Jewish teenager, Karin (Jill Haworth), with whom Kitty feels an immediate maternal kinship.

Although the movie begins with cool blond Kitty, a Presbyterian from Indiana, as its central character, she is soon joined by the passionate and dedicated Israeli freedom fighter, Ari Ben Canaan (Newman). Although his father was Jewish, Newman is not obviously Jewish in looks or mannerisms, which reinforces a major point in the story: There are Jews of all descriptions. Ari masterminds a daring mass escape by the 611 waylaid Jewish passengers aboard a boat bound for Palestine, which he commandeers by posing as a British officer. The brazen act of defiance, a symbol of Jewish resistance, is designed to capture public attention and send a message to the United Nations, which is about to vote on the proposal to partition Palestine.

Kitty gets caught up in the action, acting as a liaison between Ari and the British general she has befriended. Played by Ralph Richardson, the general is a decent bloke, sympathetic to the Jewish cause, unlike his next-in-command, a blatant bigot played by Peter Lawford. In one delicious scene, Lawford boasts that he can always spot a Jew, while staring directly into the blue eyes of Ari, disguised in a British uniform. The ship, renamed the *Exodus,* is blocked in the harbor, and the passengers stage a hunger strike as Ari negotiates for its release. The ship finally sails, with Ari, Kitty, and Karin aboard, ending a highly charged first hour of the movie, one of the longest preludes in motion picture history.

This opening action establishes a number of the movie's groundbreaking concepts. It introduces us to Ari, an aggressive, independent, handsome man of action and principle. It also conveys a Jewish sense of valor and pride. As one chess-playing passenger who serves as the group's spokesman says, "It is time for Jews to feel like human beings again." Once in Palestine, Kitty meets Ari's father Barak (played by Jewish actor Lee J. Cobb) and learns how Jewish pioneers settled in Palestine and turned the desert into green valleys. Kitty's eyes are opened to a kind of determination, purpose, and commitment she has never known. Her worldview is further shaken by Ari, with whom she becomes romantically involved—although the love affair is the least compelling aspect of the movie. "People are all the same," Kitty says, expressing the standard liberal sentiment of the time. But Ari vehemently disagrees. "People are different. They like to be different. They have a right to be different. We have to respect those differences." This may not sound remarkable today, but it is a very early onscreen expression of the notion of pluralism that has gained favor in recent years.

Karin settles in a kibbutz and declines Kitty's invitation to come to America. Ari's uncle Akiva (played by Yiddish cinema star David Opatoshu) is a leader of the Irgun terrorist organization that is taking a more violent approach to independence than Ari's more diplomatic group, the Haganah. Karin's friend Dov, a troubled, militant Auschwitz survivor played by Sal Mineo, joins the Irgun and bombs a building for the group. Akiva is arrested following the bombing. Despite their considerable philosophical differences, Ari stages a daring prison break, freeing his uncle and all the Jewish and Arab prisoners.

When the United Nations votes for partition, it is a moment of heartfelt triumph for the Jews. Their elation is short-lived, however, as the decision sets off a war between Arabs and Jews. It even drives a stake in the friendship between Ari and his Arab friend since boyhood. Karin is ambushed and killed by an Arab just outside the kibbutz. At her grave, Kitty, now armed with a gun, joins Ari in the fight that lies ahead. Ari, angered by the needless bloodshed, expresses his hope that "the day will come when Arab and Jew share this land in peace."

Exodus, filmed on location in Israel and Cyprus, offered a bold vision of its Jewish characters and made startling statements about the Jews' entitlement to a homeland following the Holocaust. American films about Israel remain a relative rarity, however. *Cast a Giant Shadow* starred a vital and virile Kirk Douglas as "Mickey" Marcus, the American World War II hero who became the first general to lead the Israeli army in 2,000 years, helping to win the War of Independence in 1948. Although well worth seeing, the 1966 film was not a big hit. *Operation Eichmann* (1961) is a rare early film that decries the horrors of the Holocaust and champions the cause of Zionism.

There are also a number of Israeli-made movies covering that nation's history. *Hill 24 Doesn't Answer Anymore* (1955), the first feature film made in Israel, covers the battle for a Jewish homeland. The Oscar-nominated *Operation Thunderbolt* (1977) deals with the daring raid on the Arab terrorists at Entebbe. *Sallah* (1966), starring Topol, is a humorous look at life in the newly formed state of Israel. *They Were Ten* (1961) looks at a group of nineteenth century settlers of Eretz Israel, while Israeli director Uri Barbash's American-made *Unsettled Land* (1988) depicts the struggles of pioneers in the 1920s.

Exodus remains the definitive film about the creation of Israel, however. Preminger built his groundbreaking reputation through the strong stand he took in *Exodus*. He became famous for challenging prevailing wisdom, defying sexual censorship, ignoring racism (by creating two all-black films in the 1950s, *Carmen Jones* and *Porgy and Bess*), and exploring taboo subjects such as drug addiction. It is not surprising that he chose to champion the Zionist cause and create a vital and potent new screen image of the Jew. What is surprising is how well his progressive efforts were received by the American public.

The critical acclaim and commercial success of *Exodus* indicated that Americans were ready to respect and admire clearly identified Jewish characters. *Exodus* lived up to its title. It led Jews out of screen obscurity and into newfound freedom in films of the future.

10

Ben-Hur

Metro-Goldwyn-Mayer (1959)
CAST: Charlton Heston, Stephen Boyd, Jack Hawkins, Haya Harareet
DIRECTED BY: William Wyler
212 minutes [Not rated]

The Ten Commandments

Paramount Pictures (1956)
CAST: Charlton Heston, Yul Brynner, Anne Baxter,
Edward G. Robinson, John Derek
DIRECTED BY: Cecil B. De Mille
220 minutes [G]

During the 1950s, Hollywood deemed the Holocaust an unsuitable subject for a feature film, and only a handful of movies made even passing reference to the mass destruction of Europe's Jews. Sympathy for Jewish suffering during the *Shoah* was clearly, if indirectly, manifested, however, in a series of lavish religious spectacles based on stories of Jewish persecution in the ancient world, most of them taken from the Old Testament.

Released three years apart, *The Ten Commandments* and *Ben-Hur* stand as the two best examples of the big-budget biblical epics of the 1950s and bear striking similarities, including the disconcerting choice of Charlton Heston to personify Jewish heroism. *Ben-Hur,* a fictional drama based on Lew Wallace's best-selling novel about a nobly born, enslaved Jew who challenges the Roman domination of his people, is arguably the better film. *The Ten Commandments,* based on the biblical story of a nobly raised, enslaved Jew who challenges the Egyptian domination of his people, might be considered more inherently Jewish because of its sacred source material, the Book of Exodus, which covers one of the most signifigant events in Jewish history.

Tied for tenth place in this ranking of the greatest Jewish films, *Ben-Hur* and *The Ten Commandments* presented to the mainstream movie-going population a positive image of the Jewish people as unjustly persecuted and valiantly fighting for survival and freedom. Both huge hits were made by powerhouse directors and filmed on location with prestigious actors and the proverbial cast of thousands. Both were extravagantly expensive and filled with stunning state-of-the-art special effects. Both were remakes of silent films. Both ran well over three hours, and both were among the five top-grossing films of the year.

The most honored film in Academy Award history, *Ben-Hur* won a record-setting eleven Oscars in 1959, including best picture, best director, and best actor. Trailers for the widescreen extravaganza promised "the entertainment experience of a lifetime." *Ben-Hur,* the ads proclaimed, had it all: strange locales, pageantry, spectacle, violence, action, romance, and a capacity to "lift your spirit to the sky." The hyperbolic praise may overstate the case a bit, but *Ben-Hur,* which extolled the virtues of a heroic Jew who clings to his faith, to his conquered people, and to his integrity in the face of an enemy

HOLOCAUST AWARENESS   *Ben-Hur* starred Charlton Heston as a Jewish hero battling oppression in the ancient world. It stands out from the spate of religious spectacles in the 1950s that were obvious, albeit oblique, responses to the Holocaust.

seeking to destroy Judaism, stands up as grand and eloquent entertainment.

The Ten Commandments was even more heavily hyped than *Ben-Hur.* The trailers proclaimed it "the greatest motion picture of all time" and "one of the greatest adventure stories ever hurled from the pages of a book." It, too, made its relevance to recent events abundantly clear. "This is a story of the birth of freedom," the introduction begins. "Its theme is whether men are to be ruled by God's laws or by the whims of a dictator. Are men the property of the state or free souls under God? The same battle continues throughout the world today." *The Ten Commandments,* which ends with the Jews' deliverance into the promised land, carried a clear pro-Zionist message and drew an obvious comparison between Pharoah and Hitler.

As Moses, famed director Cecil B. De Mille cast Charlton Heston, a strapping, strong-jawed, stage-trained actor with an air of immutable dignity. With his patrician looks, Heston offered audiences a nonethnic, heroic image of the most influential Jew in history. Moses, who emerges as a compelling figure, begins life as a babe (played by Heston's own infant son Fraser), set adrift in a basket to escape Pharoah's decree calling for death to all newborn Hebrew males, an attempt to destroy the savior whose coming has been prophesied. Pharoah's daughter finds and adopts the baby. Thirty years later, Moses has become a valiant warrior and devoted servant of Pharoah (Cedrick Hardwick). Despite his upbringing, Moses displays compassion and charity that set him apart from his fellow Egyptians. His intrinsic values, which are presumably the product of his Hebrew heritage, make him a logical choice to succeed Pharoah, which arouses the jealousy of Pharoah's biological son, the arrogant and cruel Ramses (Yul Brynner).

When Moses learns the truth about his origins, he joins his people in slavery—which looks much like the forced labor of the concentration camps—before being cast into the wilderness. After receiving the word of God at Mount Sinai, and at the behest of Joshua (John Derek), Moses returns to Egypt to confront the all-powerful Pharoah (now Ramses) and lead the Jews from the land of their affliction, parting the Red Sea during the miraculous escape. During the forty years in the wilderness, Moses confronts the doubters in his ranks, led by the Golden Calf-making Dathan (Edward G. Robinson), and receives the Ten Commandments. The film ends with Moses striking a dramatic pose on a hillside as Joshua leads the Jews to their new home.

Like Moses, Judah Ben-Hur becomes a slave before rising up to resist the evil empire threatening his people with extinction. Released the same year Hollywood finally began to deal directly with the Holocaust in *The Diary of Anne Frank, Ben-Hur* was even more outspokenly pro-Jewish than earlier post-Holocaust epics that tacitly expressed sympathy for the more than 6 million Jews murdered in the Holocaust, including De Mille's clunky *Samson and Delilah* (1949), starring Victor Mature and Hedy Lamarr, and the elegant *David and Bathsheba,* one of the top-grossing films of 1951, starring Gregory Peck.

Ben-Hur, a revered pseudo-biblical epic set in Judea at the time of Christ, was directed by William Wyler, a German-born Jew who had good reason to respond to the Holocaust. Wyler had immigrated to America in 1922 at the age of twenty and served as production assistant on the 1926 silent film version of *Ben-Hur*. His parents remained in Germany until 1938, however, and his brother Walter spent a month in Dachau before narrowly escaping with his life. Wyler had injected anti-German sentiment into his 1942 film *Mrs. Miniver* over the objections of Louis B. Mayer. But *Ben-Hur* was Wyler's first film to focus on a Jewish character. *Funny Girl* (1968) was his second and last. In 1956, Wyler could make any movie he wanted. The most acclaimed director in Hollywood at the time, his pictures have won twice the number of Oscars awarded to films by any other director. Known as a reliable, respectable, tasteful director who elicited fine performances from his stars, Wyler was paid the largest director's fee to date for *Ben-Hur,* which grossed a then-staggering $76 million worldwide.

The Ten Commandments, the costliest film of its time, was made for $13 million and grossed more than $40 million. Nominated for six Oscars, it won only for best special effects. De Mille, the son of an Episcopalian minister and an English Jewess, had also forged a mighty reputation in Hollywood. The prolific director and producer of commercially successful films, he was known as a master storyteller and craftsman. *The Ten Commandments,* which De Mille had filmed before in 1926, was a resounding success with the public, as the silent film version had been. De Mille, however, has been criticized for creating old-fashioned, empty entertainments. As Pauline Kael observed, "De Mille made small-minded movies on a big scale."

Ben-Hur, on the other hand, has been called a thinking man's epic and an intimate epic. It is also the only biblical drama of the day to use the word "Jew" instead of "Hebrew," "Israelite," or the even more euphemistic "Danite" used a decade earlier in De Mille's *Samson and Delilah.* Jewish persecution is here tied more directly to anti-Semitism than it is in other films of the era.

Still, *Ben-Hur* complies with the standard practice of casting a gentile in the role of an historic Jewish hero, although Wyler did cast Israeli actress Haya Harareet as Ben-Hur's loyal love, Esther. Just as the 1950s' biblical epics were safely distanced in the past, the Jewish characters with whom the audience was asked to sympathize were made safe by the personification of Jewish virtue in gentile form. These religious spectacles also tended to regard the Jewish characters as incipient Christians, an attitude that is manifested most overtly in Wyler's adaptation of Wallace's 1880 novel, *Ben-Hur: A Tale of the Christ,* in which Judah becomes a follower of Christ in the film's final moments. Wyler used to joke that, "It took a Jew to make a really good movie about Christ."

When the story begins, Judea has been under the domination of Rome for a century. The Romans cannot understand these stubborn people who "are drunk on religion" and smash the Roman idols. Ben-Hur is one of the richest men of Judea and head of one of its greatest families. When his boyhood friend Massala (Stephen Boyd) returns from Rome a tribune, Ben-Hur asks his old friend to use his influence with the emperor to grant his people freedom. Massala not only rejects this request as impossible, he promotes an assimilationist agenda. "It's a Roman world. If you want to live in it you must be part of it." Urging that resistance to Rome is futile and can only lead to violence, he enlists Ben-Hur to spread the voice of reason to his people.

But Massala—a nemesis akin to Ramses in *The Ten Commandments*—is not content that Ben-Hur merely exert his influence. He wants him to name

LET MY PEOPLE GO *The Ten Commandments,* which was based on the Book of Exodus, featured patrician actor Charlton Heston as Moses, the most influential figure in Jewish history, who leads his people out of slavery.

names, to betray those who do not comply—an obvious reference to the actions of the House Un-American Activities Committee, which was still exerting its pernicious influence when the film was released. Ben-Hur refuses. He goes home, puts on a yarmulke, and ritualistically washes his hands, thus demonstrating his allegiance to Jewish faith.

Wrongly accused of attempted murder, Ben-Hur is assigned to rowing Roman barges along with other chained, numbered slaves. When the ship sinks, number 41 (Ben-Hur) saves the life of its captain. The grateful consul adopts Ben-Hur and trains him as a champion charioteer. Thus, the Jewish prince turned galley slave returns to Judea as a Roman consul, a title he inherits from his adoptive father. He seeks in vain for his mother and sister, who have become lepers during their five-year dungeon confinement and are now living in misery in the Valley of the Lepers.

Believing them dead, Ben-Hur is bent on revenge. He races against Massala in a chariot race, sponsored by a sympathetic sheik who also hates the Romans and wants to see them defeated by a Jew. Ben-Hur scores a symbolic victory for his people and settles a personal vendetta in the famous nine-minute chariot race, which still stands as one of the most exciting action sequences of all time. Hailed as a hero, Ben-Hur is again exhorted to join "the great future" of Rome. (Rome is frequently associated with Nazi Germany both through language and fascist imagery.) Ben-Hur, however, recognizes the evil tyranny of the empire, which seeks to conquer and consume the world. He will not forsake his people.

Ben-Hur finds his family and, at Esther's urging, takes them to see "the rabbi who says love is more powerful than hate." After witnessing the Romans' crucifixion of Christ, Ben-Hur's sister and mother are cured, and Ben-Hur accepts Jesus as the son of God. This ending ensured its appeal to Christian audiences. It also emphasized the historic connection between Judaism and Christianity, reminding viewers of the Jewish origin of many teachings central to the now-dominant religion. The film thus exhorts tolerance and solidarity, reminding Christians of their own oppression by a powerful majority. Still, Ben-Hur's last-minute conversion is apt to cause discomfort in some viewers, especially after spending the preceding three and half hours following a proud and defiant Jew who says, "I believe in the future of my people."

Ben-Hur and *The Ten Commandments* represent a genre Hollywood is no longer able to make with any success. Recent years have seen disappointing attempts, such as *King David* (1985) and TV's *Masada* (1981). Although far from radical by today's standards, both *Ben-Hur* and *The Ten Commandments* made bold statements in the timid, conservative era of McCarthyism. *The Ten Commandments* was certainly the only film of the all-American 1950s in which the *sh'ma* could be heard, recited in Hebrew.

11

Crossing Delancey

Warner Bros. (1988)
CAST: Amy Irving, Peter Riegert, Reizl Bozyk, Sylvia Miles, Jeroen Krabbe
DIRECTED BY: Joan Micklin Silver
97 minutes [PG]

Joan Micklin Silver made her feature film debut documenting the hustle and bustle of Hester Street circa 1896. Turning a corner in time, the director took a stroll down present day Delancey Street in her second look at Jewish life, an even more accomplished and refreshing romantic comedy. Silver, the daughter of Russian-Jewish immigrants, finds much has changed on the Lower East Side, but that the central issues challenging its Jewish population remain the same. Like the zeitgeist-attuned *Hester Street* (1975), *Crossing Delancey* questions the assimilationist agenda that typically informs Hollywood movies. Although Silver's output has been slim, it has been choice, and her distinctly female perspective on the Jewish experience offers a unique counterpoint to the male voices that dominate the movies. Among the handful of films to her credit, Silver boasts two of the finest movies examining the high price of assimilation. Both woman-centered, clash-of-values stories are deftly comic yet astute, politically provocative as well as emotionally evocative.

In the charming and deceptively low-key *Hester Street,* Silver explored the culture shock experienced by Gitl (Oscar nominee Carol Kane), a greenhorn who joins her *nogoodnik* husband in America. Although her husband has quickly become a "regulah Yenkee," Gitl decides she is not so eager to forsake Jewish tradition to become an American. Her solution is an accommodation to modern life that does not sacrifice her identity or integrity.

In 1988's *Crossing Delancey,* adapted by Susan Sandler from her play, Izzy (Amy Irving) is Gitl's spiritual cousin, although the journey she makes is in reverse. Gitl, who moves toward modern self-determination and independence, finds a balance between assimilation and tradition by making some minor adjustments to American life. Izzy, who has already achieved self-reliance, takes a step back toward the past to create balance in her all-too-modern life.

Both highly original films put a feminist spin on the issue of assimilation, arriving at similiar conclusions. Gitl decides not to tear herself up by her roots;

MATCHMAKER, MATCHMAKER   Amy Irving, center, plays a single woman who initially protests when her Bubby (Reizl Bozyk, left) enlists the aid of a matchmaker (Sylvia Miles), but reluctantly comes to appreciate the outcome in *Crossing Delancey*.

Izzy returns to her roots. Both women find personal fulfillment by altering the narrow way they define their world.

Izzy lives uptown in a nice, rent-controlled apartment and works for "the last real bookstore in New York," which puts her in contact with the Manhattan literati. She has plenty of bright friends and a married boyfriend who comes around whenever he has a fight with his wife. Smart, liberated, and successful, Izzy still has a close relationship with her beloved Bubby, who lives on the lower east side and thinks any woman who "lives alone like a dog" must be hiding a terrible loneliness. At thirty-three, Izzy claims she's in no rush to get married. But if the right man were to come along . . .

When Izzy first meets pickle man Sam (Peter Riegert), he's obviously all wrong. Sam, who runs the pickle store he inherited from his late father and who goes to *shul* every morning, is too Old World, too traditional, too unsophisticated for Izzy. Sure, he's a nice guy, but what do they have in common? As it turns out, more than she thinks. Izzy dismisses him out of hand as a suitable mate, in part because her Bubby has hired a matchmaker (the incomparable Sylvia Miles) to arrange the introduction. "It's not how I do things," she protests. "It's not how I live."

One of Silver's great accomplishments in this utterly captivating and compelling film is that we initially share Izzy's skepticism. But as she begins to reassess her hasty judgment, so do we. Sam looks better and better as the movie goes on. He's more than what he first seems, and we feel a little guilty for underestimating him. Silver and screenwriter Sandler effectively motivate Izzy's change of heart with a series of encounters. Izzy carries on a flirtation with a charming, worldly but self-involved and arrogant author (Jeroen Krabbe), only to discover how manipulative he is. She also attends the *bris* of her friend's baby, which seems to awaken a longing in her. Her friend, who is single, got tired of waiting for Mr. Right. Her other best friend, played by Suzzy Roche (whose band, the Roches, provides the hip but haunting musical score), is openly disgusted by "the appalling lack of single, desirable men" in New York, and stable, sincere Sam looks pretty good to her.

As Izzy slowly comes around and recognizes her need for connection with her heritage, Sam challenges her assumptions—and ours. "You think my world is so small, so provincial? You think it defines me?" he asks Izzy. Although he's adoring, romantic, and steadfast, Sam is not about to be taken for a fool. He's direct and decent, qualities we come to appreciate along with Izzy. He emerges as one of the screen's most positive Jewish men, an unlikely romantic hero whose hands smell of pickle juice.

Irving, a very appealing actress, makes a convincing case for Izzy's reluctance, portraying her confusion and ambivalence. Riegert shrewdly refrains from revealing too much too soon, allowing us to gradually warm to his character. Reizl Bozyk, once a star on the Yiddish vaudeville stage, gives a very showy performance as the outspoken Bubby, who is endearing and aggravating at the same time.

While *Hester Street,* based on the first novel by *Forward* founder and long-time editor Abraham Cahan, asked Jewish audiences to look back at the difficult choices first generation Jews faced as they struggled to make it in the New World, *Crossing Delancey* asks us to take stock of where we are now. Its appeal for all audiences lies in the suggestion that we need to find ways to simplify our increasingly complex lives, to get our priorities straight and establish personal and communal connections that ground us. For Jewish viewers, it also warns that in our rush to express our individuality and embrace our independence, we may underestimate the importance of our *Yiddishkeit.* The film reminds Jews of the enduring cultural values all too often discarded along the immigrant trail, values that might well help guide us on our crazy journey.

12

The Golem

Hollywood Select Video (1920)
CAST: Paul Wegener, Albert Steinruck, Ernst Deutsch, Lyda Salmonova
DIRECTED BY: Paul Wegener and Carl Boese
90 minutes [Not rated]

A seminal silent film widely heralded as an early and unusually fine example of German expressionism, *The Golem* helped to establish the German cinema's international reputation for innovation, artistry, and technical proficiency. Along with Robert Wiene's *The Cabinet of Dr. Caligari* (1920), Fritz Lang's *Der Müde Tod* (1921), and F. W. Murnau's *Nosferatu* (1924), *The Golem* reflects the social unrest, chaos, and gloom of Germany following its defeat in World War I and foreshadows the nation's pending political nightmare.

Based on an ancient Jewish legend about a rabbi who seeks to protect his people from persecution by bringing to life a powerful clay figure that eventually runs amok, *The Golem* set the standard for horror films for years to come and directly influenced the *Frankenstein* films in both style and content. Paul Wegener, a man of massive build and large features, played the golem, a figure whose lumbering gait and mute intractability—as well as his undoing by a child to whom he shows tenderness—were imitated in the 1931 version of *Frankenstein* starring Boris Karloff.

Cowriter and codirector Wegener, who had become a leading character actor with Max Reinhardt's Deutsches Theater since joining the famed Berlin company in 1906, made his screen debut playing dual roles in 1913's *The Student from Prague*. This variation of the Faust legend with a supernatural theme featured a scene set in a Jewish graveyard, establishing a link between Judaism and the occult. The following year, Wegener explored the theme of Jewish mysticism more fully in the first of three versions of *The Golem* he was to create. The 1914 film, which has not survived, takes place long after the rabbi's death, when the golem is excavated and brought back to life. In 1917, Wegener directed *Der Golem und die Täenzerin,* a comic film about the making of the 1914 *The Golem.*

After World War I, Wegener reunited with coscreenwriter Henrik Galeen on his acclaimed, innovative remake, *Der Golem: Wie Er in die Welt Kam (The*

COLOSSUS OF THE CINEMA   German silent film giant Paul Wegener plundered a medieval Jewish legend in his third screen version of *The Golem,* in which he played the mythical monster brought to life by rabbi Judah Ben Loew (Albert Steinruck, center) to rescue the imperiled Jews of Prague.

Golem: How He Came Into the World), enhanced by art direction by the famed architect Hans Poelzig and cinematography by Karl Freund. Set in the sixteenth century, the story follows the creation of a golem (unformed mass) by Rabbi Judah Loew to protect the Jews after they are exiled. In this 1920 classic, Wegener remained true to the legend, drawing on the most famous version of the medieval folktale, *The Golem of Prague.* The formula for creating a golem first appeared in the sixth century in the *Sefer Yezirah,* and the first tales concerning its creation centered on Rabbi Elijah of Chelm but later shifted to Judah Loew ben Bazalel (1513–1609). The renowned rabbi had indeed successfully defended his people from the hostile clergy and government of Prague, well known as a center of occult activity, which is what drew Emperor Rudolph II to the city from Vienna.

Wegener, who went on to participate in propaganda films during the Nazi era and was named Actor of the State, has been criticized for fostering the image of the Jew as a strange and exotic "other," possessing powers that threaten public safety. The film, however, makes it quite clear that the Jews are victims of unjust persecution and that the rabbi resorts to magic out of desperation. Although *The Golem* does not have a profound Jewish sensibility—and in fact is distinctly Germanic in its romantic obsession with death and destruction—it is true to the story, the invention of a powerless, oppressed people who imagine for themselves a savior whose unholy creation leads them into even greater peril. The legend also reflects mainstream Judaism's fear of kabbalah, which resulted in the suppression of the Jewish mystical tradition now enjoying a revival.

Just as the Jewish legend on which it is based conveys the ultimate danger of summoning evil forces even for self-preservation, the pre-Nazi film prophetically suggests the difficulty of controlling a monster once it has been created. The film is also eerily, if uninentionally, prophetic in its depiction of a Jewish persecution based on the belief that Jews pose a danger "to the lives and property of their fellow men." While the film foreshadows events to come in Nazi Germany, it is unlikely that Wegener intended his film as a warning, unlike Fritz Lang's *The Testament of Dr. Mabuse* (1933), which put Hitler's words into the mouth of a pathological criminal and served as a metaphor for the danger that was about to engulf Germany.

Although Wegener later said he did not set out to make an expressionistic film but rather sought to tell a story with visual images, his use of chiaroscuro lighting (strong contrast between light and dark), of onscreen lighting sources (including a menorah in the synagogue), of oblique angles and striking shapes, and of Gothic sets featuring featuring narrow streets, crooked staircases, and pointed roofs, were all characteristic of German expressionism, now considered the pinnacle of film art at the time.

When *The Golem* played in New York in 1921, the *New York Times* review praised its visual quality, its exceptional acting, and the "most expressive settings yet seen in this country." The review also contained an odd disclaimer: "The story is said to be based on an old Jewish legend, but it is no part of orthodox Jewish tradition, surely."

The legend of the golem, famously recorded in a 1982 adaptation by Isaac Bashevis Singer and a number of award-winning children's books, inspired a 1936 French film, *Le Golem,* directed by Julien Duvivier, and a 1966 French television production by Jean Kerchbron. The golem later lumbered through an Israeli drama by Ilan Eldad and was brought to life by Roddy MacDowell in 1967's *It,* filmed in England. The success of *The Golem* led to another classic film inspired by a supernatural Jewish folktale in which disaster follows when a Jew uses his kabbalistic powers to summon Satan. *The Dybbuk,* a 1937 Yiddish film that became an international success, was based on S. Ansky's celebrated play combining shtetl folklore and hasidic legend. In this beautifully rendered portrait of pre-Holocaust Eastern European Jewish life, a lovesick yeshiva student dies when he attempts to call on the dark powers of kabbalah and his migrating soul enters the body of his beloved.

In *The Golem,* the revered kabbalist Rabbi Loew (Albert Steinruck) is similarly distraught when he hears of the emperor's edict banishing the Jews, who live apart from the Christian population behind large gates in the ghetto. Having already read in the stars that disaster is imminent, Rabbi Loew is determined to save his people, who are accused of practicing black magic. Rabbi Loew compels Satanic powers to reveal the magic word that will bring the golem he molds of clay to life. Wearing a tall wizard's hat, he causes a ring of fire to engulf him and to dance in the air around him. A mask appears, breathing smoke, and reveals the word, *Aemaet* (the Hebrew word for truth, more commonly spelled *emet*), which the rabbi writes on paper and inserts into a star of David that is placed on the golem's chest.

The rabbi brings the golem to court, where he attempts to elicit sympathy from the superstitious emperor by magically projecting moving images of "our people's history." The castle begins to collapse when the court laughs at the sight of Moses in the wilderness, and the golem is brought in to save the emperor in return for his pardon of the Jews. The golem's work being done, the rabbi removes the star and renders the creature inert.

The rabbi's daughter Miriam (Wegener's wife Lyda Salmonova), who has secretly fallen in love with the Christian courtier Flavius, is caught in a compromising position with her lover, and the rabbi's assistant, enraged with jealousy, brings the golem back to life to get rid of his gentile rival. The golem throws Flavius from the rooftop, then sets fire to the rabbi's house, and drags Miriam by the hair through the streets. Wandering outside the ghetto gates, he meets some gentile children. One little girl offers him an apple, and as he gently picks the child up in his arms, she removes his magic talisman, and the golem returns to lifeless clay.

The Golem features one fleeting negative Jewish stereotype: a greedy servant who is bribed by Flavius to bring Miriam his letter. But Flavius is by far the most sinister and foolish character in the drama, which generally conveys sympathy for the predicament of the Jews and respect for the power of their teachings.

13

Au Revoir, Les Enfants

Orion Classics (1987)
Cast: Gaspard Manesse, Raphael Fejito
Directed by: Louis Malle
103 minutes [PG]

Forty years before he wrote and directed *Au Revoir, Les Enfants,* Louis Malle stood in an icy school courtyard watching the Gestapo haul away the headmaster of his Catholic boarding school and three Jewish students the priests were sheltering under false names. Malle has said he waited so long to record the seminal event from his youth, which had haunted him throughout his life, because he was too frightened of its power to deal with it.

Malle's international hit is one of the very best in a series of excellent Holocaust dramas depicting a young Jew in peril. A surprising number of French films dealing with the Holocaust era focus on the plight of a Jewish child. Perhaps because children in jeopardy naturally evoke audience sympathy, they are often presented as victims of Nazi persecution. Certainly, their inherent innocence makes them a fitting symbol for the innocent Jews who died in the Holocaust. The French may simply feel pity for the 1.5 millon children murdered by the Nazis or even feel guilty about how readily the Vichy government handed the nation's Jewish children over to the Gestapo. Whatever the reason for this common theme, the best films of this subgenre evoke more than easy pity. They invite us to contemplate the terrible bond that links victims and witnesses.

Malle's autobiographical drama tells the story of a young Jewish boy sheltered by Christians in the countryside of Nazi-occupied France. A similar scenario unfolds in Claude Berri's *The Two of Us* (1968), which was also based on its director's own childhood. French filmmaker Michel Drach also recorded his traumatic boyhood escape from Nazi-occupied France in *Les Violons du Bal* (1974), turning his story of persecution into a poignant personal film. Like Berri's heartwarming and humorous story about a Jewish boy who hides his identity from the antiSemitic old farmer who shelters and adores him, *Au Revoir, Les Enfants* is a heartfelt story of a friendship complicated by the precarious position of the Jew in hiding.

Julien Quentin (Gaspard Manesse), filling in for the young Malle, is the pampered son in a wealthy Parisian family who is sent to a private school in the countryside in 1943. Only vaguely aware of Jewish persecution, Julien asks his older brother what the Jews are guilty of. "Of being smarter than us and of crucifying Christ," his brother tells him, attributing anti-Semitism to envy and ignorance. When a new boy arrives in school, Julien finds himself curiously drawn to him. He's not sure what to make of the intelligent, sensitive, mysterious Jean Bonnet (Raphael Fejito) and senses something is amiss. Secretly examining Jean's belongings, he finds the name Jean Kippelstein written in a book. Realizing that Jean is a Jew in hiding, Julien befriends the boy who is fated to perish in Auschwitz.

In reality, Malle did not befriend any of the Jewish boys being hidden at his school or even realize that they were Jewish. But imagining how he might have felt if he had gave him the dramatic framework on which to hang his

THE HIDDEN JEW   Gaspard Manesse, left, plays a Christian schoolboy in Nazi-occupied France who discovers his classmate (Raphael Fejito) is a Jew being sheltered at his Catholic boarding school in Louis Malle's revered autobiographical drama, *Au Revoir, Les Enfants.*

traumatic memory. The responsibility that comes with the knowledge of Jean's terrible secret becomes the theme of the film, which Malle underscores by having Julien inadvertently betray Jean with a backward glance that points him out to the Gestapo. It is a split second that will cause Julien guilt for the rest of his life. The film, which focuses on Julien's horror and helplessness in the face of a great tragedy that has suddenly become quite personal, builds slowly and surely to its understated yet devastating finale.

Malle was no doubt wise in waiting until he summoned the emotional strength for this unburdening and acquired the artistic maturity to do his subject justice. Hailed as a masterpiece, the Oscar-nominated *Au Revoir, Les Enfants* won numerous international awards, including three Cesars (the French equivalent of the Oscar), and restored the late director's declining reputation. *Au Revoir, Les Enfants* is widely regarded as Malle's best film, beautifully performed by two unknown actors and directed with quiet assurance. *Lacombe, Lucien,* his 1974 film dealing with the relationship between a French collaborator and a Jewish woman, is also highly regarded, although it generated controversy at the time of its release because it did not portray its Jewish characters with complete sympathy.

Jean, on the other hand, is the object of the audience's total sympathy. He is shown to be gifted and valiant. Ironically, he is the only student in this religious institution who prays with utter devotion—albeit secretly in his bed at night. This scene, which Julien witnesses, also reveals that although Jean is forced to hide his Jewish identity, he has not lost it. Similarly, the young hero of Berri's film washes in private so no one will see that he is circumcised, yet maintains his Jewish pride by tricking his kindly adoptive "grandpa" into revealing the absurdity of his prejudice.

This underlying theme of children whose sense of Jewish identification becomes intensified when they are forced to hide their identity surfaces as a major issue in *David* (1979), another autobiographical Holocaust drama based on a boyhood spent in hiding. *David,* the first German Holocaust film to be directed by a Jew (Peter Lilienthal), offers a haunting and proudly pro-Jewish, first-person account of a young man who becomes "the last Jew in Berlin." But as fine a portrait of desperation and resilience as *David* is, *Au Revoir, Les Enfants* is remarkable because it does not ask us to imagine ourselves in the ultimately unimaginable position of the victim. Rather, the story is told from the perspective of the horrified, powerless, yet guilt-stricken bystander. A tale of lost innocence, *Au Revoir, Les Enfants* is, above all, a story about national shame made personal.

14

Almonds and Raisins: A History of the Yiddish Cinema

Brook Productions (1988)
DIRECTED BY: Russ Karel
90 minutes [Not rated]

The Jazz Singer changed the course of motion picture history, ushering in the age of sound. A melodrama about a cantor's son who chooses show business over singing in *shul,* the first talkie proved particularly popular with Jewish audiences, who enjoyed seeing their experience reflected on the screen. The success of *The Jazz Singer* led to a new cottage industry in the cinema, the Yiddish film.

Almonds and Raisins: A History of the Yiddish Cinema is ranked among the best Jewish films not because it is a brilliant documentary, but because it so ably pays homage to this vibrant and varied Jewish art form and chronicles the brief but rich period in which it flourished. Between 1927 and 1939, more than 300 feature films were produced for the booming Yiddish-speaking market. By 1920, New York City had become the largest Jewish city in the world, a haven for more than 1.5 million refugees from Eastern Europe. Yiddish films found a large and appreciative audience among these first generation immigrants struggling to forge a new life in the *freiland.*

Filmmakers Russ Karel and David Elstein offer an overview of this often neglected domain of expressly Jewish films. The documentary is especially useful in guiding the viewer to the classics of the Yiddish cinema, which are put into historical and cultural context in this sampling of unique films steeped in Jewish values. Narrated by Orson Welles, *Almonds and Raisins: A History of the Yiddish Cinema* features film clips from the most notable Yiddish films, most of which are now available on video. The illuminating documentary pointedly contrasts Yiddish films—made by Jews for Jews—with Hollywood films, which expressed the assimilationist values of the Jewish moguls who ran the major studios and produced movies primarily geared for a gentile audience.

The Jazz Singer, for example, is the story of a young man (Al Jolson, whose life inspired the film) who fulfills the immigrant dream of success at

THE YIDDISH HELEN HAYES Molly Picon stars in the popular Yiddish musical *Yidl Mitn Fiddle,* one of the films tributed in *Almonds and Raisins: A History of the Yiddish Cinema,* which examines movies made by Jews expressly for a Jewish audience. (National Center for Jewish Film)

the price of his Jewish identity. Although his ability to make it in the New World is presented as a triumph in the film, to many first generation Jews who saw the movie, it was nothing less than a tragedy. *The Cantor's Son,* released in the *mamaloschen* in 1937, was a direct rebuke to *The Jazz Singer.* One of many Yiddish films that examined the pressure to assimilate for material gain, *The Cantor's Son* warned of the dangers of gentile influence. In the Yiddish version, popular singer Moishe Oysher, on whose life the film was based, resists the temptations of fame and rejects the option of intermarriage to return to his homeland and his roots.

The survey begins with 1932's *Uncle Moses,* the story of a young radical intellectual who runs into a conflict with the title character, a successful immigrant who has brought his entire village to America to share in his short-lived happiness. *Green Fields* (1937), Edgar Ulmer's acclaimed screen adaptation of Peretz Hirchbein's 1916 play, depicts a disaffected yeshiva student who finds the light of truth in a return to the land rather than in the synagogue. Codirected by Jacob Ben-Ami, this low-budget, artful but unprententious film, shot in five days on a New Jersey farm, conveyed a need for roots, a desire for purpose, and a respect for nature. Politically progressive and artistically dignified, *Green Fields* was declared an instant classic.

Also highly regarded, *The Dybbuk* (1937), based on S. Ansky's celebrated Yiddish play, took an expressionistic and mystical approach in its depiction of folklore, superstition, and religion. Inspired by shtetl folktales and hasidic legends, the supernatural story concerns a lovesick yeshiva student who calls on kabbalistic powers, dies, and returns as a spirit inhabiting the body of his beloved. Similarly successful, *Tevye* (1939), based on eight Sholem Aleichem stories written between 1895 and 1915 that were later immortalized on stage and screen as *Fiddler on the Roof,* was the only Yiddish film with an overtly pro-Zionist message. Famed Yiddish Art Theater director and star Maurice Shwartz wrote, directed, and played the title role, a man whose *tsuris* rivals that of Job.

Joseph Green's hugely popular *Yidl Mitn Fiddle* (1936), starring Molly Picon, mixed folklore, humor, and music. Its pre-*Yentl* plot concerned a young fiddle player who disguises herself as a man and falls in love with a fellow fiddler. Filmed in Poland, it was one of many Yiddish films to reflect the immigrants' nostalgia for the shtetl life they had left behind for the poverty and hardships of the ghetto. The first true international hit of the Yiddish cinema, it launched the screen career of stage star Picon, known as the Yiddish Helen Hayes. (Hayes, hearing this, told Picon she'd be pleased to be known as the *shiksa* Molly Picon.) The talents of the popular pint-sized actress, perfectly cast as the ungainly gamine, were featured again in Green's *Mamele* (1938), the tale of a plucky "little mother" who cares for her ungrateful siblings and unappreciative father. The consummate Yiddish comedienne was well cast in this Cinderella story, a vivacious Yiddish variation of Hollywood's screwball comedies of the 1930s.

Green's final film, *A Brivele der Mamen* (1939), filmed back to back with *Mamele* in Poland, detailed the grim reality of the immigrants' new life and expressed the sorrow of their crushed dreams. Following the outbreak of war in 1939, production in Poland stopped and, by 1941, the American Yiddish cinema came to an end.

Yiddish films are filled with the leave-takings, separations, and parental losses that characterized immigrant life. The Yiddish cinema also offered comforting images of the religious ceremonies that bonded communities and families. Many of the films featured musical interludes that added to the pathos of the stories or provided comic relief. Although most of the films were melodramas with romantic and domestic themes, Yiddish filmmakers dabbled in other genres as well, including the Western. (Although the clip is not identified in the film, the Western was *The Yiddische Cowboy*. For a more in-depth examination of the specific films, see J. Hoberman's excellent book, *Bridge of Light: Yiddish Film Between Two Worlds.*)

Almonds and Raisins: A History of the Yiddish Cinema includes interviews with noted Yiddish film actors Herschel Bernardi (who made his debut as a child in *Green Fields*), Zvee Scooler, Leo Fuchs, Miriam Kressyler, and director Joseph Green. These surviving stars reflect on a time when the new Jews of America sought refuge at the movies, where their worst fears and fondest hopes were played out in the only language they understood.

15

Enemies, a Love Story

Morgan Creek (1989)
CAST: Lena Olin, Ron Silver, Anjelica Huston, Margaret Sophie Stein,
Alan King, Judith Malina
DIRECTED BY: Paul Mazursky
119 minutes [R]

There are no people in Isaac Bashevis Singer's first novel set in America, only ghosts. These Holocaust survivors are the walking dead, bodies futilely flapping like headless chickens, their severed souls condemned to eternal torment. *Enemies, a Love Story,* written in Yiddish in 1966 and published in English in 1972, deals with the Holocaust's legacy of emotional pain. Still, as its title promises, this tragicomedy is a love story, a last gasp of agonizing, exhilarating passion.

Of the many films attempting to portray the post-traumatic effects of the Holocaust, Paul Mazursky's adaptation of Singer's complex story comes closest to evoking the survivors' lingering despair. The only adaptation of material by Singer that does the great Yiddish writer justice, *Enemies, a Love Story* is an almost perfectly realized screen translation. Paul Mazursky, who directed, cowrote, and played a small role in the film, has created a work of poignance, pathos, bitterness, and heartbreak. The performances are first-rate, and the Oscar-nominated script, coauthored by Mazursky and Roger Simon, captures the tragicomic tone of the book. The plaintive, wailing but lively klezmer music that runs through the movie provides a fitting accompaniment to the haunting film, rated among the greatest Jewish films for its substance as well as artistic excellence.

Herman Broder (Ron Silver), the polygamous hero of *Enemies, a Love Story,* is a man whose psyche has been shattered. Herman spent the war years hiding in a hayloft (the movie opens with a nightmare memory of his discovery by Nazis) protected by the family servant, a Polish peasant named Yadwiga (Margaret Sophie Stein). It is now 1949, and Herman is living in Coney Island with Yadwiga, whom he has married out of gratitude. Herman tells his simple bride, the only non-Jewish character in the story, that he is a traveling book salesman in order to justify his frequent overnight absences. He

TRAGIC SEX FARCE Based on a novel by Isaac Bashevis Singer, *Enemies, a Love Story* depicts the predicament of a psychically scarred Holocaust survivor (Ron Silver) whose wife (Anjelica Huston), presumed dead, returns to further complicate his fragmented existence.

spends these nights with his mistress, Masha (Lena Olin), a psychically scarred survivor of the camps who lives with her mother (Judith Malina). Herman actually works as a ghostwriter (with the emphasis on ghost) for a rich, vulgar, and fatuous rabbi (Alan King), a symbol of assimilationist success.

Herman cannot leave the helpless and adoring Yadwiga, to whom he feels bound by honor, and he cannot live without the beyond-help and disdainful Masha, with whom he is bound by shared pain. Only in their desperate love-making does Herman feel alive again. With Masha, he is able to forget his torment, if only for a few brief moments. Herman's attentions are further splintered when his first wife, long presumed dead, rises from the ashes. Tamara (Oscar-nominee Anjelica Huston) was shot twice and fell into a mass grave but crawled out after dark and escaped. Their reunion is tense, however, and not just because Herman has married a non-Jewish peasant. Herman and Tamara had something less than a happy marriage before enduring their separate traumas. Tamara no longer has any feelings for Herman; she claims she has no feelings at all. Nevertheless, they are bound by the past and turn to each other for comfort.

Tamara rightly describes Herman as "a lost man." She tells him, "The truth is, you're still hiding in the hayloft." "Yes," he replies. "Dat's the truth." Herman, who feels abandoned by a God who "doesn't care," can no longer find any meaning in life. He has lost all hope, purpose, and will. Unmoored, he goes whichever way the wind blows him. Masha, a volatile, jealous, and profoundly disturbed woman of great intelligence and terrible passion, does not believe Tamara is alive. When Masha becomes pregnant, she demands that Herman marry her. Although he already has two wives, he is helpless to argue and marries her, although the pregnancy turns out to have been imagined. Meanwhile, Yadwiga, who has longed to become a Jew and have a child by Herman, does become pregnant.

A sex farce steeped in suffering and sorrow, this film describes the ways people need each other. Hungry for a human connection that cannot save them, the characters cling to one another like drowning victims pulling each other under, unable to let go.

In his only film dealing with the Holocaust, Mazursky is able to evoke the intensity of the characters' damaged psychic state, yet the film never becomes hysterical or mawkish. The characters may be foolish and deluded, but Mazursky allows them their dignity. He respects their grief and guilt, without wallowing in their misery. Mazursky, whose films almost always deal with Jewish themes and characters, was named best director by the New York Film Critics Circle for his graceful direction.

Enemies, a Love Story is a gripping and wrenching film, but it is tempered with wit and irony. Writing a speech for the rabbi, Herman pauses to note, "If the Talmud is such a great book, why doesn't it explain what a man should do with three wives?" Ironically, it is the convert Yadwiga who maintains not only faith but an attachment to Judaism. She reprimands Herman for not observing the Sabbath, and when Herman slaps her after refusing to attend Yom Kippur services, she cries in genuine anguish and astonishment, "Herman, you have hit me on the holiest day of the year!"

Like many other Holocaust survivors who have made strong impressions on the screen, most notably the title characters in *The Pawnbroker* and *Madame Rosa,* Herman's faith has been shaken, much like Singer's was. *Enemies, a Love Story* examines the devastating effect of the Holocaust on Jewish religion, a subject explored even more fully in *The Quarrel.*

The actors inhabit their characters completely, giving subtle yet deeply felt performances. Silver, an unlikely Lothario, portrays Herman's delirious confusion and turmoil, which is grounded in a painful self-awareness. He sees his ridiculous situation clearly and yet is unable to do anything about it. He has lost his will as well as his faith. Olin and Huston, neither of whom is Jewish, are also excellent. Olin evokes Masha's intoxicating sensuality and destructive despair; Huston suggests the weight of Tamara's tragic loss. Stein plays the optimistic Yadwiga with beguiling sincerity.

From his window, Herman gazes at the Ferris wheel at Coney Island. The whirling Wonder Wheel serves as an apt metaphor for this dizzying story about the cycle of life and death. In the end, Herman has disappeared, and Masha has killed herself. But Tamara and Yadwiga are raising Herman's child, whom they have named Masha. The crazy world keeps turning after all.

16

The Great Dictator

The Charles Chaplin Film Corporation (1940)
CAST: Charles Chaplin, Paulette Goddard, Jack Oakie
DIRECTED BY: Charles Chaplin
128 minutes [Not rated]

The Hollywood studios, owned and operated almost exclusively by Jews, stood silent as Hitler instituted a program of state-sanctioned anti-Semitism during the 1930s. In fact, as the Jews of Germany were stripped of citizenship and its attendant rights, the Jewish moguls who controlled the motion picture industry responded by all but obliterating Jews from the screen as well.

Ironically, the only film of the era to confront the rise of fascism in Europe head-on as well as to openly attack the antiSemitic policies that formed the core of Hitler's agenda was made by Charlie Chaplin, who was not Jewish. Chaplin wrote, directed, produced, and starred in *The Great Dictator,* which costarred his then-wife, Jewish actress Paulette Goddard (born Pauline Marion Levee). Chaplin plays two roles in the scathing satire, appearing as the megalomaniacal tyrant Adenoid Hynkel (Hitler) as well as a Jewish barber—the only overtly Jewish character of his career. The movie culminates in a case of mistaken identity, rife with irony, when the Jewish barber and "The Fooey" (The Führer) change places.

Chaplin's popularity, independent status, and financial security placed him in the rare position of being able to make a film on a controversial subject if he chose to. After careful deliberation and a good many warnings against undertaking such a polemical project, "the colossus of the cinema"—as Chaplin was dubbed by the *New York Times*—decided to make *The Great Dictator,* which viciously satirized Hitler and condemned his persecution of the Jews. Chaplin spent $2 million of his own money to create a film American officials warned him would inevitably be banned. As it turned out, *The Great Dictator* was banned only by Hitler, who prohibited its screening in Nazi Germany.

Chaplin took a great risk championing a cause that was by no means universally endorsed by the American public. Even after war broke out shortly before the filming of *The Great Dictator* began, Americans were divided into isolationist and interventionist camps, and the American government was offi-

ADENOID HYNKEL Charles Chaplin wrote and directed the only movie of the Holocaust era to directly attack Hitler's program of Jewish persecution, *The Great Dictator,* in which Chaplin plays "Der Fooey" as well as his lookalike, a Jewish barber.

cially neutral. The daring nature of Chaplin's full-front cinematic assault on the madness of the Third Reich indeed caused quite a furor. The pre-publicity assured the film instant notoriety and afforded it must-see status. The most overtly political film of Chaplin's career, *The Great Dictator* was also his greatest financial success. The biggest hit of the year, the film earned Oscar nominations for best actor, screenplay, and picture. The movie met with mixed reviews, however, and its release coincided with the beginning of the beloved comic's decline in popularity.

This fall from favor may have been related to Chaplin's decision to take such a strong stand in a time of timidity. It could, however, be connected to another risk Chaplin took with *The Great Dictator,* his first talking picture. More than a decade after the advent of sound in 1927, Chaplin was still resisting dialogue. But after the release of *Modern Times* in 1936, Chaplin decided he could no longer prolong the inevitable. The world would finally hear Chaplin's voice. Chaplin wanted to be sure that when he spoke he had something to say. Although his previous films were not without social significance, the auteur was not known as a political filmmaker. What he chose to say in *The Great Dictator,* however, was just what one might expect from the Little Tramp.

Film scholars have often noted that the Little Tramp resembles a Jewish stock figure, the ostracized outcast, an outsider who survives by his ingenuity, and whose dignity and compassion remain intact despite repeated humiliations at the hands of authority figures. It was quite fitting for the Little Tramp to open his mouth and speak up for the underdogs being trampled under the stamped boot of totalitarianism. Chaplin, whose sentiments were inextricably bound to those of his popular screen persona, found he could not stand idly by while human rights—and lives—were brutally annihilated.

The Great Dictator opens with titles informing us that "Between the wars liberty took a nose dive and humanity was kicked around somewhat." We then meet a hapless Jewish soldier (Chaplin) in World War I, whose comic exploits in battle end in a plane crash that leaves him with amnesia. The nameless Jewish barber languishes in a hospital, blissfully unaware of current events in his native Tomania—a word choice that suggests a sickening madness—through which Hynkel and his storm troopers are now goosestepping. Upon his escape, the little Jew returns to his barbershop, the windows now smeared with the word *Jew,* and is baffled to find himself an endangered species.

Meanwhile, back at the Reichstag, Hynkel delivers a rousing speech to the "sons and daughters of the double cross," accompanied by his henchmen Garbitsch (a reference to Goebbels) and Herring (a reference to Goering and to a Jewish delicacy). Although Chaplin employs only German gibberish, to great comic effect, the hateful essence of the speech is clear. Hynkel's Teutonic ranting and raving, filled with such expressions as "Wiener Schnitzel," "Katzenjammer Kids," and "Free Sprechen Shtunk," is a dead-on spoof of Hitler's vitriolic speech-making style. Following the address, Garbitsch (Henry Daniell) advises him that "violence against the Jews might take the people's minds off their stomachs," and Hynkel agrees to make even more trouble for the Jews in the ghetto. Thus, Chaplin depicts not only the persecution of the Jews but suggests the political motive for their scapegoating.

The rest of the film cuts back and forth between the increasingly absurd antics of the demented dictator and the plight of the Jewish barber and the brave young Jewess he loves (Goddard). The lovers are eventually aided by Schultz (Reginald Gardiner), who defects from Hynkel's corps because he cannot stomach the "stupid, ruthless persecution of innocent people." Hynkel invades the neighboring country of Austerlich (Austria) and engages in a rivalry with Napaloni (Mussolini), the tyrant of Bacteria, played as a bumbling buffoon with an Italian accent by Jack Oakie.

The movie's finale finds the Jewish barber, now masquerading as Hynkel, making a speech broadcast live on radio. Chaplin composed a searing six-minute speech denouncing "the brutes who have risen to power" and exhorting the people to "fight for a decent world, a world of reason." This impassioned plea ends the film, which leaves the fate of its characters unresolved.

The Great Dictator is filled with displays of Chaplin's classic comic brilliance, most famously a balletic sequence involving Hynkel and a balloon globe, set to music by Wagner, the anti-Semitic composer who served as the musical mascot of the Nazi party. In a hilarious scene counterpointing this parody of the power-mad dictator, the barber shaves a customer in perfect time to Brahms's Hungarian Dance Number 5. Chaplin mocks Hitler's rabid racism, his stupidity and duplicity, and his utter lack of humanity, noting that he displays "the hatred of the unloved." That Chaplin manages to tackle such a serious subject with humor without becoming tasteless is quite a triumph.

Still, the movie raises the question of whether such monstrous evil and monumental suffering are suitable subjects for satire. In his autobiography, written with the benefit of hindsight, Chaplin said that, although he felt at the time that Hitler must be laughed at, had he known the full extent of the atrocities to come, he would not have tried to deflate Hitler with comedy. Much of the movie's bitter humor is indeed uncomfortably prophetic. The Jewish barber learns that business is slow because "most of the men are in concentration camps," so he tries his hand at a beauty parlor. There is even a mention of a new lethal "gas," which foreshadows one of the gruesome methods employed in the Final Solution.

Despite such chilling foreshadowing of the Holocaust, *The Great Dictator* is far from unrelentingly grim. By juxtaposing the two characters' stories, which are given equal screen time, Chaplin is able to balance his stinging satire of insane evil with the sweetness and pathos that typically categorize his films. *The Great Dictator* continued to generate controversy and to find an audience long after its release. Chaplin went on to become more politically active and soon came to be identified as a leftist social critic.

Although following America's entry into the war, Hollywood began cranking out war pictures that were vaguely antifascist, they rarely made more than a passing mention of the Jewish persecution that was about to spring into full-blown genocide. Famed German–Jewish expatriate Ernst Lubitsch was one of the only Hollywood directors at the time to touch on the anti-Semitism of the Third Reich. His classic 1942 comedy, *To Be or Not to Be,* which was also criticized as tasteless for satirizing the Nazi menace, starred Jewish comic Jack Benny and Carole Lombard as Polish theater stars who execute a daring ruse to save the Polish underground. Although created by Jews, *To Be or Not to Be,* remade by Mel Brooks in 1983, featured only a minor Jewish character.

The Great Dictator remains by far the most outspokenly anti-Nazi film of its day—and of the next two decades. Although a comedy, *The Great Dictator* expressed the moral outrage of American Jews and all those sympathetic citizens who rallied around them during those dark days. The movie puts to shame the Hollywood Jews who did not add their voices to Chaplin's lone cry for sanity in a world gone mad.

17

The Apprenticeship of Duddy Kravitz

Paramount Pictures (1974)
CAST: Richard Dreyfuss, Jack Warden, Randy Quaid, Joseph Wiseman,
Micheline Lanctot, Henry Ramer
DIRECTED BY: Ted Kotcheff
121 minutes [PG]

Duddy Kravitz is one of the most provocative and vivid characters in Jewish literature and film. A schemer, a hustler, a *tummler,* a *gonif,* a nobody who wants to be a somebody, Duddy is driven by burning ambition. His ambition, in turn, is fueled by feelings of insecurity and a desire to prove his worth. While some viewers are appalled by Duddy's craven materialism, his unethical business practices, and his unmasked aggression, others react sympathetically to his ingenuity and enthusiasm, his defiance in the face of anti-Semitism, and his eagerness to please. Most viewers, however, are torn between admiration and disdain for this complicated, conniving character, which is what makes Duddy so intriguing.

The Apprenticeship of Duddy Kravitz is based on the celebrated fourth novel by Canadian writer Mordecai Richler, written in 1959 and set in Montreal in the late 1940s. Richler also wrote the Oscar-nominated screenplay for this invigorating film directed by Ted Kotcheff, which was one of the first international hits to come out of Canada during the 1970s and the winner of the Berlin Film Festival's prize for best film.

The Apprenticeship of Duddy Kravitz depicts an undeniably unattractive Jewish quality: a desire to achieve material success at all costs. But the sardonic screenplay, like the book, goes to great lengths to explain its root cause, to place Duddy's obsessive drive in the larger context of the Jewish immigrant experience.

Duddy (Richard Dreyfuss) is just a "*pisher* of 19" according to his coarse, cab-driving father Max (Jack Warden). His rich and refined Uncle Benjy (Joseph Wiseman) calls him a *pusherke,* a pushy Jew. But Duddy describes himself as a real comer, a *macher* in the making. He's on his way to becoming a big shot, and nothing will stop him. Crude and crass, Duddy may not have any class or taste, but he knows how to schmooze, he's got chutzpah, and he is loaded with money-making inspiration. A self-taught expert at playing the angles, Duddy is a study in determination.

Duddy has been raised on his father's stories of the Boy Wonder, Jerry Dingleman (Henry Ramer), a local punk who built an empire from nothing. Max, a part-time pimp who will do anything for a buck, considers the drug-dealing gangster a local boy who made good. Max is a second generation, working-class Jew still struggling in vain to get ahead—an example of the Jewish immigrant who has adopted the American ethic and its emphasis on material gain. Duddy also embraces this perversion of Jewish values—with a vengeance. His grandfather (Zvee Scooler), however, is still rooted in Old World values, desiring permanence and security but clinging to a moral code that places personal integrity above wealth. Duddy adores the old man, the only person in his family who has ever appreciated him, and takes heed when his *Zaida* tells him that a man without land is nothing.

Duddy takes a summer job as a waiter at a Jewish resort, where he is scorned by the snooty college crowd of Jewish summer waiters who have climbed a few rungs higher on the socioeconomic ladder than Duddy. "It's cretinous little money-grubbers like Kravitz who cause anti-Semitism," sneers a tennis-playing McGill medical student. Later, Uncle Benjy reiterates this derision, telling Duddy he's "a little Jewboy on the make. You make me ashamed."

Duddy finds a kindred spirit and future mentor among the vulgar, greedy, nouveau riche guests. Mr. Farber (Joe Silver), a prosperous scrap yard owner, coaches Duddy in the ways of the business world. It's every man for himself, screw or be screwed, Duddy learns from this dubious teacher, who advises him to trust no one—a sentiment that comes from centuries of persecution. Duddy indeed takes advantage of people, psychologically justifying his actions as revenge for his own historic abuse. Duddy is an underdog who bites back. "The Jew has no friends," cautions Mr. Farber, who underscores his "us against them" mentality by referring to the prevailing and presumably hostile social establishment as "the white man." Indeed, when Duddy discovers a beautiful lake and decides to buy the surrounding land and develop it, he finds that the farmers who own the property won't sell to a Jew. Duddy enlists his gentile girlfriend Yvette (Micheline Lanctot) to purchase the land for him, and he sets about raising the required capital.

Duddy's most creative fund-raising venture involves the creation of a motion picture company, Dudley Kane Enterprises, that films weddings and bar mitzvahs. The grand plan is almost ruined by the dissolute director (Denholm Elliott) Duddy takes as a partner, a pretentious has-been who claims he couldn't make it in Hollywood because he didn't speak Yiddish, an antiSemitic reference to the Jewish domination of Hollywood. The editorialized film of the

Farber bar mitzvah—produced from the perspective of an outsider who completely misreads the ceremony—proves outrageously hilarious, the film's comic highlight. The scene also serves a symbolic function, echoing Duddy's misreading of his grandfather and his distortion of traditional Jewish values.

Duddy runs into serious problems when he hires Virgil (Randy Quaid), the dopey and trusting Texas version of the *schlimazel,* and allows him to drive a truck even though he's an epileptic—a member of another maligned minority and the object of discrimination. When the inevitable tragedy strikes, Duddy is forced to face his irresponsible, unscrupulous actions. Although shaken, Duddy eventually returns to his scheming ways and succeeds in buying the land with money stolen from Virgil. He is spurred on by competition from the Boy Wonder, whom Duddy now gleefully dismisses as a *schnorrer.* Duddy, whose name is a diminutive of David, symbolically slays the giant gangster.

The victory is hollow, however, as Duddy loses the approval of his grandfather, the person he has most wanted to please, as well as the love and respect of Yvette, a decent woman Duddy has failed to appreciate because she's not Jewish. The look on Duddy's face at the film's conclusion conveys that he has lost much more than he has gained. He has debased himself and his heritage; and although he has achieved wealth, he has become morally bankrupt.

Dreyfuss, an actor who has consistently applied his distinctly Jewish persona to a wide variety of roles, was just beginning to make a name for himself when he was cast in this career-making part. Dreyfuss gives a fabulously shaded performance as the likable loser. His Duddy is charming and annoying, vulnerable and arrogant, nervy and nervous. He knows his limitations, knows that others laugh at him or feel superior to him. This self-awareness is affecting, as is his active devotion to the very members of his family who dismiss and deride him.

Duddy may be a swindler, but he is also capable of brutal honesty. Meeting with a wealthy W.A.S.P. tycoon who clearly disapproves of his nakedly grasping hunger for money, Duddy points to a portrait on the mansion wall, noting that no doubt his ancestor's fingernails are not so clean. Each generation has had to claw its way up, Duddy realizes, so that the next generation can enjoy the luxury of taking the high moral ground. Duddy is far from admirable, but the film clearly depicts the social, economic, and psychological forces that shape him. Like the antihero of Budd Schulberg's famed novel, *What Makes Sammy Run?,* Duddy falls victim to the American dream and the dilemma of assimilation. His brother Lennie (Allen Rosenthal) has taken the more approved road, studying to become a doctor, but he is quick to shed his Jewish identity, which is also depicted as a grave mistake.

THE PUSHY JEW   Richard Dreyfuss plays an aggressive hustler who has adopted the materialistic values of his father, Jack Warden, in *The Apprenticeship of Duddy Kravitz*.

Richler consciously explored issues of Jewish identity and the crisis of assimilation in subsequent books such as *Joshua Then and Now,* the story of an aggressive, defiant, and complex Jew who crashes W.A.S.P. society, which was made into a film starring James Woods and Alan Arkin in 1985. Richler, along with director Kotcheff, plumbs the depth of the Jewish psyche in *The Apprenticeship of Duddy Kravitz.* The knowing film is a cautionary tale that depicts a low point in the contemporary Jewish experience, which it regards with dismay tempered by understanding.

18

Blazing Saddles

Warner Bros. (1974)
CAST: Gene Wilder, Cleavon Little, Harvey Korman, Madeline Kahn
DIRECTED BY: Mel Brooks
93 minutes [R]

Armed with outrageous irreverence and borsht-belt humor, Mel Brooks brazenly galloped onto the hallowed ground of the movie Western with this scattershot comedy that took unsteady aim at everything from Hollywood movie conventions to the racism inherent in the pioneer ethic. *Blazing Saddles* laid to rest the romantic myth of the Old West, winning the adulation of middle America even as it ran roughshod over her sacred icons.

Brooks's first big hit as well as his most successful film, *Blazing Saddles* earned $45 million at the box office in North America alone, was the most-viewed movie on its first year of release on HBO, and is still on many critics' short list of Hollywood's all-time funniest films, although *The Producers* is considered by some to be a superior, or at least more original, comedy. The unapologetically Jewish writer and director had burst onto the American movie scene in 1968 with *The Producers,* an audacious and edgy black comedy starring Jewish comics Zero Mostel and Gene Wilder playing two stock Jewish figures, the scheming shyster and the timid accountant. The producers stage an egregious Nazi musical as a scam, but the plan backfires when *Springtime for Hitler* becomes a hit. Although Brooks's daring screenplay won an Oscar, the broad farce was only a modest success.

Brooks hit his stride with *Blazing Saddles* and proceeded to forge a lucrative, if wildly uneven, career parodying movie genres. By taking the familiar Western formula—decent, stout-hearted white folks settling the lawless West—and turning it on its head, the deliriously multicultural movie was perfectly suited to the anarchic attitudes of its time. A mad, mad, mad, mad Western, *Blazing Saddles* applied a zany and satirical Jewish sensibility to the stock story of a one-horse—and one Baskin-Robbins flavor—frontier town saved from the bad guys by the good guys. In the topsy-turvy universe of Brooks's Wild West, however, the good guys are the very ethnic minorities so conspiciously absent from Westerns.

Brooks's oddball heroes are the black sheriff, Bart (Cleavon Little) and his Jewish sidekick, the has-been gunslinger Jim (Gene Wilder), known in better days as the Waco Kid. The bad guys are led by avaricious land baron Hedley Lamarr (Harvey Korman), who is trying to buy up a town that is soon to be a rich railroad stop, and his bigoted cowboy henchman Taggart, played by Western icon Slim Pickens, one of the few non-Jewish actors in the cast. In this revisionist Western, even the Indians are Jews. When Bart's family—segregated from the white pioneers and forced to ride at the back of the wagon train—is attacked by Indians, the chief (played by Brooks in full feather) expresses surprise at finding *schvartzers* taking part in the westward expansion. Speaking Yiddish, he tells them to go in health.

The encounter between Bart's black family and the Yiddish-speaking Indians is not simply an expression of solidarity between two oppressed, marginalized minorities, however. It also suggests the tension that exists between the two historic victims of discrimination. There is some debate as to whether the term *schvartzer* is derogatory (controversial comic Jackie Mason defends his use of the word by noting that it is the only word in the Yiddish language for black), but the final comment by the chief clearly conveys the sense that blacks are even lower on the totem pole than Jews *or* Indians. "They're even darker than we are," the chief observes with a shudder of disgust—or is it pity?—after the family rides on unmolested.

Outcasts eventually unite in *Blazing Saddles,* which culminates in a triumphant alliance between oppressed black, Chinese, and Irish railroad workers and the initially reluctant, racist townfolk. Significantly, the victory is one of brain over brawn, as Bart shrewdly and imaginatively devises a plan to fool the forces that Lamarr has marshaled against them. Brooks gets in another lick against prejudice by having Lamarr hire a posse composed of Arabs, Nazis, Hell's Angels, and klansmen.

Although Brooks generally gets full credit for *Blazing Saddles,* in fact it is the product of an alliance between black and Jewish comics. Richard Pryor collaborated with Brooks on the screenplay, along with a handful of Jewish writers: Norman Steinberg, Alan Unger, and then-unknown Andrew Bergman, who gets story credit as well. (Bergman went on to write *The In-Laws* and to write and direct *The Freshman* and *Honeymoon in Vegas.*) Pryor brings his sense of political outrage to the film, which deals more specifically with bigotry than Brooks's other films, all of which have a strong social conscience and are marked by the perspective of the alienated, disenfranchised outsider. Brooks rounds up his usual suspects—hypocrisy, intolerance, and greed—but slaps them around with more than usual vigor in this politically barbed parody.

The Western, which had already fallen from favor due to its association with imperialism and genocide, was ripe for parody, and Brooks knew whom

THE YIDDISHE COWBOY   In Mel Brooks's myth-shattering spoof of the Hollywood Western, *Blazing Saddles,* Gene Wilder and Cleavon Little represent two ethnic minorities typically absent from the genre.

to enlist for the job. No doubt inspired by the success of the irreverent comic Western *Cat Ballou,* released in 1965, Brooks took great glee in trampling sanctified American historical myths. Although the subversive mentality of *Blazing Saddles* no doubt contributed to its popularity in 1973, its wide appeal also rested on its less sophisticated elements. Brooks has always displayed a strong sophomoric streak, relying heavily on scatological humor and slapstick. This vulgarity, coupled with a reliance on cultural clichés and ethnic stereo-types, has made Brooks unpopular in some circles. Although he is fiercely, compulsively Jewish, Brooks makes some Jewish viewers uncomfortable.

Brooks, ever the naughty little boy shocking his parents with references to unmentionable boldily functions, was surely the brains behind the famous symphony of flatulence that accompanies a campfire dinner of beans. The most memorable moment of Brooksian physical comedy comes when the humongous henchman Mongo (Alex Karras) punches a horse. Brooks's trade-mark bawdy sex comedy is provided by chanteuse Lilly Von Shtup (whose last name even non-Jews will recognize as the Yiddish term for sexual inter-course), who parodies sleepy sensuality in her Brooks-composed song, "I'm

So Tired." Shtup is hilariously enacted by Brooks's regular Madeline Kahn playing an ennui-laden Marlene Dietrich clone who finds long-awaited sexual satisfaction with the well-endowed Bart. (Offensive cultural clichés run rampant in Brooks's anything-goes universe.)

The show-biz references are also pure Brooks, including the climactic confrontation between a Busby-Berkeley production directed by a swishy gay choreographer (Dom DeLuise) and the zealous Western actors, whose final brawl spills off the movie set in an eruption of anarchy. Brooks wrote several musical numbers for *Blazing Saddles,* and was nominated for an Oscar for the movie's theme song. (An arguably better song, and his most quintessentially Jewish one, however, is "Hope for the Best, Expect the Worst," the theme song of his least Jewish movie, *The Twelve Chairs.*)

Brooks appears in a second role as the cross-eyed, pea-brained, sex-addled Governor Lepetomane who is manipulated by shrewd and greedy Hedley Lamarr. Lamarr establishes his Jewish identification very early, by calling the yokel Taggart "a provincial *putz.*" Later, Taggart improbably suggests driving out the townfolk by killing the first-born male in every household. Lamarr rejects the plan as "too Jewish." Appointing a black sheriff, he decides, is a much better way to send the prejudiced townspeople running.

There are no specific references to the Waco Kid's Jewish identity, just as there are none in *The Producers,* in which the word "Jew" is curiously never uttered. Nevertheless, the casting of well-known Jewish comedy actor Wilder, who plays the voice of reason with impish humor, establishes his ethnic identity. Born Jerry Silberman, the son of a Russian immigrant, Wilder went on to costar with Pryor in several successful comedies and to star in and cowrite Brooks's *Young Frankenstein.* In 1979, Wilder starred in another very funny Jewish Western, *The Frisco Kid,* playing an Orthodox Polish rabbi who travels across the Wild West in the company of an outlaw (half-Jewish actor Harrison Ford).

One of Brooks's many implicitly Jewish characters, the Waco Kid forms a fast friendship with Bart that is based on shared outsider status and a deep disdain for discrimination. Taking a well-aimed shot at the pioneer myth, the fast-on-the-draw Waco Kid tells Bart, "You have to remember, these are simple farmers, people of the land, the common clay of the New West. You know, morons." In the end, Bart and the Waco Kid successfully foil Lamarr's plan to "stamp out runaway decency in the West." Champions of justice and ethnic diversity, they ride off into the sunset together—in a limo.

19

Chariots of Fire

Warner Bros./Ladd (1981)
CAST: Ben Cross, Ian Charleson, Alice Krige, Nigel Havers, John Gielgud
DIRECTED BY: Hugh Hudson
123 minutes [PG]

One of the screen's most eloquent and thorough depictions of anti-Semitism as the motivating force behind the Jewish drive to succeed, *Chariots of Fire* is not so much a sports story as a character drama examining the spirit that inspires two runners competing in the 1924 Olympics. The acclaimed drama is also unusually explicit in its depiction of the dichotomy between Jew and Christian. The Jew and the Christian excel for very different reasons, which are attributed to their religious backgrounds in this uncommonly open examination of class divisions and ethnic barriers in 1920s England. Based on a true story, director Hugh Hudson's British drama won Oscars for best picture, best script, and best score, and earned rapturous reviews.

Harold Abrahams (Ben Cross), the son of Lithuanian Jews, is a Cambridge University student who is acutely aware of the anti-Semitism around him. "England is Christian and Anglo-Saxon, and so are her corridors of power," he tells a fellow student. "Those who stalk them guard them with jealousy and venom." His friend asks if he plans to grin and bear it. "No," Harold says. "I'm going to take them on, all of them, one by one, and run them off their feet."

Eric Liddell (Ian Charleson) is the Scottish son of a missionary who plans to follow in his father's footsteps and return to China, where he was born. First, however, he plans to set an example of Christian might by winning an Olympic medal. His devout sister Jenny worries that running will distract him from his calling. "God made me for a purpose, for China," he reassures her. "But he also made me fast. When I run, I feel His pleasure. When I win, I honor Him."

Harold is driven by a need to prove himself, while Eric is divinely inspired. For Harold, running is a compulsion, a weapon. "Against what?" his girlfriend Sybil (Alice Krige) wants to know. "Being Jewish, I suppose," he admits. For Harold, running is vindication. For Eric, it is an act of devotion. Eric feels it is his sacred duty to put his talents to good use. The reasons the men run, which are clearly delineated in this provocative period piece, are as diametrically opposed as the men themselves. Harold is arrogant, Eric humble. Harold is intense and combative. "He has a go at anyone who stands in his way," a friend says. Eric is serene and self-effacing, although equally determined.

Harold is not the only one aware of his outsider status. "Imagine what it means to a man like Harold to have this chance at immortality," his friend Lord Lindsay (Nigel Havers) says. "It's a matter of life and death." Indeed, when Harold is beaten for the first time in his life, by Eric in the 100 meters, he is devastated. Nor does Harold merely imagine the anti-Semitism he describes as "an ache, a helplessness, and an anger I feel in the cold reluctance of a hand-shake." The Master of Trinity College (John Gielgud) often evinces antiSemitic attitudes. He says Harold's father is a financier. "What does that mean?" his snobbish colleague (Lindsay Anderson) wants to know. "I imagine he lends money," he says with a tone of disapproval. "Exactly," the other old boy replies.

"He's defensive, as 'they' invariably are," the headmaster continues. Later, after Harold hires a private trainer, the half-Italian, half-Arab coach Sam Muss-

RUN FOR YOUR LIFE   Ben Cross plays a runner competing in the 1924 Olympics whose burning desire to win is fueled by the anti-Semitism that bars him from England's corridors of power in the Oscar-winning *Chariots of Fire*.

abini (Ian Holm), the don calls Harold in for a chiding. He accuses Harold of running for personal glory rather than out of loyalty to the school. His approach has been "too plebian," he's told. "You are a member of the elite and expected to behave as such." Harold responds that he runs for his family, his university, and his country, and he bitterly resents the suggestion that because he is a Jew he must be acting out of self-interest. When he leaves the room, the old man shakes his head. "There goes your Semite," he says coolly. "Different God, different mountaintops."

Interestingly, Eric's loyalty is also challenged in the course of the film. When he refuses to run in the 100-meters qualifying heat on the Sabbath, the Prince of Wales joins in the pressure group formed to get him to change his mind. He is accused of not placing the desire to bring honor to his country first. Indeed, Eric honors God above king and refuses to compromise his principles. Lord Lindsay, who has already won a medal in the hurdles, salvages the situation by offering him his place in the 400 meters.

Although dramatically the film has been headed for another confrontation between Eric and Harold, history causes the story to veer in a different direction. The two men are no longer in conflict. Their stories run parallel to each other and will not be allowed to collide in a climactic race that will prove the superiority of one over the other. Both the Jew and the Christian can and do win. Perhaps to further this sense of equality, *Chariots of Fire* only hints at one important piece of historical information: Harold Abrahams converted to Christianity later in his life.

In comparing and contrasting the two runners, however, the film portrays Eric in a more favorable light. It has been criticized for suggesting that Eric is a more noble character than Harold, which may be true. Harold, however, is the more interesting and compelling character, played with intensity by Ben Cross (born Bernard Cross). As critic David Denby points out, "More of us will be drawn to the tormented Abrahams" than to the saintly Liddell. Harold evokes our sympathy more than Eric because he needs it more. And he earns our respect for overcoming obstacles Eric never encountered.

Like many films that deal with anti-Semitism, *Chariots of Fire* is safely set in the past. *Quiz Show,* an excellent look at the subtle social forces at work in television, is set in the 1950s. So, too, is *School Ties,* a teen film that exposes anti-Semitism at a posh private school. *The Fixer,* based on the Pulitzer Prize–winning novel by Bernard Malamud, is set in turn of the century Czarist Russia. *Betrayed* is a rare exception that tackles the subject of virulent and violent anti-Semitism in America today.

Chariots of Fire may distance itself somewhat by looking at an earlier era, but it does suggest that attitudes so deeply ingrained in the dominant culture will not change quickly or easily.

20

Body and Soul

NTA/Enterprise Studios (1947)
Cast: John Garfield, Lilli Palmer, Anne Revere, Canada Lee
Directed by: Robert Rossen
104 minutes [Not rated]

"In Europe, the Nazis are killing people like us because of their religion," the grocer Shimen tells defending middleweight champion Charlie Davis on the eve of his challenge match. "But here Charlie Davis is a champion. So you'll win, retire, and be proud." This speech drives the stake of guilt through the Jewish boxer's heart. The fix is in, and Davis has already agreed to go down. He has bet every last penny against himself and plans to retire with his winnings.

Body and Soul, a hard-hitting classic widely honored as the definitive boxing film, was the only proudly pro-Jewish post-Holocaust of the late 1940s film to actually center on a Jewish character played by a Jewish actor, Oscar-nominee John Garfield. Charlie Davis is a businessman who fights strictly for the money and who knows boxing is a mob-run racket. He also knows that if he doesn't take a dive, he may end up with a bullet in his head—an ending director Robert Rossen advocated but was persuaded to reject by screenwriter Abraham Polonsky.

Will Davis betray his persecuted people, for whom he offers a glimmer of hope? Will he prize money over honor? Will he lose the woman he loves (Lilli Palmer) and disappoint his long-suffering mother (Anne Revere), who has always urged him "to fight for something"? In our hearts, we know Davis will not roll over. He will defy the forces of oppression and redeem himself. Any other outcome would be unthinkable in this knockout boxing film released in 1947 and set a few years earlier. With the Holocaust fresh in the American public's mind, *Body and Soul* sent out a message of Jewish resilience and integrity. The film expressed faith in the future of the savaged Jewish people, represented by the fictional boxer. Davis has taken a beating, but he will not be defeated. He has allowed himself to be a victim, but he will end his career a victor. His body has been punished, but he will save his soul.

be ruined by the hearings, despite having no official party affiliation. Deemed guilty by association, Garfield had knowingly hired many Communist sympathizers to work on *Body and Soul*. The film was considered offensive not so much for its depiction of corruption in a capitalistic society but for assembling like-minded leftists to work on the "subversive" project. Garfield was blacklisted after refusing to name names and died in 1952 at age thirty-nine, brokenhearted by the inability to work and beset by pressing legal problems.

Body and Soul, which was ineffectually remade in 1981 with Leon Isaac Kennedy cast in the lead, was a commercial and critical success and is considered one of Rossen's finest social dramas. *Body and Soul* used boxing as a metaphor for exploitation, a theme that would be echoed in future films, including *On the Waterfront, The Champ, Somebody Up There Likes Me, Rocky,* and the most recent film to feature a Jewish pugilist, *Triumph of the Spirit.* None surpasses *Body and Soul,* however, a film that offered American audiences a heroic Jewish fighter in a time of desperate need.

21

The Pawnbroker

American International Pictures (1965)
CAST: Rod Steiger, Brock Peters, Jaimie Sanchez, Geraldine Fitzgerald
DIRECTED BY: Sidney Lumet
116 minutes [Not rated]

The Pawnbroker was the first American fiction film to feature scenes set in a Nazi concentration camp and among the first to deal with the heritage of the horror it so harrowingly re-creates. By far the most hard-hitting Holocaust film to date upon its release in 1965, *The Pawnbroker* remains a tough film to watch today, long after the Holocaust has become a commonly explored screen topic, and still ranks high on the list of films examining the ongoing pain that plagues survivors of the *Shoah*.

Sol Nazerman (Rod Steiger), who runs a pawnshop in Harlem, is a survivor in name only. His soul perished in the camps, where his wife and children died, and he is now among the walking dead, a man without pity or passion, suffering a grief too intense to be borne. Wrapped in a shroud of indifference, Sol has cut himself off from life. He treats people with unilateral disdain, refusing all attempts at communication and appeals for compassion. Triggered by the twenty-fifth anniversary of his wife's death, repressed memories come flooding back over the course of several traumatic days, sending Sol reeling into a new awareness of his agony. His long-buried guilt at having failed to save his family heaves up with volcanic fury.

When a black prostitute bares her breast to entice him, Sol sees his naked wife prostituted by Nazis as he stands helpless. Riding on the subway, he is plunged back into the cattle cars, where he is no longer able to hold his young son, who slips off Sol's shoulders to his death. (In the respected 1961 book by Jewish novelist Edward Lewis Wallant on which the movie is based, the boy drowns in human feces.) When a young man tries to escape a beating by climbing a chain link fence, Sol remembers the death of his friend, who flung himself on a barbed wire fence in anguish, calling for his wife Tessie, with whom Sol is currently having a loveless affair.

The defiantly downbeat movie belongs to an era when films were suddenly allowed to be ugly, brutal, painful, and real, films like *Midnight Cowboy* and *Bonnie and Clyde*. *The Pawnbroker* does not end with Sol's miraculous spiritual resurrection. There is no redemption, no healing, no embrace of life, merely a suggestion that Sol will no longer be able to seek solace in isolation and denial. He will live with and in his pain.

Filmed in black and white, with evocative cinematography that suggests early German expressionism in its use of light, shadows, and dramatic camera angles, and a jangly, dissonant score by Quincy Jones, *The Pawnbroker* was novel in terms of style as well as substance. A prisoner of the past, Sol is often shot through the bars on his tomb-like pawnshop, where he doles out dollars to his pathetic customers with chillingly cold detachment. Unable to feel kinship with the suffering he witnesses, Sol finally begins to recognize his own participation in oppression when he learns that the black gangster who owns the pawnshop (Brock Peters) makes most of his money running black whorehouses. In addition to being one of the first films to directly confront the Holocaust, *The Pawnbroker* was also one of the first to take a hard look at ghetto life and to convey tensions between Jews and blacks.

Adapted by Morton Fine and David Friedkin, *The Pawnbroker* was inde-

HERITAGE OF HORROR   Rod Steiger played a traumatized Holocaust survivor in the 1965 release of *The Pawnbroker,* a dark drama about a man wrapped in a protective shroud of indifference to the suffering around him.

pendently produced and distributed by Ely Landau after it was rejected by the major studios. Landau initially hired Arthur Hiller to direct, but replaced him with another Jewish-American director, Sidney Lumet, whose sensibility proved well-suited to the drama. Lumet's father, the Yiddish stage star Baruch Lumet, plays the ailing father of Sol's friend who died on the fence. With *The Pawnbroker,* Lumet proved his willingness to experiment and to tackle tough subjects and his ability to elicit riveting performances from powerhouse actors. Best known for three stories of modern alienation and moral crisis, *Serpico, Network,* and *The Verdict,* Lumet went on to explore Jewish themes in *Bye Bye Braverman* (1968), *Just Tell Me What You Want* (1980), *Daniel* (1983), *Garbo Talks* (1984), and *A Stranger Among Us* (1992).

Rod Steiger, nominated for an Oscar for his potent performance in *The Pawnbroker,* won the best actor prize at the Berlin International Film Festival and was chosen best actor by the British Academy Awards. Steiger is able to convey the fathomless well of torment that Sol has sealed off. It is a monumental acting challenge to play displaced pain, desolation, and isolation, and to let the audience see what the character works so hard to keep hidden. Steiger, who was equally magnificent as a hasidic rebbe in *The Chosen* (also produced by Landau), rises to the challenge with this frightening study in dehumanization.

On one level, the tough-minded movie addresses a question central to the Jewish experience regarding the psychological effects of senseless suffering. Although Sol's alienation may be tied to a specifically Jewish experience, his emotional estrangement is not a uniquely Jewish reaction. Sol is locked in his private cell of torment, but he is not alone in his misery. On a larger level, the film evokes the spiritual crisis of humankind in an age of unspeakable cruelty.

The Pawnbroker, like the novel, is filled with religious symbolism. Sol's Puerto Rican assistant is named Jesus Ortiz (Jaime Sanchez), and although the movie downplays the father–son relationship of the book, it is Jesus who dies for Sol's sins—and salvation. In the movie's memorable final scene, a reference to the crucifixion of Christ that was not in the book, Sol slowly pushes the palm of his hand down on a sharp spindle, forcing himself to feel the pain he can no longer escape. He then wanders into the street to rejoin the downtrodden masses.

22

Goodbye Columbus

Paramount Pictures (1969)
CAST: Richard Benjamin, Ali MacGraw, Jack Klugman, Nan Martin
DIRECTED BY: Larry Peerce
105 minutes [PG]

Philip Roth's career reached a critical crescendo just as all hell broke loose in America. The 1969 release of *Goodbye Columbus,* based on his first novella, coincided with the publication of his hugely popular novel, *Portnoy's Complaint.* Although not without their detractors, the book and the film were widely acclaimed, solidifying Roth's reputation as the premier chronicler of the contemporary Jewish identity crisis.

Goodbye Columbus charts the conflict between two Jewish generations and two socioeconomic classes, revealing the failings of all concerned. One of the few films of the time to focus exclusively—although not flatteringly—on Jewish characters and themes, the movie was a surprise hit, partly because audiences were hungry for ethnic diversity and for honest appraisals of modern life that challenged prevailing wisdom and questioned sanctified institutions. Even more significantly, its protagonist was perfectly attuned to the zeitgeist.

Like the Jewish hero of *The Graduate* (1967), Neil Klugman (Richard Benjamin) is searching for self-definition without much success. He admits he finds everything ridiculous. To both generational figureheads, the get-ahead world of their parents appears absurd. Old values have lost their meaning, but what exactly has replaced them? Nothing, except a gnawing sense that there must be more to life. But what? The money-grubbing pursuit of materialistic success, represented in *The Graduate* by plastics, in *Goodbye Columbus* by plumbing fixtures, is repellent to these existential heroes. But the alternatives—living in a commune, dropping out and tuning in, adopting radical politics, joining an ashram—seem equally silly to the sensible Jewish protagonists.

Apathetic, ambivalent, and indecisive, these disaffected young men know what they don't want but aren't sure what it is they do want. Love is the (apparent) answer in *The Graduate,* but is only a temporary solution for Neil in *Goodbye Columbus.* A truly mixed up character, Neil has mixed feelings

THE COUNTRY CLUB SET Richard Benjamin, as a disaffected and conflicted iconoclast who engages in a summer romance with pampered and privileged Brenda Patimkin (Ali MacGraw), was embraced by the public as a hero attuned to the times in *Goodbye Columbus*.

about everything. He is contemptuous of wealth but finds no romance in poverty either. There's certainly nothing noble about the cramped apartment he shares in Newark with his Old World-style Aunt Gladys and Uncle Max. Everywhere he looks, he sees emptiness and failure of one kind or another. Cynical and detached, Neil is a bundle of contradictions. His surname may mean "smart man" but he's not such a clever fellow.

Neil is attracted to pampered princess Brenda Patimkin (Ali MacGraw), with whom he enjoys an ill-fated summer romance, because she has attained the status and privilege imparted by the kind of financial success his family has failed to achieve. But he is also appalled by the conspicuous consumption Brenda takes for granted. He simultaneously resents, envies, and adores Brenda, whom he mocks at every turn. Indeed, the nouveau riche world of the Patimkins is rendered as grotesquely vulgar, reflecting Neil's jaundiced view. The movie's caustic portrait of raging consumerism in the Jewish country club crowd caused considerable consternation and discomfort in some quarters, and the movie was labeled an example of Jewish self-hatred, just as charges of self-hatred had greeted Roth's National Book Award–winning collection of stories that included *Goodbye Columbus* in 1959.

These allegations were hurled with even more vehemence against *Portnoy's Complaint* a decade later. The 1972 screen adaptation of *Portnoy's Complaint* was indeed an artless, tasteless, and ugly film. Both Roth adaptations were part of an antifamily, antiestablishment trend. In the late 1960s, highly critical images of Jewish home life emerged in films such as the quirky crime drama *No Way to Treat a Lady* (1968), starring George Segal as a nebbish cop and Eileen Heckert as his smothering mother, and the even more egregious cult classic *Where's Poppa?* (1970), starring Segal as a frustrated mama's boy whose monstrous mother is played by Ruth Gordon.

Goodbye Columbus leaves no doubt that Roth takes a dim view of suburban affluence, which he regards as spiritually hollow. Like many other American Jewish writers, Roth is concerned with the high price of success and the cost of assimilation. Roth goes further than other writers, however, in his harsh assessment of American Jewry's cultural crisis. Roth's despairing vision of errant values is recreated, warts and all, by director Larry Peerce, screenwriter Arnold Schulman, editor Ralph Rosenblum, and producer Robert Evans, all of whom are Jewish. The film has been accused of going overboard by depicting some of the Jewish characters as gluttonous, crass, crude, greedy, and garish philistines, most notably in the wedding scene that serves as the film's comic climax.

Although *Goodbye Columbus* does reinforce negative stereotypes of the upwardly mobile Jew, it tempers its criticism with affection for some of the characters. Mr. Patimkin (wonderfully played by Jack Klugman), in particular, emerges as a generous and loving man whose pride in his children is palpable and touching. He knows that the *naches* he gets from his children is the most valuable thing in life. He may indulge his children too much, but this overindulgence clearly comes from his own years of doing without.

The movie also fairly allows both sides of the generational conflict to be heard and honored. Mr. Patimkin is understandably baffled and insulted by the younger generation that fails to respect his years of hard work and the pride he takes in having created a fortune from *bubkes*. He's not about to feel guilty for enjoying his hard-earned money. His enjoyment of life is presented as another virtue, one that actually makes him superior to Neil, a *kvetch* whose fault-finding, whining, and mocking humor keep him removed from life. Unlike Neil, Mr. Patimkin is no hypocrite. He's direct, decent, sentimental, and unpretentious. He has not lost his moral grounding in the move away from traditional Jewish life. When his wife complains that Brenda should be dating a boy from a good family, he asks how she knows Neil is not from a good family. To her, of course, "good" means rich and respectable. To him, it means decent, loving, and hard-working. He may be materialistic, but he does not judge others by their financial success.

Mr. Patimkin is also people-smart. He wisely advises his social-climbing, status-conscious wife (Nan Martin) to leave Brenda alone or she'll marry a ditch digger just to spite her. In fact, Brenda is, at least in part, dating Neil to defy her manipulative mother, who does not approve of this aloof young man who works at the Newark Public Library and appears to have no ambitions. Mrs. Patimkin rightly senses his scorn for the family whose hospitality he nevertheless accepts.

What attracts Neil to Brenda, aside from her wealth, is much more complex. Brenda, a student at Radcliffe, is pretty, assertive, confident, smart, shallow, and vain. She's had her nose fixed, and Neil teases her constantly about fixing anything else that might be wrong with her. From a feminist perspective, the film makes a potent point about the Jewish woman needing to be "fixed" in order to be acceptable to the Jewish male or accepted by society. Neil's mean-spirited ribbing is also hypocritical, because he is attracted to the athletic, vivacious, and vacuous Brenda precisely because she conforms to gentile standards of beauty and behavior. With Brenda, he can have his *shiksa* fantasy cake without the guilt. (MacGraw was raised Episcopalian but has a Jewish grandfather.) With his conquest of Brenda, he can sample the fruits of the American dream—which he does literally by raiding the Patimkin's rec room fridge—while pretending to find them distasteful.

Although Brenda appears to be independent and liberated (she sleeps with Neil and swims nude at a party), in the end, Neil discovers Brenda is inextricably bound to her family. Perhaps she is tied by love. Maybe she is merely financially dependent on them. Possibly she shares their values, enjoys their lifestyle, and hoped Neil would join her family and her world. Neil, however, is not a joiner. As the movie ends, Neil walks down the street alone, away from Brenda. He has added one more thing to the list of what he does not want. Who knows what he's walking toward or what direction his life will take? The movie may not suggest any solutions to Neil's dilemma, but many viewers can identify with his confusion and isolation.

23

Bugsy

Tristar Pictures (1991)
CAST: Warren Beatty, Annette Bening, Harvey Keitel, Ben Kingsley,
Elliot Gould
DIRECTED BY: Barry Levinson
135 minutes [R]

A tale of love, sex, murder, larceny, and spiraling construction costs, *Bugsy* is the ostensible biography of legendary Jewish gangster Benjamin Siegel. Nominated for ten Academy Awards, the curious character drama refashioned the volatile gangland thug into a doomed dreamer and reimagined his violent life as a tragic love story. Siegel's story was improbably reshaped as a vehicle for actor Warren Beatty, who was not only not Jewish but already ten years older than Siegel when he was executed by fellow mobsters at age forty-one. All around, *Bugsy* was a work of considerable chutzpah.

Producer Beatty's calculated gamble paid off handsomely, however, due in equal measure to Barry Levinson's skillful direction and its enigmatic and colorful subject. *Bugsy* is arguably the most successful and certainly the most unusual Jewish gangster film, a category that boasts some heavy competition. Indeed, of all the notorious Jewish mobsters who dominated organized crime in the first half of the century, Siegel was easily the most flamboyant. A glamorous celebrity gangster who hung out with Hollywood movie stars, Siegel was a dapper dresser, an inveterate ladies' man, and a cold-blooded killer whose insane, murderous rages earned him the hated nickname *Bugsy*, which no one dared call him to his face. The Lower East Side pimp turned underworld czar was a key player in the birth of the modern mob, along with his childhood pals Meyer Lansky (born Maier Suchowljansky in Poland) and Charles "Lucky" Luciano.

In 1935, Siegel was sent by the syndicate to run the rackets in L.A., where he met another pal from the old neighborhood, rising movie star George Raft, and befriended Gary Cooper, Cary Grant, Howard Hughes, Jean Harlow, and Clark Gable. In 1945, Siegel was given the go-ahead to realize his grandiose plan to acquire a casino under construction in the Las Vegas desert. Cost overruns and suspicions of embezzlement put him in dutch with the mob and he was rubbed out at the Hollywood home of his starlet girlfriend, Virginia Hill, in 1947.

Beatty had been interested in the story of the debonair mobster with the hair-trigger temper since he'd been a child. In 1984, he commissioned a script from James Toback, whose screenplays for *The Gambler* and *Fingers* have a Jewish subtext. Toback wrote twenty-five drafts, based on Dean Jennings' novel, *We Only Kill Each Other: The Life and Bad Times of Bugsy Siegel,* before the perfectionistic star was satisfied. Beatty brazenly undertook the role of a romantic visionary in the revisionist film. Although an experienced director himself, Beatty hired Oscar-winning director Barry Levinson (*Rain Man*) to helm the production. Levinson, who is Jewish, had come under fire for deleting all Jewish references from his semiautobiographical drama about an immigrant family, *Avalon.* Similarly, in *Bugsy,* Siegel's Jewish background is not a big issue. The word "Jew" is spoken only once, when Siegel announces his mad plan to assassinate Mussolini because he and Hitler are "trying to knock off every Jew in the world."

Beatty, who speaks with a slight New York twang, subtly suggests his character's Jewishness, which is conveyed less by mannerisms than by his personality profile. Siegel stays nominally rooted in his past by maintaining his marriage to Esta, a warm, maternal Jewish matron played by Wendy Philips. *Bugsy* is filled with a handful of more obviously Jewish characterizations, reflecting a trend toward overt ethnicity that began surfacing in a host of Jewish gangster films that followed the 1974 release of *The Godfather, Part II.* In Francis Ford Coppola's classic sequel, Lee Strasberg played a Jewish underworld tycoon modeled on Siegel's partner, Meyer Lansky. It was quickly followed in 1975 by a film dubbed *The Jewish Godfather,* Menahem Golan's portrait of Louis Buchalter, *Lepke,* starring Tony Curtis.

In 1984, Sergio Leone's sprawling opus documenting the rise of a fictitious Jewish mob, *Once Upon a Time in America,* hit the screens in a badly cut version and was later restored and redeemed. In 1991, the year *Bugsy* was released, Siegel popped up in two other films. The youth-oriented *Mobsters* details the Jewish brains and Italian brawn alliance of masterminds Siegel (Richard Grieco) and Lansky (Patrick Dempsey) with tough guys Lucky Luciano and Frank Costello. Armand Assante played Siegel in *The Marrying Man,* bringing the total of non-Jewish actors to play Siegel in 1991 to three. Also in 1991, Dustin Hoffman added his portrayal of mobster Dutch Schultz, born Arthur Flegenheimer, to the Jewish gangster ouvre in the intriguing adaptation of E. L. Doctorow's novel, *Billy Bathgate.* In 1995, Martin Scorsese revisited Siegel's creation, Las Vegas, with *Casino,* a true story based on the life of gambling czar Lefty Rosenthal, played by Robert De Niro.

Bugsy is also peopled with infamous Jewish gangsters, played with relish

CELEBRITY GANGSTER   In *Bugsy*, Warren Beatty adds his unique interpretation of the infamous crime czar Benjamin Siegel to the long and illustrious list of Jewish gangsters immortalized on screen.

by three character actors well suited to their parts. Ben Kingsley (*Schindler's List, Murderers Among Us: The Simon Wiesenthal Story*) is marvelous as Meyer Lansky. Kingsley, who is half-Jewish and half-Indian, plays Lansky as a dignified gentleman who speaks with a broad accent and conveys cautious, Old Worldly wisdom. The movie only hints at the strong friendship that bound these two men. The proudly Jewish Lansky, who had used his mob muscle to ship arms to Israel during the War for Independence and sent thugs to break up German American Bund meetings in the 1930s, became the richest and most powerful as well as prudent Jewish gangster, outliving all of his cohorts in crime.

Harvey Keitel—coincidentally the only Jewish actor ever to have played Siegel, in the 1974 TV movie *The Virginia Hill Story*—is also effectively cast as Mickey Cohen, Siegel's rough and ready henchman. Mickey, who says "*oy*" a lot, is the flip side of gentleman gangster Lansky, a feisty, fearless hustler. Despite his rough manners, Mickey proves a man of good sense and old-fashioned sentiment. (In reality, Cohen was known as a gangster of unusual depravity and cunning.) Elliott Gould also makes a strong impression as

Siegel's old buddy and dim-witted button man, Harry Greenberg, for whom Bugsy has a soft spot. In the film, it is with great reluctance that Siegel slays the informer Greenberg, when in fact Siegel reportedly relished ferreting him out and organizing his execution.

This is not the film's only revision of history. Although *Bugsy* shows Siegel being killed before the Flamingo has a chance to flourish, the gangland slaying actually took place after the casino was profitably up and running, although it went on to even greater success under the management of the two Jewish gangsters who succeeded Siegel. Also, the casino was not Siegel's invention, as the film indicates, but was already under construction when Siegel took it over.

All of these changes serve to sentimentalize Siegel. *Bugsy,* after all, is a love story, the core of which is the stormy, passionate relationship between Siegel and the tempestuous Virginia Hill (Annette Bening), a long-legged actress whose nickname, the Flamingo, graced the casino Siegel built in the desert. Hill, who in real life suffered from manic depression and detested the casino named in her honor, is vividly portrayed by Bening as a grasping moll redeemed by her love for Siegel.

In *Bugsy,* Las Vegas is a brainstorm that becomes Siegel's obsession—and his undoing. Siegel is depicted as an obsessive type, and although the film does not directly connect his personality with his heritage, it is easy to read Jewish traits in his nature, particularly his stated desire to "build something," to make something that will last. The project brings out both the best and the worst in Siegel, a megalomaniacal, single-minded perfectionist. Siegel is an extravagant, impetuous, restless soul whose desire for permanence turns him into a misunderstood failure, a victim of mercenary forces.

Beatty plays Siegel as a little bit of a *nebbish,* an often awkward and endearingly flustered, vulnerable person constantly seeking to overcome his shyness and feelings of inadequacy. He uses a tongue twister to improve his diction and uses a sun lamp to maintain his year-round tan. A sweet man—when not enraged—Siegel valiantly defends the honor of his shady lady love. A bundle of contradictions, Siegel emerges as a fascinating and appealing character, surely far less menacing than the real deadly dandy. Its title notwithstanding, the starstruck Siegel would surely have been flattered by *Bugsy.*

24

Cabaret

Allied Artists (1972)
CAST: Liza Minnelli, Michael York, Joel Grey, Marisa Berenson,
Fritz Wepper, Helmut Griem
DIRECTED BY: Bob Fosse
128 minutes [PG]

Played out against the ominous background of the incipient Nazi menace, an allegorical story of doomed love is thrown into sharp relief in this smashing screen adaptation of the 1966 Broadway musical hit. Clear-eyed and lucid, *Cabaret* slices to the heart of the creeping horror with razor-sharp skill, providing a gut-level understanding of the era.

One of the most overtly political movie musicals ever produced by Hollywood and one of the best evocations of the early Nazi era made in any country, *Cabaret* is set in decadent Berlin as Hitler is poised to seize power. In the foreground of this tale of multiple deceptions and ever-deepening corruption is the odd-couple relationship between Sally Bowles (Liza Minnelli), a devil-may-care, amoral American singer, and a straightlaced and marginally more principled English university student, Brian Roberts (Michael York), who arrives in Berlin at the film's opening and slowly finds himself seduced by the adorably outrageous Sally and the tantalizing debauchery of the era. The story's main subplot concerns the complicated relationship between two Jewish lovers.

Using bold strokes, Jewish director and choreographer Bob Fosse (*Lenny, All That Jazz*) details a dizzying world about to spin out of control. The permissiveness of the time is about to give way to repressiveness and moral anarchy of an entirely different, and deadly, order. Fosse's stylish, visually dazzling 1972 screen version benefits from an incisive, unsentimental screenplay by Jay Presson Allen (*Funny Girl*), a female screenwriter who beefed up the character of Sally Bowles, a deluded and self-absorbed free spirit seeking fame and fortune in 1931 Berlin. Sally, a role tailor-made for Minnelli, is maddening yet endearing, a vulnerable waif in wolf's clothing who charms and appalls us. So, too, does the cabaret fascinate and repel us.

The film's title locale, a cabaret known as the Kit Kat Klub, provides a potent metaphor for the volatile political situation. The theater is a place of elaborate deceptions and deliberate, desperate illusions, and while it appears to be a refuge from the insanity outside its doors, it actually reflects the growing danger and depravity of the world around it. Each song relates directly to the plot as well as to the story's larger social context. The musical numbers are intercut with dramatic scenes, heightening the visceral effect of the songs as well as the emotional power of the drama.

Based on the *Goodbye to Berlin* stories written by Christopher Isherwood in 1939, later turned into a play and film titled *I Am a Camera, Cabaret* was reshaped into an artistically and commercially successful stage musical by John Kander and Fred Ebb. Fosse's screen adaptation of the darkly entertaining musical was also a ripping success, winning eight Oscars, including direction, score, and cinematography. Liza Minnelli won a best actress Oscar and Joel Grey was named best supporting actor for his role as the malevolent M.C.—a part that is entirely sung and danced. Repeating his Tony Award–winning stage performance, Grey (born Joel Katz) creates an enigmatic character whose lewd, leering wickedness both embodies the insidious malice of Nazism and thumbs its nose at it. The ambiguity is intensified by the casting of this Jewish actor who often sounds a little like Al Jolson.

Although the two principal characters are gentile, the story's secondary romance concerns the equally problematic affair between Fritz (Fritz Wepper), a German gigolo, and the very wealthy Jewess he pursues for her money but comes to truly love. The heiress Natalia Landauer (Marisa Berenson) appears cool, aloof, dignifed, and prudish, but eventually she returns his affections. Natalia decides that because of escalating anti-Semitism she cannot marry him, however. Fritz is thus forced to reveal his secret: He is also a Jew. Fritz has taken the prudent, if cowardly, course of passing as a gentile in order to smooth his social and financial way. Following his confession, Fritz and Natalia are married in a Jewish ceremony. Their fate, however, remains uncertain.

Interestingly, although the characters of Natalia and Fritz appeared in Isherwood's source material as well as the subsequent stage and film adaptations, they were deleted from the Broadway musical. They were reinstated by Allen, who was wise enough to appreciate that these Jewish characters were crucial to a story headed for the Holocaust.

Cabaret also features the decadent but utterly captivating German aristocrat Max (Helmut Griem), who represents the hedonism and nihilism of the times. This bisexual baron, who seduces both Sally and Brian, initially dismisses the Nazis as a bunch of hoodlums who are presently useful in ridding Germany of Communists and who can be easily gotten rid of after they have served their purpose. In one of the movie's most chilling scenes, Brian and Max stop in a country beer garden where an angelic looking German youth begins singing "Tomorrow Belongs to Me." As the camera slowly pulls back, we see the swastika on his armband and his Hitler Youth uniform. As the stirring song continues, Germans of all ages begin to rise and sing in unison this hymn to Hitler. As Max and Brian flee in disgust, Brian asks his friend if he still thinks the Nazis can be controlled. He gets no answer. *Cabaret* is a film of clever contradictions and contrasts, such as a beautiful boy singing a grotesque Nazi anthem.

Brian, who allows himself to be corrupted but is eventually sickened by the moral decay around him, wants Sally to return to Cambridge with him. She chooses, instead, to go on pretending and denying reality, to try to be a

LIFE IS A CABARET   Liza Minelli and Joel Grey play entertainers at the Kit Kat Klub—the title locale of *Cabaret*—which appears to be a haven from the gathering Nazi storm in 1931 Berlin but actually reflects the deadly menace about to engulf Germany.

star at all costs. Brian, whose eyes are opened to Sally's fatal delusions as well as to the darkening storm clouds in Germany, leaves Berlin sadder but wiser at the film's bitter end.

Several equally brilliant but less commercial European films also successfully portray the rise of Nazism. Luchino Visconti's *The Damned* (1969) is an intense Jacobean-style tragedy that charts the rise of a depraved family of German industrialists in the Third Reich. *The Tin Drum* (1979), Volker Schlondorff's Oscar-winning adaptation of the Günter Grass novel, is a viscerally striking, symbolic drama expressing the abomination of Nazism. Istvan Szabo's magnificent, Oscar-winning biographical tale of corruption and compromise, *Mephisto,* is the true story of an actor who makes a Faustian bargain with the Nazi devil.

Few American films, however, are concerned with the events leading to the Holocaust. A rare exception, Stanley Kramer's *Ship of Fools* (1965), based on Katherine Anne Porter's novel, views the Nazi menace via a group of passengers on a 1933 transatlantic voyage.

Cabaret focuses more on Hitler's anti-Semitic agenda than any of these films, however, and offers a stinging indictment of bystanders like Sally who turned a blind eye on the brutality around them.

25

Crimes and Misdemeanors

Orion Pictures (1989)
CAST: Woody Allen, Mia Farrow, Anjelica Huston, Martin Landau,
Sam Waterston, Jerry Orbach
DIRECTED BY: Woody Allen
104 minutes [PG-13]

There are two stories told in tandem in *Crimes and Misdemeanors,* a complex morality tale that ranks as the cinema's most rigorous exploration of Jewish values and ethics as well as Woody Allen's most ambitious, accomplished, and thoroughly Jewish film to date.

The first story—the one in which the crime is committed—concerns a respected Jewish doctor (Martin Landau) whose unstable mistress (Anjelica Huston) threatens to blow the whistle on his sexual indiscretions and financial improprieties. Rather than allow his life to be ruined by a neurotic woman, Judah heeds the advice of his gangster brother (Jerry Orbach) and has her murdered. In the second tale—the one with the misdemeanor—Woody Allen plays Clifford, a principled but poor documentary filmmaker trapped in a loveless marriage to a woman (Joanna Gleason) with two very different brothers. One is the rich, sleazy TV producer Lester (Alan Alda), the other the compassionate and decent rabbi Ben (Sam Waterston). Clifford, hired to direct a self-serving profile of Lester, falls in love with Hallie (Mia Farrow), the show's producer. Hallie, who happens to be the only non-Jewish character in the entire story, commits the misdemeanor. She picks the wrong guy. True, marrying a buffoon instead of the nice guy who deserves her is not a punishable offense in the eyes of the law, but it is a truly terrible betrayal in Allen's eyes.

In *Crimes and Misdemeanors,* ranked among the greatest Jewish films for both its rigorous examination of Jewish values and its artistic excellence, Allen weaves a rich but somber-hued tapestry of transgressions depicting a profoundly unjust world. In Allen's screenplay, the wrong guy gets the girl as well as the unmerited glory, the most exemplary human being in the story goes blind, and the faithless killer gets away with murder. This sobering scenario prompted some critics to castigate Allen for creating a bleak portrait of

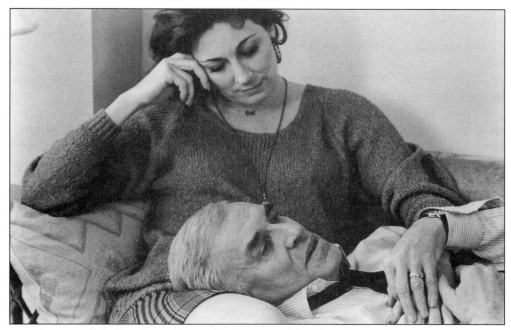

THE EYES OF GOD   Martin Landau plays a deluded and desperate ophthamologist who murders his mistress (Anjelica Huston) in Woody Allen's *Crimes and Misdemeanors,* in which the only character with clear moral vision is a rabbi.

a godless universe where sin goes unpunished and goodness is not rewarded. Indeed, Allen's theme is that life is not fair. However, although Allen's subject is the cruel injustice of life, his vision is not as despairing as it might seem on the surface.

Although we are meant to feel fate's sting when the venerable rabbi goes blind, when we last see him—proudly dancing with his daughter at her wedding—we know that he does not view his blindness as a tragedy, and we would be wrong to pity him. A man so strongly guided by the inner compass of his faith will easily find his way through the world without his eyes. The different way we choose to look at things is, in fact, the larger theme of *Crimes and Misdemeanors,* nominated for Oscars for best director and screenplay. Allen's deadly serious yet often painfully funny script also won the Writers' Guild of America's award for original screenplay. Alda, who oozes the kind of shallow insincerity Allen detests, won several supporting actor awards for his wry comic performance. Landau, nominated for a best supporting actor Oscar, revived his career with this gripping portrait of moral ruin.

"There is a fundamental difference in the way we view the world," Ben tells Judah, who has confessed his problems to the rabbi. "I see a moral structure, a higher power, forgiveness," Ben says, adding that this sense of ethical order lets us know how to live. The rabbi, ironically, is the only person to see things clearly, the only one who can see past the apparent injustice to the larger meaning and obligation of life. He is the moral center of the story, and the fact that he is a rabbi is quite remarkable considering that Allen rarely gives any credence to Judaism as a religion.

Vision is a recurring metaphor in Allen's mature and masterfully acted drama of betrayals small and large. Judah is an *ophthalmologist* who remembers that as a child his religious father repeatedly told him, "The *eyes* of God are on us always." "Without the law it is all *darkness*," the rabbi says. When Judah first meets his future mistress, she tells him that the *eyes* are the mirror of the soul. Later, when he goes to check on her murdered body, one of the *headlights* on his car is out. Clifford jokes with Hallie when she tells him her marriage was a case of love at first *sight.* "Maybe you should have taken a closer *look,*" he says.

Maybe we should all take a closer look. "We define ourselves by the choices we make," Ben says at the film's conclusion, offering the audience another way of looking at the characters. True, Judah is not caught. In fact, he claims that the whole experience has brought him back to his faith and his family. Despite his claims, however, Judah is a sham. He is what he always was: a weak, pathetic worm. And while the smarmy hack Lester has succeeded in fooling seemingly smart and sensible Hallie into thinking he's sweet and sincere, we doubt the deception will last forever. Although Lester will probably go on making gobs of money, we know he will never earn the respect of anyone whose opinion matters.

Nor is Clifford's defeat complete. He is indeed heartbroken by Hallie's choice of Lester and feels betrayed by the suicide of a noted Jewish scholar whose life-affirming philosophy he so admired (loosely based on Primo Levi). But Clifford holds onto his self-respect. He will not be overcome by bitterness, loneliness, or cynicism. In the end, the film leaves no doubt that God knows the difference between a *mensch* and a putz. So does Allen, and so do we.

26

The Last Angry Man

Columbia Pictures (1959)
CAST: Paul Muni, Luther Adler, David Wayne, Nancy Pollack
DIRECTED BY: Daniel Mann
100 minutes [Not rated]

Paul Muni gave the final performance of his professional life playing the dedicated, defiant doctor in *The Last Angry Man.* This proudly pro-Jewish film offered a refreshing break from the safe, de-Semitized Jews that populated the Hollywood cinema of the 1950s, inaugurating a trend toward overt ethnicity that was to flourish in the coming decade. The stirring and still effective social drama directly links its main character's morality to his Jewish heritage, presenting audiences with the sympathetic but unsentimental image of a devoted Jewish healer. The complex role in this stirring saga of Jewish principles put to the test served as a fitting finale for Muni, not only because the character's values closely matched his own but because it offered the actor the chance to play the most expressly Jewish part of his screen career.

Muni, who changed his name from Muni Weisenfreund when he came to Hollywood in 1929, had been a star of the Yiddish stage and frequently played Jewish characters on Broadway. In film, however, he was best known for playing a Mexican statesman (*Juarez*), a French scientist (*The Story of Louis Pasteur*), a French author (*The Life of Emile Zola*), an Italian-American gangster (*Scarface*), a Chinese farmer (*The Good Earth*), and Don Juan, Napoleon, and Schubert (*Seven Faces*). Known as a man of many faces, Muni also adopted a disguise in *The Last Angry Man,* but this time one closer to his own origins. Dr. Sam Abelman is an elderly doctor who has devoted his life to his patients. After forty-five years, he still lives and works in the ethnically mixed, crime-ridden Brownsville section of Brooklyn, where his impoverished patients are often unable to pay for the care he lavishes on them.

Dr. Abelman is a proud, honorable man who lives by the highest principles. An angel of mercy to those in need, he is blind to race and class divisions. A sweet old man he's not, however. He speaks his mind, railing against whatever he deems unjust and whomever he feels is unworthy. His favorite insult is to call someone a galoot, by which he means "someone who takes and gives nothing in return." A rebel with a cause, Abelman has been stubbornly "fighting the whole world" his entire life. His loyal wife Sarah (Nancy Pollock) knows why he's so cantankerous. "Poverty, hypocrisy, cruelty—that's what he's angry about," she says.

An article written about this selfless healer by his nephew Morton (Joby Baker), headlined "Good Samaritan of the Slums," attracts the interest of a down-on-his-luck television producer, Woodrow Thrasher (David Wayne), who is looking for real-life heroes for a documentary-style TV program. At first, Abelman is not interested in being honored for doing what he feels every doctor should do. He hates television and is afraid he'll be made to look foolish or, worse, self-serving. When Abelman is eventually persuaded to appear, the inevitable problems arise. Although Abelman does not solve Thrasher's career crisis, some of his integrity does rub off on the callow hustler. *The Last Angry Man* is representative of the common screen scenario in which a worthy Jew edifies and uplifts a gentile, becoming the catalyst for his

MAN OF MANY FACES   Paul Muni, right, a socially concerned Jewish actor who donned many disguises in his distinguished career, transformed himself into an altruistic and idealistic Jewish doctor in *The Last Angry Man.*

moral redemption. (See *Reversal of Fortune* for more discussion of the "Jews to the Rescue" film phenomenon.)

Interestingly, Muni's most famous role, the title character in *The Life of Emile Zola,* also offered a variation of this image of the Jew as savior. In this revered classic, Emile Zola achieves spiritual salvation by rescuing Alfred Dreyfus, the Jewish captain wrongly convicted of treason in an infamous case of anti-Semitic scapegoating. The socially committed actor eagerly undertook the part of Zola in the 1937 Oscar-winning historical drama, which was clearly meant as a rebuke to the anti-Semitic persecutions of the Third Reich.

Muni's progressive political beliefs were also reflected in Abelman, who is contrasted to his old medical school friend Max Vogel (Luther Adler), a successful Park Avenue specialist. The two men clearly love each other, although Abelman constantly *kibitzes* his colleague, who has made very different choices about how and why he practices medicine. Vogel endures the ribbing because Abelman, who serves as his conscience, is his link to his past and his lost idealism.

Based on the novel by Gerald Green, who also wrote the screenplay, *The Last Angry Man* is a character study that extols Jewish values without turning its main character into a warm and fuzzy, cute, and cuddly old coot. Director Daniel Mann, who earned a reputation for eliciting strong performances from his actors in films such as *Come Back, Little Sheba, The Rose Tattoo,* and *Butterfield Eight,* went on to make TV's acclaimed 1980 Holocaust drama *Playing for Time.* Green also turned to television as the author of the famed 1978 miniseries *Holocaust.*

In lesser hands, the character of Abelman might be rendered merely quaint or, worse, saintly. But Muni, who was much more than a mere master of dialects (rivaled only by Meryl Streep), brings great depth of feeling to the part. His sincerity is absolutely convincing. Muni, who was nominated for an Oscar for his first film, *The Valiant,* was nominated again for his last performance. In between, he was nominated for *I Am a Fugitive From a Chain Gang* and won for *The Story of Louis Pasteur. The Last Angry Man* holds up as well as, if not better than, any of Muni's earlier social dramas. For Jewish audiences, it has additional appeal, offering viewers a glimpse of Muni in a role close to his own heart and heritage.

27

The Outside Chance of Maximilian Glick

Northern Lights Media Corporation (1988)
CAST: Saul Rubinek, Noam Zylberman, Jan Rubes
DIRECTED BY: Allan Goldstein
96 minutes [G]

"Where there's oxygen, there are Jews," Maximilian Glick informs us at the beginning of this captivating Canadian film, explaining the unlikely presence of a small outpost of hardy Jews breathing the frosty air in a small town outside Winnipeg.

An utterly charming coming-of-age comedy about a boy approaching bar mitzvah in 1963, *The Outside Chance of Maximilian Glick* is one of the very best Jewish family films. This little-known gem is compassionate, clever, and knowing, a warm, witty, and embracing look at the trials and tribulations of a twelve-year-old boy precariously balanced between the safe confines of childhood and the terrifying liberation of adulthood. A must-see for Jewish families with preteens, it compares favorably with better-known examples of the growing-up-Jewish genre, including Woody Allen's *Radio Days,* Neil Simon's *Brighton Beach Memoirs,* and Diane Keaton's *Unstrung Heroes.*

Maximilian (Noam Zylberman) is not only the smartest kid in his class but a piano prodigy to boot, which has not exactly done wonders for his social life. His problems are compounded by his overly attentive family. He lives with his mother, father, bubby, and zaidy, all of whom smother him with well-intentioned concern. Like so many Jewish movie males before and after him, Max is torn between his need for autonomy and his desire to live up to his parents' expectations.

"Hasn't anyone around here ever heard of the concept of free will?" Maximilian grumbles good-naturedly as his family directs his every move. A philosophical and likable lad, Maximilian has a highly developed sense of humor, which serves as a buffer against the indignities humorously heaped upon him. Wise beyond his years, Maximilian shrewdly reasons that "Jews don't beget children, they build them. It comes from all those years when they had nothing else to build." Maximilian also struggles to forge his own identity and gain acceptance in a Christian world that eyes him warily. He is smart enough to see that prejudice cuts both ways, however. He knows that his family is just as bigoted as their neighbors, with whom they live in a superficial harmony rife with tension. When Maximilian is teamed up with the pretty and talented Polish girl Celia for a four-handed piano competition, his family objects to the friendship that blossoms. "You're better than she is," his grandmother tells him. "I didn't build a synagogue to have my grandson marry a *shiksa* in," his strong-willed grandfather adds.

Forbidden to see Celia, Maximilian continues to practice in secret, aided by his piano teacher, who is married to a Japanese woman and knows something about intolerance. Another form of bias rears its head when the town's beloved rabbi is killed in a crash with a hay truck. A new rabbi is quickly hired, sight unseen. When he arrives, the small Jewish community is dismayed to find that in their haste they have hired a Hasid. The subject of inter-Jewish prejudice, which rarely surfaces in films, is here handled with dry humor.

Saul Rubinek gives a marvelous performance as the humble Hasid who arrives to take over Maximilian's bar mitzvah education. Rubinek went on to play another Hasidic rabbi in *The Quarrel,* a Canadian film about matters of faith that also deals with differences of opinion within the Jewish tradition. At first, Maximilian thinks this oddly dressed Orthodox Jew, who prays in a snowy cornfield and tells jokes when he is expected to dispense wisdom, is yet another curse on his troubled young life. But Rabbi Tittelman proves an unexpected ally. A frustrated comic who does not quite fit the hasidic mold himself, the renegade rebbe introduces Maximilian to the joys of *Yiddishkeit* and to the liberating power of pluralism. His lesson is that we can enjoy each other without compromising our own unique individuality.

Glick, whose name means luck in Yiddish, has the good fortune to be mentored by a true *mensch.* The friendship between a boy and his rabbi has never been so touchingly rendered on film as it is in this expertly acted and shrewdly crafted comedy by director Allan Goldstein. In turn, Maximilian teaches the rabbi something about the importance of following one's dreams. When Rabbi Tittelman sheds his beard and sidelocks to try his hand at comedy, he retains his Jewish identity, reinforcing the idea that one does not have to reject cultural identification in the pursuit of personal expression.

The Outside Chance of Maximilian Glick, which won the Toronto and Vancouver film festivals' awards for best Canadian feature film of 1988 but was given only a limited release in the United States, pokes gentle fun at Jewish family life while ultimately honoring the traditionally close bond between parent and child. It is an affecting and affectionate story about the inevitable triumph of love once mutual respect is established. "We're a family. We'll work this thing out," Maximilian's father tells him.

In the end, Maximilian drives a hard bargain with his parents, finding a way to win his family's approval by appealing to their best instincts. We have no doubt, as Maximilian delivers his bar mitzvah sermon from the *bima*, that he will be a very good man and the best kind of Jew.

GROWING UP JEWISH   *The Outside Chance of Maximilian Glick,* a Canadian coming-of-age comedy that failed to receive the recognition it deserved, stars Saul Rubinek as an unorthodox hasidic rabbi who undertakes the title character's bar mitzvah education.

28

The Revolt of Job

MGM/UA Home Entertainment (1983)
CAST: Ferenc Zenthe, Hedl Temessy, Gabor Feher
DIRECTED BY: Imre Gyongyossy and Barna Kabay
97 minutes [Not rated]

Children are commonly featured in films about the Holocaust, perhaps because they are symbols of innocence and arouse automatic sympathy in viewers. But while the preponderance of child-centered Holocaust films depict Jewish children protected by Christians, *The Revolt of Job* features the reverse scenario.

In this touching film set in the Hungarian countryside during World War II, a childless Jewish couple adopts a gentile child so that they will have an heir. Unlike many Jews of the era who refused to believe they were in grave danger, Job (Ferenc Zenthe) and Roza (Hedl Temessy) are well aware that their days are numbered. Adopting an orphan is their way of defying death, of ensuring that a son will survive them and inherit all that they have worked to accumulate. "We have outwitted the philistine dolt Hitler," Job exults in this beautifully acted, Oscar-nominated drama, perhaps the best foreign film about the Holocaust not based on a true story. In its focus on an unusual relationship between a Jew and a Christian, it also resembles two other noteworthy fictional foreign Holocaust films: *The Shop on Main Street,* a 1965 Oscar-winning Czech drama about the relationship between an elderly Jewish woman and the Czech peasant assigned to take over her "Aryanized" shop; and Agnieszka Holland's 1985 German-language drama about a Polish peasant who shelters and exploits a sophisticated Jewish woman, *Angry Harvest.*

All of these provocative and ironic films examine role reversals and explore issues of personal responsibility and the temptation of power. Unlike many Holocaust films that focus on survival, these films reflect the dominant reality of the event, acknowledging the tragic fate of the vast majority of Europe's Jews. *The Revolt of Job* does not provide viewers with an emotionally uplifting ending, but the heartwrenching story is tinged with humor and profound affection.

Job's unconventional but practical decision is born of desperation by a long-suffering man who knows his death is imminent. "I can't die without

DESPERATE MEASURES   In a last-ditch effort at symbolic survival, Job and Rosa (Ferenc Zenthe and Hedi Temessy) adopt a gentile boy as an heir to their heritage in the Oscar-nominated Hungarian film *The Revolt of Job*.

knowing that a descendent will survive me. Our whole life has been a struggle for an heir," says the severely-tested Job, who has buried seven children. "I'd like to raise one man for the Lord," the religious man adds. Jews are forbidden to adopt any child, let alone a Christian one, of course. But times are hard, and the director of the local orphanage is willing to risk the illegal trade of a boy no one else wants for two fat calves. Job selects a wild and unruly lad because, he says, he sees the spark of life in him, transplanted from the calves.

Lacko (Gabor Feher) is indeed a handful, but he soon settles into life on his new parents' prosperous farm and develops a genuine affection for the kind and caring couple. Although his parents teach him to say he's not a Jew, Lacko feels such kinship with his family that he wants to be Jewish too. His parents make sure he learns Christian prayers, but they eventually allow him to join their Jewish observances. They also pass on important teachings, telling their child that God is to be found in all acts of love.

As anti-Semitism escalates in their rustic and formerly peaceful town, where they once enjoyed the privilege and security of wealth and continue to act as benefactors to the financially less fortunate among them, *The Revolt of Job* builds to its inevitable conclusion. Lacko, about to be orphaned a second time, watches in helpless bewilderment as his mother and father are taken away in a cart with the other Jews from the village. Some of the villagers gloat as the Jews, whose position they obviously resent, are taken away; while other neighbors show their solidarity for their departing friends. In 1944, the final credits inform us, 600,000 Jews were deported from Hungary, and 500,000 never returned.

The Revolt of Job, which enjoyed success on the American art film circuit, is a German-Hungarian coproduction directed by Imre Gyongyossy and Barna Kabay. Although the Hungarian directors and coscreenwriters are not Jewish, the story has autobiographical origins. During the war, Gyongyossy was left for a time with an elderly Jewish farming couple whose sudden, unexplained arrest by armed police, he has said, has haunted him ever since. That child-like sense of mystification at a terrible, unfathomable tragedy is well communicated in *The Revolt of Job,* which is permeated with a sense of loss. The film conveys deep affection for Job and Roza, who are observed by Lacko practicing their faith with great beauty and joy. "Do not give in to the sin of despair," Roza tells Job when the boy falls deathly ill with diphtheria, emphasizing the Jewish resilience of spirit and perseverance of faith that their adoption of Lacko represents. Someone must be left to wait for the Messiah, Job tells the boy as they are taken away, pretending not to know their son so he will be spared.

Lacko, left well provided for and ensconced with the family's decent servants, will surely mourn his saviors, and in that sense, he assumes the usual child's role as innocent victim. But Lacko serves a more complicated function in this story of a man valiantly, and perhaps futilely, fighting for his heritage. Although we might question the resignation with which Job and Roza accept their destruction, we also recognize that Lacko is an ingenious survival tactic at a time when Jews survived any way they could, even if it is only the symbolic survival of leaving something of value behind. The memory of Job and Roza's life will not die with them. Lacko, a Jew in his heart, is more than an heir to a fortune of love. He has also been left with a terrible burden. He has been charged with the responsibility of bearing witness.

29

Homicide

Triumph Releasing Corporation (1991)
CAST: Joe Mantegna, William H. Macy, Ving Rhames
DIRECTED BY: David Mamet
102 minutes [R]

In the course of a murder investigation, homicide detective Bobby Gold makes an unexpected discovery: his Jewish identity. Gold has always been the first cop through the door, although he doesn't know why he insists on putting himself in harm's way. He finally figures out the reason for his bravado. As a Jew, he constantly has to prove himself. It's not enough to be as good as the black or Irish cops; he has to be better than the other policemen, who regard him with suspicion nonetheless.

Gold has several such startling revelations in *Homicide,* a taut, eccentric, character-driven crime drama written and directed by famed Jewish playwright and screenwriter David Mamet. *Homicide* reflects the experience of an increasing number of Jews today who have reconnected with their cultural or religious roots. One of the best of numerous movies of recent years to center on a Jewish identity crisis or deal with disaffected Jews struggling with the question of what it means to be Jewish, *Homicide* heads a notable list that includes *Joshua Then and Now, Leon the Pig Farmer, Unstrung Heroes, Willie and Phil,* and *Next Stop, Greenwich Village.* Typically, the characters find some sort of comfortable balance between tradition and modernity, connection and independence. In some cases, characters redefine themselves along more Jewish lines, most memorably in *The Way We Were* and *Crossing Delancey.*

But of all the movie Jews struggling to find their places in the world, none is more intriguing or complex than Gold, who regards his newly discovered Jewishness with a mixture of horror and exhilaration, ambiguity and angst, resentment and relief. For years, Bobby Gold (Joe Mantegna) has ignored or denied his Jewish heritage. He defines himself exclusively by his work, into which he pours his devout passion. His tribe is the police force. He has even absorbed the anti-Semitic attitudes that pervade his profession, and he does not recognize the prejudices that have rubbed off on him as self-hatred.

Things change when he stumbles upon a case involving the murder of an elderly Jewish woman who owned a candy store in a black inner-city neighborhood. At first, he regards the case he has been handed as a nuisance. He and his partner Sully (William Macy) are deeply involved in another, much more high-profile case involving a dangerous black criminal (Ving Rhames). But as Gold becomes involved with the murdered woman's family, his loyalties are divided. The family changes a number of his misconceptions. At first, he dismisses the Kleins as paranoid. But he learns the truth of the old maxim, "Just because you're paranoid doesn't mean they aren't out to get you."

He also finds that not all Jews are passive victims who contribute to the prejudice against them, as he has been led to believe. At first, he thinks Mrs. Klein was asking for trouble by staying in the black neighborhood. He finds a poster that reads "Crime is caused by the ghetto. The ghetto is caused by the Jews." He almost buys the thesis. In fact, however, he discovers the hate-mongering leaflet was created and distributed by white supremacists who, of course, despise Jews and blacks equally.

Gold is surprised to find that "the old Jew broad," as he disrespectfully refers to Mrs. Klein, once ran guns for Israel and is still considered a hero in the Jewish homeland. He becomes involved with a group of Zionists who continue to engage in covert action against anti-Semitism. This dangerous, glamorous image of Jews as warriors refutes his earlier preconception of the wealthy, passive Jew who buys protection. It all adds up to quite an awakening, one that shakes him to the core. Gold discovers that nothing he has done, or can do, will erase the anti-Semitism in the largely black police department. Even the black criminal he corners calls him "a smart kike," echoing the incendiary slur of the black deputy mayor's assistant at the film's opening.

He realizes that his specifically Jewish verbal skills, his ability to talk to people and empathize with "how the bad guys felt," have made him useful. A hostage negotiator, he's called "the Orator" and "the Mouthpiece." But the other cops, he comes to understand, always felt he was a "pussy" because he was a Jew. In returning to his roots, Gold begins to see himself as part of history. He acknowledges his need to "be part of something," and he moves to establish a more authentic sense of self.

Mamet, who admits he has always felt like an outsider and acknowledges a great longing to belong, has said the story was inspired by his experience as an American Jew growing up not feeling sufficiently Jewish *or* American. Like many of his previous films, *Homicide* deals with what Mamet calls "problems of reconciliation and self-worth."

Gold, an assimilated, secular Jew who doesn't know the difference betwen Hebrew and Yiddish, is openly pitied by the cultured, proudly Jewish Klein

IDENTITY CRISIS   David Mamet wrote and directed *Homicide,* starring Joe Mantegna as a Jewish cop who reconnects with the heritage he has long denied.

family he initially treats with scorn. "Do you belong nowhere?" Mrs. Klein's granddaughter asks after overhearing a phone conversation in which he expresses hostility toward the family. In addition to its social and cultural questions, *Homicide* directly deals with the political issue of racial tensions between Jews and blacks. Mrs. Klein, who once put her children through school by running the candy store in what was then an ethnically diverse neighborhood, is murdered because of persistent anti-Semitic rumors that she kept a fortune in the basement. Not since *The Pawnbroker* has the complex situation of the Jewish merchant in the black ghetto been so thoroughly explored.

The third film written and directed by Mamet, *Homicide* is a dark drama of loss and disillusionment that ends not with resolution but with a series of betrayals that shatter Gold's past connections and future affiliations. Gold fails in his sworn duties and pays dearly for his defection. However natural and even laudable his desire for cultural connection and community may be, it has led to his destruction. Such is the nature of Mamet's amoral universe. The disturbing drama ends without solace and with scant hope. Gold indeed is a man who belongs nowhere.

Mamet is a Pulitzer Prize–winning playwright (*Glengarry Glen Ross, The Disappearance of the Jews, Speed-the-Plow, The Old Neighborhood*), an Oscar-winning screenwriter (*The Verdict, The Postman Always Rings Twice, The*

Untouchables, We're No Angels, Hoffa), and an accomplished director (*House of Games, Things Change*). He has brought a Jewish sensibility—particularly a sense of otherness—to a number of projects and has written about his Jewish heritage in essays. *Homicide*, however, is his first overtly Jewish film. Mamet, who has become religious in recent years, is also known for his allegiances and long-standing relationships. Mantegna is to Mamet what De Niro is to Scorsese. The two men have worked together off and on, on stage and in film, since 1977. Mantegna, an Italian-American who has played Jewish characters on several occasions, embodies Mamet's tough, urban, ethnic, conflicted characters, men grappling with crises of spirit and career. Mantegna is especially adept at handling Mamet's elliptical, mannered prose. William Macy, who plays Gold's best buddy Sully, has also appeared in three other Mamet films: *House of Games, Things Change*, and *Oleanna*.

Mamet's somber, seamy world is typically peopled with lonely, defeated, and defiant men and, less frequently, women struggling to find their balance in unsettling times. The awakening of Gold's Jewish identity is no quick fix for his alienation, but the challenging and absorbing movie does show the psychological danger of repressing such potentially meaningful cultural associations.

30

Madame Rosa

Hen's Tooth Video and Vestron Video (1977)
CAST: Simone Signoret, Samy Ben Youb, Claude Dauphin
DIRECTED BY: Moshe Mizrahi
105 minutes [PG]

Winner of the Academy Award for best foreign film of 1977, *Madame Rosa (La Vie Devant Soi)* is the poignant tale of an ailing, aging, retired Jewish prostitute. One of the best portraits of a Holocaust survivor, *Madame Rosa* also offers a unique and unquestioningly positive look at the Jewish maternal instinct. The living embodiment of compassion, Madame Rosa (Simone Signoret) supports herself by taking in the children of younger Parisian prostitutes. "The kids of whores are kids too," she reasons.

A survivor of Auschwitz, Madame Rosa is a tender-hearted soul who cares deeply for each of her children, most of whom are unwanted. Madame Rosa has formed an especially strong attachment to her eldest ward, Momo (Samy Ben Youb), an Algerian boy whose parents have long since abandoned him. Momo, a troubled boy who loves her deeply, is being raised to be "a fine Moslem" under the tutelage of a local Algerian. Momo wants to know how Madame Rosa knows he's not Jewish like her, or like her other favored child, Moshe, who is being raised Jewish. Madame Rosa, who honors the ethnic and religious traditions of all her children, assures him that although his papers are false, she is positive of his heritage. "When you're in a mess, it makes no difference if you're an Arab or a Jew," she adds.

Madame Rosa has her own false papers proving she's not Jewish in case the French police come for her, as they did some thirty-five years earlier when her Jewish lover denounced her as a Jew. She also keeps a secret "Jewish hideaway" in the basement, "just in case," where she takes refuge when nightmares keep her awake. Madame Rosa's paranoia and anxiety attacks are the products of a lifetime lived on the edge. Her marginalized existence has always been precarious. Now, with her health failing and money tight, her future is more uncertain than ever. Madame Rosa has been persecuted for her heritage and ostracized for her occupation, but she has retained her compassion. Her respect for human life has perhaps been magnified by her experience.

Director Moshe Mizrahi's delicate drama of palpable desperation, adapted from a prize-winning 1975 French novel by Emile Ajar, is sentimental without becoming maudlin. Much of the credit for the film's power rests with Signoret's deeply touching portrait of a woman who has reached the end of her formidable strength. "Everything has its limits, even for Jews," she says of her endless suffering. Her body and face have been ravaged by a hard life, but she still exudes a beguiling sensuality and great warmth.

Signoret was born Simone Kaminker to a French mother and a Jewish father who fled Paris during the French Occupation. Once a great beauty, Signoret did not age gracefully. She did not hide from the camera but found dramatic use for her lost looks. She was perfectly cast in *Madame Rosa,* and won the French César for her performance, a personal triumph for the actress, who collaborated with director Mizrahi again in 1980 on *I Sent a Letter to My Love.* Mizrahi, an Israeli who makes films in Israel and France, went on to direct *Every Time We Say Goodbye,* starring Tom Hanks as an American soldier who falls in love with a Sephardic Jew in 1942 Jerusalem, and previously

THE FACE OF COMPASSION   Simone Signoret plays a Holocaust survivor who defiantly lives her life with humanity and dignity in the Oscar-winning French film *Madame Rosa.*

made *I Love You, Rosa,* a 1972 film about a Sephardic woman obligated to marry her dead husband's eleven-year-old brother.

A story of the friendship between a young boy and a surrogate grand-parent, *Madame Rosa* bears some resemblance to Claude Berri's 1968 French film *The Two of Us,* which also examines how anti-Semitism is transcended by human compassion. In its depiction of a non-Jewish child sheltered by Jews, it also resembles *The Revolt of Job,* which portrays an alliance between members of two warring cultures.

Madame Rosa is attended by another compassionate Jew, the kindly old Dr. Katz (Claude Dauphin). "He is well known in the Jewish community for his Christian charity," Momo says without intended irony. Madame Rosa, who has always treated her neighbors with respect and kindness, is also taken care of by a black transvestite prostitute and other multiethnic residents in the building. Madame Rosa's compassion does not extend to those she considers unworthy, however. She extracts her revenge on Momo's negligent Algerian father, who murdered his mother, by telling him she mistakenly has raised Momo as a Jew. Madame Rosa is a good Jew, but not a religious one. "I saw the workings of God in Auschwitz," she says, adding that she doesn't want a rabbi to officiate at her funeral. "Just bury me under a tree," she says.

Madame Rosa wants for her children what Jewish immigrant parents typically wanted: a better life. She also wants Momo to become a decent human being. "School won't make you a *mensch,*" she says. She makes Momo promise he will never "peddle his ass" or become "a fancy man," that he never contribute to human exploitation or fall victim to it himself. Madame Rosa admits she worries about her children. "You have to worry about children or they grow up to be bums," she tells Dr. Katz when he suggests that all her worrying is putting a strain on her fragile health.

In the end, Momo helps Madame Rosa die as she has lived, independent and defiant. In one of the last scenes, Momo says the *Sh'ma* with Madame Rosa. Madame Rosa has raised him well. He is, as she has said, a *gute kind.* She has done some good in the world despite all that she has unjustly suffered.

31

Driving Miss Daisy

Warner Bros. (1989)
CAST: Jessica Tandy, Morgan Freeman, Dan Aykroyd, Patti LuPone
DIRECTED BY: Bruce Beresford
99 minutes [PG]

When Daisy Werthan and her chauffeur Hoke are pulled over in rural Alabama in the late 1950s, two suspicious Southern police officers check their identification and send them on their way. "There goes an old nigger and an old Jew woman," one of the rednecks sneers to the other as they drive off. "That's one sorry sight."

A touching story tracing the unlikely twenty-five-year friendship that develops between prim and proper Miss Daisy (Jessica Tandy) and her loyal employee (Morgan Freeman), *Driving Miss Daisy* examines the uneasy relationship between members of two persecuted minorities, a complex, controversial subject rarely explored in film. The Oscar-winning drama also presents an image of the Jew not often seen on film. A genteel Southern matron who takes pride in her heritage, Miss Daisy has faults as well as virtues. Unlike the aging Jewish women in *The Cemetery Club* and *Used People*—all also played by gentiles—she is not an object of comic ridicule, however. She is a dignified character treated with respect if not unfettered admiration. Her chief failing is that while her family has secured a precarious position in the stubbornly bigoted American South, she does not fully appreciate the plight of blacks still struggling to gain a toehold.

In this beautifully acted, multi-award-winning adaptation of Alfred Uhry's play, Daisy's Jewish liberalism is put to the test—much like it is in *Majority of One,* another film about tolerance and the relationship between a mature Jewish woman and a non-Jewish man. Miss Daisy insists she is not racist, but she condescendingly refers to blacks as "they," as in "they all take things" and "they're like children." She also expects Hoke to adopt a subservient manner, which is what he is adept at doing. A bossy, proper woman, she would never think to ride in the front seat with Hoke, for example. There is considerable irony late in the film when Miss Daisy attends a dinner for Martin Luther King Jr. while Hoke waits outside in the car, listening to the speech on the radio.

Hoke may be illiterate, but he is much more aware of the discrimination that binds—or perhaps should bind—Jews and blacks than Miss Daisy is willing to admit. When the temple Miss Daisy attends regularly is bombed, Hoke tells her a story about a lynching he witnessed as a boy. She fails to see the connection. Hoke has earlier told Miss Daisy's dutiful, affable son (Dan Aykroyd) that he prefers working for Jews, perhaps because he feels an affinity based on history or because he has been treated more fairly by sympathetic, liberal Jews in the past. (His last employer was a Jewish judge.) "People be saying they're stingy and such," he says, "but don't be saying none of that 'round me."

Miss Daisy warms to her faithful, trusted servant slowly, eventually confiding in him more openly about personal matters that, as a black man, he is in a position to understand better than white Southerners of equal social standing. Miss Daisy, who does not forget her roots or her religion, disdains her daughter-in-law (Patti LuPone) for currying favor with Christians and denying her Jewishness. "If I had a nose like that I wouldn't be going around saying 'Merry Christmas,' " she says sharply. Although Miss Daisy is stubborn, fiercely private, and doggedly independent, she comes to rely on Hoke more and more as a confidant and helpmate. In a touching moment late in the film, she tells Hoke that he's her best friend. Despite the differences in their backgrounds, and perhaps because of their shared experience with adversity, they are both dignified and proud.

Alfred Uhry loosely based his three-person play on his own grandmother and her chauffeur. Even before the acclaimed drama opened in New York in 1985, the screen rights were acquired by producer Richard Zanuck, the son of the legendary Darryl Zanuck—one of the few non-Jewish moguls in Hollywood's studio days who spearheaded a number of important Jewish-themed films. Ironically, to some extent, Hollywood's attitude mirrored the reaction of the Alabama rednecks who stop Miss Daisy's car simply because a black man is driving an expensive automobile. "No one would want to see a movie about an elderly Jewish woman and an old black man," Zanuck was told when he and his partners hired Uhry to write the screenplay and shopped the project around Hollywood. One executive reportedly suggested refashioning the story as a vehicle for Eddie Murphy and Bette Midler. Eventually, Warner Bros. nervously agreed to finance the low-budget film.

Driving Miss Daisy, which opened while the play was still running in New York, was a surprise hit. Critics politely applauded the tender but prickly look at race relations in the South, which won four Oscars, including best picture. Tandy won her first best actress Oscar—at the age of eighty. Uhry won an Oscar for his adapted screenplay as well as a Writer's Guild Award. Freeman, who had played Hoke on the stage, was nominated for best supporting actor

BEST FRIENDS   In the surprise hit *Driving Miss Daisy,* an Oscar winner and one of the top films of 1989, Jessica Tandy won her first Academy Award playing a Southern Jewish widow who forms an odd alliance with her black chauffeur (Morgan Freeman).

and won a Golden Globe award as well as one from the National Board of Review. The film was nominated in eight categories and won a host of critics' awards.

Only Bruce Beresford came up empty-handed, failing to earn the best director nomination, a slight that perhaps reflects a feeling that the material was so strong it carried itself. Beresford, an Australian director who cast Richard Gere in the failed biblical epic *King David*, again cast non-Jews in the Jewish roles in *Driving Miss Daisy*. Yet he does not shy away from visually identifying Miss Daisy as Jewish. We see her playing mah-jongg and at sparsely attended services at the synagogue. Miss Daisy enjoys her position of privilege and relishes maintaining full control over her life. Despite her denial of anti-Semitism, she is also guarded and protective of her privacy. She does not like to call attention to her wealth and avoids any display she considers "vulgar," which can also be read as a reaction to having grown up in a hostile environment. Her tight-fistedness is directly related to her childhood, when her family was so poor they couldn't afford to keep a stray kitten she found.

Miss Daisy is a sad figure, really, a lonely, unbending, brittle old woman. Hoke takes her on a short but memorable journey toward greater compassion. She softens some, but her defenses and preconceptions do not melt away. Hoke respects her but remains aware of the distance between them. "How do you know how I see," he says when she questions his eyesight, "lessen you can look out my eyes?"

32

Reversal of Fortune

Warner Bros. (1990)
CAST: Jeremy Irons, Ron Silver, Glenn Close
DIRECTED BY: Barbet Schroeder
112 minutes [R]

Moments after meeting Alan Dershowitz, Claus von Bulow informs the famed lawyer that he has "the greatest respect for the intelligence and integrity of the Jewish people." The remark catches Dershowitz off guard, literally and figuratively. Bending over his briefcase, the litigator looks back at his prospective client in speechless astonishment.

Reversal of Fortune, Barbet Schroeder's astounding adaptation of the book by Dershowitz describing his defense of von Bulow, goes further than most films dealing with the relationship between a Jewish savior and the gentile he rescues, sharply delineating the vast differences between them at every turn. Much more than a murder mystery—the mystery is never, in fact, solved—*Reversal of Fortune* is a story of class and ethnicity that juxtaposes an enigmatic, Eurotrashy aristocrat with his unlikely ally, a man of the people. The invigorating film is an astute study in contrasts, ripe with contradictions and deep, dark irony. At its heart it is a delicious and devilish black comedy of manners and mores as well as a flattering profile of a famous, controversial, and outspoken modern Jewish figure.

Dershowitz, who finances worthy but unprofitable cases by representing rich clients when he feels there is a constitutional or moral issue at stake, agrees to take on von Bulow's case. His unpopular client has been tried and convicted of trying to murder his socialite wife, Sunny, who lies in a coma from which she will never awaken. Dershowitz successfully appeals the notorious case, which results in von Bulow's acquittal in a second trial.

In *Reversal of Fortune,* Dershowitz plays a role commonly assigned to screen Jews, that of the physical or spiritual savior of a gentile. This stunning film serves as a fine example of a category that might be called "Jews to the Rescue," a genre that includes numerous memorable movies. Judd Hirsch plays a Jewish psychiatrist who comes to the emotional rescue of an uptight W.A.S.P. family in *Ordinary People.* Ron Leibman is cast as a Jewish labor

CHUTZPAH   Ron Silver plays Alan Dershowitz in *Reversal of Fortune,* which continually emphasizes the culturally ingrained differences between the famed Jewish lawyer and his W.A.S.P. client, Claus von Bulow (Oscar-winner Jeremy Irons).

organizer who guides a Southern woman on her journey to self-fulfillment and political empowerment in *Norma Rae.* Rocky Graziano's rise to personal and professional success is mentored by his Jewish manager and Jewish wife in *Somebody Up There Likes Me.* In *Mr. Skeffington,* a Jewish businessman provides salvation for his vain, foolish wife (Bette Davis). A brainy Jew (Jeff Goldblum) and a brawny black (Will Smith) save the world from annihilation by aliens in *Independence Day.* A principled young Jewish woman (Jennifer Grey) teaches her lower-class gentile boyfriend to do the right thing in *Dirty Dancing.* In *The Caine Mutiny,* a Jewish lawyer (Jose Ferrer) wins justice and then holds his clients to a higher code of morality.

Dershowitz is also morally superior to the man he saves. He inhabits the opposite end of the personal and social spectrum from the philistine playboy von Bulow. Dershowitz, life force personified, is dedicated to justice, a champion of the oppressed. He is an angry, animated man who takes cases on the basis of how "pissed off" they make him. A man who puts career first, Dershowitz admits he would probably represent Hitler—if he didn't kill him first. This admission draws attention to the lawyer's relationship with von Bulow, a man who may very well be evil. Von Bulow, lazy and decadent, is the cinema's most unlikely victim. Calm, composed, and unfailingly courteous, he is so cold and calculating we easily believe him capable of murder. Surely he is guilty of something, as one of Dershowitz's students assisting him on the case observes. These high-minded students don't like von Bulow one bit, but they have to admit that even he is entitled to a fair trial.

Sunny and Claus live in a chilly, immaculate, and sterile mansion, isolated and insulated. Claus wears ear plugs and a wool scarf and hat to bed. Reserved and repressed, they epitomize a stereotype of W.A.S.P. wealth: plenty of money and no enjoyment of life. In contrast, Dershowitz lives in a modest, ramshackle home with a menorah on the mantle, plays basketball in the driveway, and eats takeout Chinese food out of the box. Warm, relaxed, direct, Dershowitz is a passionate and compassionate man of principle.

Although worlds apart, the two men seem to understand each other perfectly. When Dershowitz candidly informs von Bulow "There's one thing in your favor—everybody hates you," Claus doesn't bat an eye or miss a beat. "That's a start," he gamely replies. Later, in one of the movie's many great lines, Dershowitz tells von Bulow he's a very strange man. "You have no idea," Claus drolly responds with a sly suggestion of a smile. (Irons repeats this famous line in *The Lion King*.) This cavalier honesty is beguiling, making von Bulow one of the creepiest yet oddly charming characters in screen history. Irons's brilliant comic performance drew heaps of praise from the critics. The real Dershowitz was among Irons's most ardent admirers, telling the press that "Irons is a better Claus von Bulow than Claus von Bulow." Irons won a much deserved Oscar for his highly mannered, ambiguous performance. Close, however, was unjustly overlooked for her own bleakly brilliant portrait of ruin.

Barbet Schroeder's devastating film feeds on our fascination with the lifestyles of the rich and shameless. Schroeder, nominated for a best director Oscar, understands the delight we take upon discovering that wealthy people are morally corrupt, spiritually bankrupt, pathetically dysfunctional, and miserably unhappy. The sense of moral superiority such disclosures impart assuages our jealousy a little.

The movie is narrated by the most pathetic character of all, the hilariously misnamed Sunny, whose voice rises eerily from her comatose body. Her condition is described as "persistent vegetative," a description that fits her life before the insulin-induced coma as well. Vain, vacuous, drug-addicted, abusive, and fabulously eccentric, Sunny spent her purposeless life wrapped in a shroud of misery before her insulin overdose. Did von Bulow try to murder his miserable wife? Dershowitz himself has said that to this day he does not know, and the movie does not answer this question. Irons's sly performance hints at both guilt and innocence.

Screenwriter Nicholas Kazan (son of director Elia Kazan) crafted a cleverly structured story filled with stinging sarcasm. His strikingly sardonic screenplay is worded with utmost care. Von Bulow has been given marvelously understated lines that Irons knows just how to deliver. Challenged for his apparent lack of feeling about his wife's condition, he tells Dershowitz, "I don't wear my heart on my sleeve. We can't all be like you, Alan." This statement indicates that von Bulow is very aware of the differences between the effusive Jew and the uptight gentile. It is clear that he finds this idealistic Jew useful, even if he would never associate with such an undecorous man socially. There's a class-conscious form of anti-Semitism at work here, a double standard in which Jews, despite a recognition of their obvious talents and exploitable virtues, are regarded as inferiors. This attitude is clearly stated by von Bulow's new girlfriend (Christine Baranski), who tells Dershowitz that she advised von Bulow to hire him. " 'Get the Jew,' I said," she recalls, oblivious to any insult that might be taken.

Silver, who received accolades for his performance as the controversial, emotionally engaged, and ethical defense lawyer, plays Dershowitz as a whirlwind of energy. The son of Jewish immigrants who grew up on the Lower East Side, Silver brings a working-class quality to the part that further contrasts with von Bulow's icy affectations. Silver, himself a dedicated political activist who has been involved with numerous liberal causes, seems to have an instinctive understanding of the role, one of his very best.

The character of Dershowitz serves, as many screen Jews do, as the moral center of the story. *Reversal of Fortune* is unusual, however, in that it presents the very worst side of the W.A.S.P. world and nothing but the best of Jewish values and character.

33

Europa Europa

Orion Classics (1991)
CAST: Marco Hofschneider, Julie Delpy
DIRECTED BY: Agnieszka Holland
115 minutes [R]

A story this incredible has to be true. No one would have the temerity to make up such an unbelievable tale. Based on the autobiography of Solomon Perel, *Europa Europa* is the amazing story of a young man who survives the Holocaust by the most extreme means imaginable. Solomon's life is a series of losses, separations, and transformations that involve assumed identities, shifting allegiances, deliberate deceptions, bizarre coincidences, astounding strokes of luck, and brazen acts of chutzpah.

Agniezska Holland's adaptation of *Europa Europa: A Memoir of World War II* (published in an English translation in 1997) is one of the boldest and arguably most disconcerting Holocaust films ever made. Filled with black humor and marked by an almost surrealistic sense of absurdity, *Europa Europa* was so controversial in both subject and style that the German film establishment decided not to submit it for Academy Award consideration for best foreign film. Members of the jury called it trash and an embarrassment, but Holland charged that they simply hated the subject. After noted German film artists took out ads requesting that the academy compensate for the omission by nominating it in other categories, it received a nomination in the best adapted screenplay category, a rare honor for a foreign film. *Europa Europa* proved a great success on the American art film circuit and won a Golden Globe for best foreign film as well as a number of critics' awards.

A metaphor for the extraordinary lengths to which Jews were forced to go in order to survive the Holocaust, *Europa Europa* is a suspenseful and often terrifying drama tinged with a satiric edge. This ironic tone suits the audacious tale, but did not sit well with all viewers, some of whom felt the film did not treat its subject with enough seriousness. Some also objected to its sympathetic treatment of a Jew who conceals his Jewish identity and masquerades as a Nazi, while others saw this daring disguise as an inspirational example of a Jew outwitting his persecutors. In any case, the provocative film raises dis-

129

turbing questions about the moral dilemmas so many victims of the Holocaust faced. Not since Italian director Lina Wertmuller mixed humor and horror in *Seven Beauties* (1976), which also dealt with a man who goes to desperate measures to survive, was a Holocaust film greeted with such a mixture of praise and censure.

The dubious hero of *Europa Europa* is born in Germany in 1925 on Hitler's birthday. Solek (Marco Hofschneider) is of bar mitzvah age when his family moves to Lodz to escape the escalating persecution of Jews. When war breaks out, Solek and his older brother flee eastward. Separated from his brother, Solek is saved by Russian soldiers and sent to an orphanage for two years where he is turned into a good Communist—the first of his many incarnations.

Although his father's last words of advice are "Never forget who you are," Solek adopts an ideology that states "Religion is the opiate of the masses" and takes grateful shelter in a country that has made a pact with Hitler. When war finally reaches the orphanage, Solek is separated from the truck carrying his fleeing comrades. Arrested by the advancing German army, Solek claims to be a German of pure Aryan stock. The desperate ruse works, and the bilingual Solek proves so useful as a translator he becomes a trusted soldier. When he tries to desert, he accidentally becomes a German war hero and is sent to an elite training school for Hitler Youth.

Now sixteen, Solek again metamorphoses into his disguise, which puts him into an agonizing situation. Although he lives in mortal fear of discovery, his conscience somehow permits him to fall in love with a pretty, anti-Semitic German girl (French actress Julie Delpy), an element of the story some critics found objectionable. Forced once again to fight in the Germany army, Solek attempts to defect to the Russians, who naturally do not believe his story. Solek is about to be shot when his brother, who has just been liberated from a concentration camp, recognizes him and saves him. Together they find their way to the American side and to a new life in Israel, where Solek resolves to live forever after as a Jew.

Although his brother warns him not to tell his story because no one will believe it, the veracity of Perel's tale is underlined by the film's coda, in which the real Solomon Perel is filmed, peacefully humming *Hineh Mah Tov* with a sly smile on his face. (This updated, real-life ending, filmed in Israel, bears resemblance to the conclusion of *Schindler's List,* in which the survivors and their descendents visit Schindler's grave, accompanied by the film's actors.)

Like a number of other excellent films about the Holocaust, *Europa Europa* examines the high cost of survival. In theme it resembles *Triumph of the Spirit,* based on the experiences of a boxer who literally fought for his life in Auschwitz-Birkenau. In its fluke-of-fate subject, it bears comparison with *The Dunera Boys,* a fascinating English film about a bizarre bit of Holocaust

HIDDEN IN PLAIN SIGHT   In the international hit *Europa Europa,* Marco Hofschneider plays a Jewish teenager who survives the Holocaust by pretending to be "Aryan," a disguise so successful he is sent to an elite training school for Hitler Youth.

history. In tone, it can be compared with *The Nasty Girl,* a spirited true-life drama about a young German woman who seeks to find the truth about her hometown during the Holocaust. The story of a young Jew who comes of age surviving the horror of Nazi Germany, it is not unlike *David,* the first German Holocaust film to be directed by a German Jew.

The international success of *Europa Europa* greatly enhanced the reputation of Polish director and screenwriter Agnieszka Holland, who had previously dealt with the moral complexities of the Holocaust in the Oscar-nominated *Angry Harvest* and provided the script for Andrej Wajda's controversial, fact-based Holocaust biography, *Korczak,* released the year before *Europa Europa.* Holland, whose father was Jewish, prefers astringency to sentimentality as she deals with ethical dilemmas in her character-driven dramas.

Although the sight of a Jew in Nazi uniform is deeply unsettling, the film never lets us forget how young, confused, petrified, and traumatized Solek is. We do not have to approve of his actions in order to marvel at the grotesque absurdity of his situation.

34

The Big Fix

Universal Pictures (1978)
CAST: Richard Dreyfuss, Susan Anspach, F. Murray Abraham, Bonnie Bedelia
DIRECTED BY: Jeremy Paul Kagan
108 minutes [PG]

Woody Allen adopted Humphrey Bogart as his role model in *Play It Again, Sam* (1972) precisely because the trench-coated tough guy's confidence with women, physical courage, and cool under pressure were antithetical to the fragile, angst-ridden Jewish psyche of Allen's schlemiel character. Richard Dreyfuss plays a private eye who succeeds despite—or perhaps even because of—his Jewish qualities. Not that Moses Wine, a Jewish version of the fabled private eye featured in *The Big Fix* (1978), is so tough. Smart, yes. And just as cynical and uncompromising as Bogie's Sam Spade. But with his frizzy Jewish Afro, keen sense of humor and irony, and general disrespect for authority, Moses is no *goyish* gumshoe. Cute and cuddly, guided by *menschlichkeit* and a nose for trouble, Moses invades the hard-boiled detective territory previously inhabited by hard-drinking, no-nonsense, smack-'em-around W.A.S.P.s.

The casting of the distinctly and proudly Jewish Dreyfuss as a contemporary version of the 1940s dick reflects the era in which the film was made, when genres were routinely turned on their heads and eccentric ethnic characters replaced all-American heroes. Beginning in the late 1960s, as the cultural concepts of diversity and pluralism found their way onto the screen, overtly Jewish characters began to pop up in the unlikeliest places, from vampire movies (*The Fearless Vampire Killers, Love at First Bite*), to Westerns (*Blazing Saddles, The Frisco Kid*), to thrillers (*All the President's Men, Marathon Man*), to gangster films (*Lepke; The Godfather, Part II*), to detective dramas. In 1968, George Segal played a Jewish cop on the trail of a serial killer in the screen adaptation of William Goldman's novel, *No Way to Treat a Lady*. In 1973, Elliott Gould was cast against type as Sam Spade's spiritual cousin, Philip Marlowe, in Robert Altman's *The Long Goodbye,* playing a *schlubby,* disaffected Jewish version of Raymond Chandler's cynical private investigator.

NO GOYISH GUMSHOE Richard Dreyfuss plays Jewish private eye Moses Wine in *The Big Fix,* a genre-bending drama that invades the previously restricted detective drama territory.

Moses, who is also disaffected, is a much more specifically Jewish character than Gould's Marlowe, however, and a much more unambiguously positive figure, which is one of this relatively unknown, offbeat film's virtues. A former Berkeley radical who is no longer politically active, Moses is a burnt-out activist. Overcome by a sense of futility, which commonly replaced the idealism of the 1960s, Moses has lost his bearings. Although disillusioned, he has not lost his personal integrity, however. Scornful of materialistic success and skeptical of New Age fads, Moses still smokes a bong and plays Clue.

Unlike the earlier bachelor detectives who always worked alone, Moses is a family man at heart. He has an ex-wife (Bonnie Bedelia) and two sons, to whom he sweetly sings lullabies over the phone. He frequently takes the kids along as he works and even uses his elderly Aunt Sonya (Rita Karlin) in his investigation. A former radical herself, this Russian refugee is still an avowed socialist who has not given up the good fight. Moses' arm is in a cast—further proof that his life is in disarray—and throughout the film he offers various facetious explanations for the injury, cleverly using the disability to his advantage. Moses' deceptively casual style is reminiscent of *Columbo,* the long-running TV show that starred Jewish actor Peter Falk. The resemblance is not coincidental. Director Jeremy Paul Kagan, the son of a rabbi, began his career directing episodes of *Columbo.* Kagan, whose 1982 film *The Chosen* ranks among the very best Jewish films, has said that Moses Wine represents the kind of commitment to social change he associates with Jews and admires most in his heritage.

Moses doesn't take anything very seriously anymore, including his job, so when an old girlfriend (Susan Anspach) offers him an assignment, he agrees to take it only for the money. She is now working for a liberal mainstream candidate whose cause is being hurt by an unwanted association with a notorious radical who has gone into hiding. When Moses' old flame, with whom passion has been rekindled, is murdered, Moses takes a personal interest in solving the case.

Ironically, the trail leads Moses to another Jewish ex-activist, the former leader of the militant underground, Howard Eppis (F. Murray Abraham), who is suspected of various acts of terrorism. Modeled on Abbie Hoffman, this radical holds some surprises for Moses. Also much to his own surprise, Moses proves a gutsy gumshoe. In the process of proving himself, Moses experiences the reawakening of his political consciousness.

It should be noted, without giving away the story's clever outcome, that the movie's political message is decidedly left of center. This is a rare Hollywood film that treats the idealism of 1960s political activism with respect and acknowledges the heavy participation of Jews in the counterculture. In one stirring scene, Moses watches newsreel footage of the Chicago riots, tears streaming down his face.

Based on a novel by Roger Simon and produced by Dreyfuss, this well-acted and deceptively low-key story of renewed personal and political purpose is steeped in a rich Jewish sensibility. The movie offers a look at the dilemma faced by Jews who, living in an age of apathy, seek to honor an age-old mandate to better the world in which they live.

35

Broadway Danny Rose

Orion Pictures (1984)
CAST: Woody Allen, Mia Farrow, Nick Apollo Forte
DIRECTED BY: Woody Allen
86 minutes [PG]

Defender of the downtrodden, Broadway Danny Rose has a heart as big as Manhattan. A man of little taste but enormous faith, Danny is a theatrical manager whose clients include a one-legged tap dancer, a blind xylophone player, penguins dressed up as rabbis, a balloon folding act, a woman who plays water glasses, a one-armed juggler, a parrot that sings "I Gotta Be Me," a ventriloquist who stutters, and a dumb, fat, temperamental has-been Italian singer with a drinking problem.

Danny's misplaced optimism is amusing, but his hopefulness is touching, making *Broadway Danny Rose* one of Woody Allen's sweetest and saddest comedies. Danny is also one of Allen's most sympathetic and thoroughly Jewish characters. Danny, who calls everyone darling and means it and uses the expression "my hand to God" with equal sincerity, wouldn't hurt a fly. Ironically, in a cutthroat world, his values consign him to the role of pathetic loser. It is a role Danny plays with endearing dignity and resignation—a perfect example of the "schlemiel as hero" phenomenon identified by literary critic Sanford Pinsker.

Allen was nominated for a best directing Oscar for *Broadway Danny Rose,* and his Oscar-nominated script was named the best original screenplay by the Writers Guild of America. Allen also stars as the perpetually positive Danny in the black-and-white film, an affectionate show-biz homage to the borscht belt comics who narrate the story and serve as the film's framing device. The hilarious tale of Danny's greatest misadventure is recounted by a group of veteran comedians that includes Sandy Baron, Jackie Gale, Corbett Monica, Howie Storm, and Morty Gunty. Due in part to the presence of these real-life comics, *Broadway Danny Rose* is also one of the best movies about Jews in show business.

Trading anecdotes at the famed Carnegie Deli, the comedians recall the strictly small-time manager with a mixture of amazement, fondness, and rueful

THE SCHLEMIEL AS HERO   Woody Allen plays a luckless but likable talent agent who becomes involved with a mob-connected bombshell (Mia Farrow) in *Broadway Danny Rose,* an affectionate character study that doubles as a show-biz homage.

pity. Danny, the story goes, took a very personal approach to personal management. Years earlier, Danny had rescued and nurtured Lou Canova (Nick Apollo Forte), an over-the-hill lounge lizard who had a few hits in the 1950s. Groomed by Danny—a stage mother, rabbi, and mentor rolled into one—Lou now stands poised for a comeback. The day of Lou's big audition for a gig with Milton Berle turns into a nightmare for Danny, however, when he is assigned the thankless task of picking up Lou's mistress, Tina Vitali, wonderfully played by an almost unrecognizable Mia Farrow. Danny is supposed to be the beard so Tina can attend the show to bolster Lou's shaky confidence.

Arriving at Tina's apartment hours early, Danny finds the hotheaded, mob-connected Italian bimbo feuding with Lou on the phone, and is sent straight to the bottle. Danny follows Tina first to a fortune-teller and then to a party where mobsters mistake Danny for Tina's secret lover. Danny, who has never done anything wrong in his entire humble existence, finds himself on the run for his life.

In this Jewish morality tale, Danny, who continually protests "I didn't do anything," learns that innocence is no protection from persecution and that there is precious little justice in the world. Like Chaplin's Little Tramp, whom

Allen's schlemiels often resemble, Danny is destined to get the short end of the stick. Screenwriter Allen also has some fun spoofing Italian culture in the sure-footed screwball comedy, but he also defines his Jewish view of the world by contrasting it with a different ethnic group. Danny outlines his philosophy to Tina, telling her, "It's important to have some laughs, but you've got to suffer a little too, otherwise you miss the whole point of life." Tina counters with her own "life is short, so have fun," "screw or be screwed" philosophy, which Danny finds appalling. "That sounds like the screenplay of *Murder Incorporated*," gasps Danny, who is profoundly old-fashioned and morally conservative.

Time and time again, Danny gets into trouble for being so "insistently moral," as *New York* magazine critic David Denby aptly described him. Denby, however, goes on to lodge a curious complaint about Allen's "high Jewish self-regard," noting that Allen's "Jews are more moral than other people sentiments get a little sticky here." Allen, who is sometimes accused of Jewish self-hatred for portraying disaffected, ambivalent Jews, apparently can't win. He's either too critical or too complimentary.

Danny also quarrels with Tina about the value of guilt. "Guilt is important, otherwise you're capable of terrible things," he tells her. "I feel guilty all the time, and I never did anything. My rabbi used to say we're all guilty in the eyes of God."

"Do you believe in God?" Tina asks.

"No, but I feel guilty about it," Danny replies, expressing the idea that Jewish identity runs deeper than religious faith. In film after film, Allen asserts his conviction that a secular Jew is still very much a Jew. Danny is indeed Jewish down to his toes, a man who, wandering in the weeds, complains that he feels like Moses. Danny actually does hope to lead his clients into the promised land of success. Sadly, like Moses, he will never enter that realm himself, but the hope that springs eternal in his heart will see him through his frustrations and wanderings.

Woody Allen, who got his start writing jokes for Sid Caesar (along with Mel Brooks and Neil Simon), is but one of many film artists to pay homage to the thriving Jewish comedy tradition that nourished them. Billy Crystal's hilarious if mawkish *Mr. Saturday Night* (1992) follows the career of a fictitious Jewish comic—an amalgam of numerous real stars—over the course of fifty years. Neil Simon's award-winning comedy *The Sunshine Boys* (1975) features two quintessentially Jewish vaudeville comics, perfectly played by Walter Matthau and George Burns, who *kvetch* and *kibitz* as they stage an ill-fated comeback. Bob Fosse's *Lenny* (1975), starring Dustin Hoffman, offers a darker take on the Jewish penchant for humor as it looks at the life of Lenny Bruce, who was part of a new breed of Jewish comics. Richard Benjamin's *My Favorite Year* (1982) acknowledges the heavy Jewish participation in television's early years as it goes behind the scenes of a 1954 comedy show hosted by a Milton Berle/Sid Caesar–style comic (Joseph Bologna).

Non-Jewish directors have also dealt with the rich tradition of Jews in show business. Martin Scorsese took a break from the Italian-American milieu in *The King of Comedy* (1983), which offers a disturbing look at the comic Jewish psyche. Robert Redford's evocative and provocative *Quiz Show* (1994) is also set in the Jewish-dominated world of 1950s television. The preponderance of Jewish talent in Hollywood's early days is depicted in a number of entertaining films, most notably Joel and Ethan Coen's *Barton Fink* (1991), starring John Turturro as a Jewish playwright who goes to work for a crass studio mogul (Michael Lerner), and Howard Zieff's *Hearts of the West* (1975), starring Alan Arkin as a B movie director in the 1930s. Arkin also stars in *The Magician of Lublin* (1979), based on a novel by Isaac Bashevis Singer about a Polish performer at the turn of the century.

Biographies of famed Jewish performers also abound, including *Funny Girl, Houdini, The Benny Goodman Story,* and *The Jolson Story*. Neil Simon documented his shaky show business start in *Broadway Bound,* and Carl Reiner did the same in *Enter Laughing*.

While Jews have been amazingly sucessful in every realm of entertainment in the twentieth century, *Broadway Danny Rose* offers on offbeat look at one failure. Danny may be a classic *nebbish,* but he's also a *mensch* who places decency and kindness above success.

36

Julia

20th Century-Fox (1977)
Cast: Vanessa Redgrave, Jane Fonda, Maximilian Schell, Jason Robards
Directed by: Fred Zinnemann
118 minutes [PG]

The story of a Jewish woman who learns a lesson in courage and commitment that will inform the rest of her life and work, *Julia* is a highly suspenseful character drama and one of the most compelling films to examine social activism as an expression or extension of Jewish values. The impending Holocaust forms the backdrop of *Julia,* which champions those who took action against the rise of fascism in the 1930s. A sense of political purpose gives meaning to the life of its title character, whose valor inspires her best friend, Lilly, a character based on a fascinating Jewish literary figure.

Adapted from an allegedly autobiographical story in Lillian Hellman's second volume of memoirs, *Pentimento, a Book of Portraits* (1973), the film focuses on the close bond between the young heiress Julia (Vanessa Redgrave) and her adoring best friend Lilly (Jane Fonda). As the two starry-eyed idealists grow into womanhood, their lives move in dramatically different directions, crossing only twice. The second meeting, however, proves a pivotal crossroad in Lilly's life as she recalls the formative experience some forty years later. Screenwriter Alvin Sargent *(Ordinary People, Nuts),* who won an Oscar for his adaptation of Hellman's memoir, ably evokes a feeling of memories being replayed in the mind.

An idealized figure viewed through Lilly's admiring eyes, Julia is appalled by social injustice at an early age and goes to Europe to work for the antifascist underground, while Lilly becomes a celebrated playwright. Julia has put her life on the line to fight Hitler and asks her apolitical friend, who is busy being the toast of Broadway, to carry out a dangerous mission. Lilly swallows hard and undertakes the task, smuggling $50,000 of Julia's family money into Germany in a fur hat.

The film's message of working for the common good found a receptive audience in 1977, an era of ongoing agitation for social justice and increasing awareness of personal political responsibility. *Julia* received eight Academy

Award nominations and won three Oscars; it was also heralded for its focus on the friendship between two women who are morally valiant and self-sufficient human beings. It was, in fact, one of the first big Hollywood films to focus in a positive way on female friendship.

Oscar-nominated director Fred Zinnemann aptly describes the drama as a story about friendship and a test of courage. Zinnemann, an Austrian Jew who immigrated to America before the Nazi era, was one of the few directors to deal with the Third Reich in two early films, *Seventh Cross* (1943) and *The Search* (1948). He did not make another movie with a Jewish theme until *Julia* (1977), one of his last films before retiring. The success of his best known films, *High Noon, A Man for All Seasons,* and *From Here to Eternity—* all of which deal with tests of courage—established Zinnemann's reputation as a master craftsman who produced serious, intelligent, well-acted dramas.

While a large number of Jews during the 1930s participated in political groups that actively opposed fascism, in the film it is the non-Jewish Julia who is fighting the forces threatening the Jews with annihilation, while the Jewish Lilly is the reluctant heroine drawn into a war she does not even rec-

WOMEN OF VALOR   In Fred Zinnemann's *Julia,* Jewish writer Lillian Hellman (Jane Fonda) is persuaded by her non-Jewish friend (Oscar-winner Vanessa Redgrave) to fight Nazism by smuggling money to the Resistance in a fur hat.

ognize as her own. (In fact, Hellman was already quite actively engaged in politics.) Curiously, however, we do not learn that Lilly is Jewish until halfway through the film. When we hear the word *Jew* spoken for the first time in reference to Lilly, it comes as a bit of a shock to the audience, because we have been given no clues to her Jewish identity. The scenes of Julia's and Lilly's teenage years never show Lilly's family background, focusing instead on Julia's aristocratic upbringing. And because Lilly is played by a non-Jewish actress, we have no reason to suspect she's Jewish.

Although Hellman actively opposed anti-Semitism as well as fascism, she was a freethinking intellectual who did not have a strong sense of Jewish identification. She had no religious education and admitted she did not clearly know what being Jewish meant growing up in the genteel South. Yet, she added, she knew she'd rather be Jewish than not be. She confused matters by expressing scorn for the materialistic, vulgar, conservative Jews of Hollywood and tended not to see the importance of specific Jewish content in literature and film. She was accused of Jewish self-hatred for the negative depiction of the Jewish family in her play *My Mother, My Father and Me.* She also made contradictory statements regarding her background, stating at one time that she was almost completely unaware of her Jewishness until she became an adult, at another time claiming to have been the victim of vicious anti-Semitism as a child. *Julia* reflects Hellman's ambiguous, conflicted feelings about her Jewish heritage.

Redgrave's casting was initially protested by the studio because of her outspoken pro-Palestinian views, which executives feared would carry unwelcome associations into a movie that dealt with Jewish persecution. The misgivings were not unfounded. At the Oscar ceremony, some seventy-five members of the Jewish Defense League protested Redgrave's appearance outside the Dorothy Chandler Pavillion while a group of 200 supporters of the Palestine Liberation Organization demonstrated nearby in support of her nomination. Redgrave was delivered to the stage door in an ambulance, surrounded by bodyguards. When Redgrave won the best supporting actress Oscar, she used the occasion to make her notorious speech in support of the P.L.O., thanking those who "refused to be intimated by the threats of a small bunch of Zionist hoodlums," eliciting gasps, boos, and a smattering of applause from the audience. She went on to say that these protestors were "an insult to the stature of Jews all over the world and their great and heroic record of struggle against fascism and oppression." She ended her speech pledging to fight against anti-Semitism and fascism.

The famed Jewish screenwriter and playwright Paddy Chayefsky (*Marty, Network*), announcing the writing awards, publicly condemned Redgrave's anti-Zionist remarks, which latter drew a storm of offstage protest. Alan King, for example, told the press, "I am that Zionist hoodlum she was talking about.

It's just a pity I wasn't on the platform tonight. I would have gone for the jugular." The furor surrounding Redgrave did not die down. In 1980, Jewish groups again protested her casting as a concentration camp victim in the television drama *Playing for Time,* for which she won an Emmy.

Maximilian Schell, an actor of some stature who agreed to play a cameo role in *Julia,* received a best supporting actor nomination for his brief but memorable appearance as the antifascist operative who initially contacts Lilly on Julia's behalf. An Oscar went to Jason Robards for his portrayal of the famed writer Dashiell Hammett, who has little to do with the story. Zinnemann admits he put the character into the film primarily to counteract any suggestion of lesbianism between Julia and Lilly.

Ironically, the veracity of the story has been the subject of dispute. Hellman refused to name the real Julia, whom she claimed was still alive, and there seems to be some doubt as to whether she existed at all and if she did, if the two women ever even met. The woman who most likely served as the model for the character did not know Hellman, but they shared a mutual friend who could have told Hellman about her. Indeed, the film's Julia is a little too perfect to be believed. Pauline Kael calls the idealized character a "saintly Freudian Marxist queen," noting that only an actress of Redgrave's majesty could carry it off, as she indeed does. Fonda, who shares little screen time with Redgrave, gives a convincing performance as the brittle, nervous, hard-bitten, insecure Lilly, a much more complex character.

Like many post-Holocaust films, *Julia* glosses over the issue of anti-Semitism and de-emphasizes the Holocaust as a specifically Jewish event by downplaying the jeopardy of European Jewry. The second and last time the word *Jew* is spoken Lilly asks Julia if the money will be used to rescue Jews. Julia says that about half are Jews, the rest are "political people" of all backgrounds. Although it is unfortunate that the film goes to great pains to point out it is not "just" the Jews who are in peril, the movie does establish that many Jews, along with non-Jews, actively fought Hitler. This image of Jewish resistance offers a refutation of the common cinematic image of Jews going like lambs to the slaughter, abandoned by their fellow Jews.

37

Marathon Man

Paramount Pictures (1976)
CAST: Dustin Hoffman, Laurence Olivier, Roy Scheider, Marthe Keller
DIRECTED BY: John Schlesinger
125 minutes [R]

The Holocaust officially ended with the liberation of the Nazi death camps in 1945, but the heritage of the horror lives on. The extent to which the Jewish genocide continues to haunt the public's imagination is evident in the growing abundance of historical Holocaust films examining the tragic events of the era.

The posttraumatic terror and dread that scarred the culture's psyche was also vividly manifested in a series of fictional films of the 1970s focusing on ongoing Nazi activity. The best of the lot, *Marathon Man,* drives home the harrowing point that the Nazi menace still stalks our world. Although the taut, terrifying thriller is not a serious examination of the Holocaust, it serves as a striking reminder that many of those responsible for the atrocities were never brought to justice.

Dr. Josef Mengele, the sadistic Nazi physician who conducted barbaric experiments on prisoners at Auschwitz and oversaw the camp's life-or-death selection process, emerged as the nefarious villain in two films of the 1970s. In the suspenseful *Marathon Man,* a character clearly modeled on Mengele engages in a battle of wits and will with a Jewish graduate student, Babe Levy (Dustin Hoffman). Mengele reappeared two years later in *The Boys From Brazil,* a paranoid thriller starring Gregory Peck as the deranged doctor. Coincidentally, Laurence Olivier, nominated for an Oscar for his performance as the medical madman in *Marathon Man,* turned up again in *The Boys From Brazil,* playing a Nazi-hunter based on Simon Wiesenthal, for which he received another nomination.

Although both films are pure fantasy, the repellent image of the unpunished and unrepentant Nazi reflected reality. In fact, Mengele, who was never captured, could easily have seen both films. The man responsible for 2.5 million murders was still alive and well and living in Brazil when the movies were released. He is believed to have died a peaceful death in 1979, having lived his life as a free man. Additionally, both Mengele-inspired films were

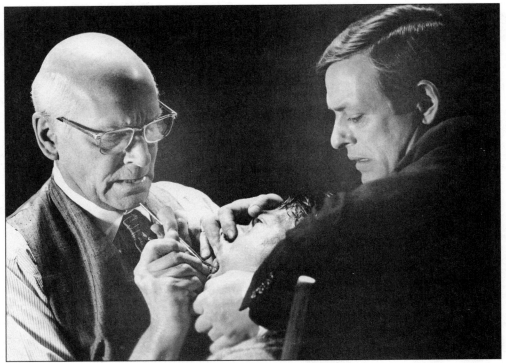

Is It Safe?   In *Marathon Man,* a Jewish graduate student (Dustin Hoffman) is tortured by a notorious Nazi doctor modeled on Joseph Mengele, played by Laurence Olivier, left, who went on to play Simon Wiesenthal opposite Gregory Peck as Mengele in *The Boys From Brazil.*

based on books by popular Jewish authors. *Marathon Man* is based on the novel by William Goldman, who wrote the screenplay as well, and *The Boys From Brazil* was taken from the book by Ira Levin. The Nazi menace was exhumed in two other films of the 1970s, both also adaptations of literary works. *The Odessa File,* a fact-based but fictional 1974 thriller detailing a thriving secret network protecting ex-Nazis, was based on a novel by Frederick Forsyth. Director Arthur Hiller's acclaimed 1975 screen adaptation of Robert Shaw's play *The Man in the Glass Booth* is an even more fascinating, complex, and literate Nazi-hunting drama featuring Oscar-nominee Maximilian Schell as a man who might be a Jewish survivor or a camp commandant.

Marathon Man envisions the Mengele figure as aging but still brutal—although not as diabolical as he is in the sillier and more fantastical *The Boys From Brazil.* Anti-Semitism is not an overt issue in the film, as it is in *The Boys From Brazil,* for which *Marathon Man* might well be faulted. It is significant, however, that the ex-Nazi engages in a fight to the finish with a Jew. Innocent of any crime, and indeed ignorant of the reasons for his persecution, Babe functions as a symbol for the Jewish victims of the Holocaust.

Director John Schlesinger, an English Jew, reunited with his *Midnight Cowboy* star for this nightmarish tale of persecution and vengeance. Hoffman rarely plays explicitly Jewish characters (his performance as comic Lenny Bruce in Bob Fosse's *Lenny* was an exception), but many of his roles carry strong Jewish undercurrents. Babe Levy possesses qualities that can be linked to his background. Babe is nervous, compulsive, and competitive. Anxious and eager, he is also tenacious. A graduate student at Columbia University training to run his first marathon, Babe is haunted by the memory of his famous historian father, who, hounded by McCarthyites, was driven to suicide when Babe was a boy. Babe's older brother, Doc (Roy Scheider), is now an agent working for a shadowy secret service organization known as the Division.

The Division has formed a relationship with Christian Szell (Olivier), a former death camp doctor known as the White Angel. (Mengele was known as the Angel of Death.) When Szell's brother is killed in an accident caused by a violent conflict with a Jewish cabbie at the film's opening, Szell comes to New York from South America to retrieve the fortune in diamonds, stolen from Jewish concentration camp prisoners, which he has stashed in a safety deposit box. Afraid of being robbed after leaving the bank, Szell kills Doc, who knows about the diamonds. Before he dies, Doc staggers to Babe's apartment, and Szell therefore suspects that Babe now also knows of his hidden wealth.

In the famous scene of dental torture, Szell, who perfected his technique extracting gold teeth from Jewish victims, subjects Babe to incredible pain to determine whether his brother told him anything before dying. (He didn't.) "Is it safe?" he keeps asking the baffled Babe, who is a "wrong man" cut from the Hitchcock hero mold. In the end, it is Babe's ability to withstand pain and his endurance—products of his running as well as his heritage—that allow him to triumph over his Nazi persecutor.

Szell is chillingly portrayed by Golden Globe-winning Olivier, whose sinister performance was so memorable it hindered audience acceptance of him as Simon Wiesenthal in *The Boys From Brazil*. Wiesenthal, who plays a small role in *The Odessa File* as well, later reappeared on the screen in two TV movies: excellent *The Murderers Among Us: The Simon Wiesenthal Story* (1989), starring Ben Kingsley, and the 1990 adaptation of Wiesenthal's book, *Max and Helen*, starring Martin Landau as Wiesenthal.

Marathon Man, in which Mengele serves as a symbol of demonic evil, evokes the horrors of the past. It warns of the ongoing threat of anti-Semitic fanaticism while allowing the Jew vicarious revenge and a cathartic victory. Like a number of fantasies of the era, *Marathon Man* seeks to redress the wrongs of history by symbolically restoring power to the Jewish victims of the Holocaust who suffered terribly but, unlike Babe, were not able to defeat their enemy.

38

A Majority of One

Warner Bros. (1962)
CAST: Rosalind Russell, Alec Guinness
DIRECTED BY: Mervyn LeRoy
149 minutes [Not rated]

Bertha Jacoby (Rosalind Russell), a Jewish widow living in Brooklyn, gets a chance at late-life romance when she meets a wealthy widower. A learned and religious man, he shares with Bertha a deep respect for tradition and ritual. He values family highly, prizes community, and honors his ancestors. Like Bertha, he has lost a child in the war. A proper, formal man, he treats her with respect. There's only one thing wrong with Bertha's suitor. He's not Jewish. In fact, he's Japanese.

A Jewish–gentile love story with a twist, *A Majority of One* is also a meditation on the nature of prejudice. The prefeminist film is about Jewish liberal values put to the test. Bertha passes with flying colors, embodying the social ideals of her heritage while maintaining her connection to her family and roots. Like so many of the screen's Jewish women, she strikes a balance between tradition and modernity.

Based on the Broadway play by Leonard Spigelgass, who also wrote the screen adaptation, *A Majority of One* offers an extremely positive, respectful look at both cultures, with an emphasis on the warm Jewish world of Mrs. Jacoby. Bertha is a kind, caring, loving, understanding, unpretentious, and sensible woman. She may have lived in Brooklyn all her life, but she adapts quickly and is open to the strange Japanese customs she encounters when she accompanies her daughter and diplomat son-in-law to Japan. Shown her Japanese-style bathtub, she shrugs and says, "Listen, if dat's the vay you do it, I'll try." The film rarely has any fun at her expense. She proves to be wise, practical, independent, and intelligent. Unlike numerous Jewish movie mothers, she does not interfere, meddle, dominate, or lay guilt on her children. Rather, she is nurturing and supportive, although no pushover. She is revealed to be less bigoted than her children, who pay lip service to egalitarian ideals but balk at the idea of intermarriage.

This unambiguously positive image of the Jewish mother makes *A Major-*

ity of One a relative rarity and is the prime reason for its inclusion in this ranking of great Jewish films. Bertha is a far cry from the grasping, closed-minded materialistic mothers of *Marjorie Morningstar* or *Goodbye Columbus*. She is light-years removed from the interfering, infantalizing mothers of *Where's Poppa?, Portnoy's Complaint,* and the *Oedipus Wrecks* segment of *New York Stories*. She couldn't be more different from the critical, dominating mothers of *No Way to Treat a Lady* and *Enter Laughing* or the guilt-tripping, overprotective matrons of *Next Stop, Greenwich Village,* or *Flirting With Disaster*. Neither does she resemble the long-suffering, manipulative mom of *I Love You, Alice B. Toklas*. Although she is utterly devoted, she is not like the cold, self-sacrificing martyrs of *Broadway Bound, Brighton Beach Memoirs,* or *Used People*.

Bertha may be unusual, but she is not unique among warm, nurturing, supportive, and independent Jewish movie mothers. Julie Kavner plays a distinctly wonderful modern mother in Nora Ephron's *This Is My Life,* and Anne Bancroft stars as an eccentric and liberated but devoted mother in *Garbo Talks*.

MY YIDDISHE MAMA   Rosalind Russell plays one of the screen's most unambivalently positive and uncommonly broad-minded Jewish mothers in *A Majority of One,* costarring Madlyn Rhue and Ray Danton as her daughter and son-in-law.

Russell, who earlier in her career specialized in playing headstrong career women in screwball comedies, was an unusual choice to play the Brooklyn *balaboste,* a part that had been played by Gertrude Berg on the stage. Mrs. Jacoby keeps a kosher home and uses Yiddish expressions such as *gonif, meshuga, tsuris, kvelling,* and *schlemiel.* Russell affects an accent and relies on intonations and mannerisms to make Mrs. Jacoby as Jewish as possible. The role is a bit of a reach for Russell, but her costar stretches even farther. Alec Guinness—whose characters include an Arab prince, Marcus Aurelius, a pope, Hitler, and Obi-wan Kenobi—has a good go playing the dignified Japanese gentleman, but his disguise is not entirely convincing.

Acclaimed Jewish director Mervyn LeRoy, who made this rare, overtly Jewish film late in his long career, had previously tackled the subject of intolerance in an Oscar-winning documentary he directed in 1945 *The House I Live In.* LeRoy, perhaps best known as the producer of *The Wizard of Oz,* steeps the odd-couple love story in Jewish and Japanese customs. He makes the film as specific as possible, illustrating the differences between the two cultures while establishing underlying similarities. Although the film comes down on the side of intermarriage, much like earlier proassimilationist movies, the affectionate and proudly Jewish film was an early part of the trend toward presenting fully defined ethnic characters that began in the 1960s.

A Majority of One, a comforting comedy that should have special appeal for older audiences, is a bit sentimental and certainly safe by today's standards, but it treats its characters with dignity, compassion, and gentle humor, valuable qualities in any age.

39

Oliver!

Columbia Pictures (1968)
CAST: Ron Moody, Mark Lester, Jack Wild
DIRECTED BY: Carol Reed
153 minutes [G]

Fagin is among the most memorable, and notorious, Jewish characters ever drawn by a writer's pen. Ever since Charles Dickens published an 1839 novel about a workhouse orphan who falls into a den of thieves, the nefarious character has been the object of considerable censure.

In 1960, Fagin reemerged as a charming, conniving, quixotic, irrepressible rogue in Lionel Bart's stage musical, *Oliver!,* which became an international stage hit and broke London box office records. Criticized by purists for its "jollification" of Dickens, *Oliver!* took a more kindly view of all the characters, especially Fagin, who now took center stage. Carol Reed's 1968 screen adaptation of *Oliver!* continues the deliberate attempt to turn Fagin into a more sympathetic character, reflecting the increasing sensitivity to ethnic images in the 1960s. Still, the popular movie musical caused a bit of consternation for perpetuating a negative Jewish stereotype.

Second only to Shylock in fame and controversy, Dickens's infamous Fagin is a greedy, scheming, self-serving, cruel crimelord who presides over a pack of pint-size pickpockets in nineteenth-century London. Like the despised merchant of Venice, Fagin is an outcast who has managed to eke out a living. Although the story illustrates the liberal view that poverty breeds crime, Fagin—who is arrested, tried, and condemned to death—is not regarded as a victim of the social system but as a corrupting influence on society. Dickens's depiction of the grasping Jew who exploits young boys was representative of the widespread anti-Semitism of his time and place.

Dickens's classic has been adapted for the screen numerous times, beginning with seven silent film versions. Until 1968, when *Oliver!* burst onto the screen with a tragicomic Fagin who was more lovable rascal than despicable villain, movies tended to present Fagin as the vile man Dickens conceived, with one consistent alteration. While Dickens deridingly referred to Fagin as "the Jew" several hundred times in the book, the screen versions do not state the

obvious. Rather, they make the character's Jewishness clear with makeup, speech, and mannerisms. Lon Chaney, sporting blackened teeth, long dirty fingernails, a large putty nose, and a greasy beard, played Fagin in the popular 1922 version of *Oliver Twist* starring Jackie Coogan. Irving Pichel played a less stereotypical villain in the first talking version, made in 1933 with Dickie Moore in the title role.

Alec Guinness returned to Dickens's grotesque conception of the evil Jew when he was cast as Fagin in David Lean's acclaimed 1948 version, which drew considerable fire from Jewish quarters for perpetuating the negative stereotype of the filthy, corrupt, money-hungry Jewish miser. Guinness, with a grossly exaggerated hook nose, played Fagin as alternately sinister and servile. His performance was deemed so offensive that a number of Jewish organizations attempted to ban the British film from American theaters. They succeeded in delaying the film's release until 1951, when it was shown with several of Fagin's scenes cut. The reviews were uniformly favorable, although a number of critics took exception to the unflattering portrayal of Fagin.

Director Carol Reed, who had proved himself a sympathetic chronicler of Jewish life, was nearing the end of a long and luminous career when he signed on to direct *Oliver!* Known for well-acted, technically adept, keenly observed, intelligent, warm, and restrained films, Reed had been especially successful with adaptations, including *A Kid for Two Farthings* (1955), his tenderly rendered screen version of Wolf Mankowitz's novel set in the Jewish East End of postwar London.

Reed's hugely popular film version of *Oliver!* won six Academy Awards, including best picture and best director. It is for its entertainment value as well as its inventive reassessment of Fagin that it ranks among the greatest Jewish films. Ron Moody (born Ronald Moodnick), who originated the role of Fagin on the stage, was given top billing in Reed's lively, robust musical and earned an Oscar nomination for his vivid performance. Moody's portrayal stands as the screen's most beguiling interpretation of the role, although George C. Scott offered some stiff competition in the 1982 TV movie, as did Richard Dreyfuss in Disney's 1997 small-screen adaptation, neither of which make specific reference to Fagin's Jewish identity. Moody's Fagin sports a scraggly beard, a lean visage, and eyes that burn with greed. His unsavory appearance aside, he is presented as a playful sort, mischievous rather than malicious, and prone to moments of rueful reflection. The boys adore him, and he is especially fond of Oliver (Mark Lester), whom he tries to protect from Bill Sikes (Oliver Reed), the story's true dastardly villain. This Fagin opposes violence, worries about his future, and expresses genuine human emotion.

Although there are no verbal references to Fagin's ethnic identity in *Oliver!,* there are many visual and auditory hints. The music that accompanies Fagin's songs has an unmistakable Eastern European flavor, with mandolin and clarinet strongly suggesting klezmer music. Moody allows a slight Jewish accent to creep into his English speech, especially in the song "I'm Reviewing the Situation." Through mannerisms and inflections, Moody makes it clear that Fagin is Jewish. Fagin is the colorful centerpiece in *Oliver!,* which went to great lengths to rectify previous depictions of the character. Most significantly, Fagin does not die in *Oliver!* as he does in Dickens's novel. Instead, he dances off into the sunset with the Artful Dodger. Starting from scratch once again, Fagin has been reimagined as a crafty survivor who somehow always manages to land on his feet.

40

Down and Out in Beverly Hills

Touchstone Pictures (1986)
CAST: Richard Dreyfuss, Bette Midler, Nick Nolte, Little Richard
DIRECTED BY: Paul Mazursky
103 minutes [R]

Jerry Baskin is a member of a dispossessed group, a wanderer, an outsider, an object of fear, existing on the edge of a society that scorns him. Funny thing is, he's not a Jew. He's a homeless man who is taken in by the fabulously wealthy Whiteman family, who ensconce him in the cabana and undertake his rehabilitation. Ironically, Jerry effects even greater changes in his self-appointed Jewish saviors than they do in him. Jerry (Nick Nolte) is one of only three characters in *Down and Out in Beverly Hills* who are not Jewish. Another is the Mexican maid (Elizabeth Peña), an illegal alien pursuing the American dream in the land of opportunity, who also assumes a role historically played by the Jew. Finally, there's the Whiteman's neighbor, black record producer Orvis Goodnight (Little Richard), another outsider who is envious of the Whiteman's recently acquired status.

Director and cowriter Paul Mazursky turns the tables on tradition in his comic Jewish success story, a box office hit that reflects an ambiguity about modern Jewish life that percolates through films of the 1980s and 1990s. Poised somewhere between antagonism and affection, Mazursky speaks for a large number of contemporary Jews. His willingness to examine the failings as well to celebrate the virtues of his heritage is refreshing, even though the implied criticism of Jewish mores and values in his movies makes some viewers uncomfortable. Mazursky (*Blume in Love; An Unmarried Woman; Scenes From a Mall; Enemies, a Love Story*), whose perceptive films almost always feature Jewish characters, documented his own bid for independence in the disarming *Next Stop, Greenwich Village* and examined the relationship between an idealistic Jew and his Italian buddy in a wonderful tale of an emergent Jewish identity, *Willie and Phil.*

In the crazy inverted universe of *Down and Out in Beverly Hills,* the Whitemans are at the top of the totem pole. They have made it. They have it made. Or do they? Dave Whiteman (Richard Dreyfuss) has made millions sell-

CULTURAL CRISIS   Richard Dreyfuss and Bette Midler are paired in *Down and Out in Beverly Hills,* Paul Mazursky's comic examination of shifting values in a Jewish nouveau riche family.

ing clothes hangers to Holiday Inns. He drives a white Rolls Royce, lives in sunny, palatial splendor, and has his Thanksgiving dinner catered—his turkey is bigger than Mel Brooks's, the caterer assures him. Still, there's not enough white meat. And Dave can't get his mind off the less fortunate.

There's more *tsuris* in Dave's life. His dog hates him, his wife Barbara (Bette Midler) won't sleep with him, his son, Max (Evan Richards), can't talk to him, and his daughter, Jenny (Tracy Nelson), has an eating disorder. So much for family togetherness, the staple of traditional Jewish life. Dave also feels guilty about his wealth, is worried about his kids, and is clearly uncomfortable slinking downstairs to sleep with the maid when Barbara dismisses his sexual overtures with "You're such a *noodge.*"

The Whitemans are familiar, albeit comically exaggerated, figures in contemporary Jewish fiction and film. In their desire to succeed, to break the cycle of poverty and persecution, they have mistakenly embraced materialism as a new Jewish value. They have left much behind in their flight from tradition. They have achieved the American dream but it has not made them happy. Assimilation has come at a high cost. They may now be at the center of American life, but they are still wandering, still searching, still yearning— another familiar Jewish phenomenon. Barbara studies with a yogi. Unable to relax, she's looking for inner peace and spiritual fulfillment, and like so many Jews, she's looking outside Judaism. A grownup Jewish-American princess, she's more concerned about her dog, Matisse, than her children, and hires a pet therapist (played by Mazursky's own analyst, Donald F. Muhich, who also played a shrink in Mazursky's *Blume in Love*) for the neurotic pooch.

When Jerry, despondent over the disappearance of his own beloved dog, Kerouac, decides to end his life by filling his pockets with rocks and jumping into the Whitemans' pool, Dave rushes to the rescue. "Dial 911, dial 911!" he keeps shouting as he races to his pool, oblivious of the mobile phone clutched in his hand. He pulls out the drowning man and performs mouth-to-mouth resuscitation, over his wife's protests that he'll get a disease from the filthy derelict. "He's a human being," insists Dave, who has not lost his compassion or his Jewish identification with the underdog. "He's a disgusting human being," Barbara responds. She's horrified when Dave, still high from his act of heroism, decides he enjoys feeling virtuous and takes on the bum as an improvement project. Honoring the Jewish commandment to welcome the stranger, Dave sees poor, unfortunate Jerry as his chance to perform a mitzvah. Indeed, sharing his bounty alleviates some of Dave's guilt.

Jerry cleans up nicely, as it turns out. He shares his sad history with the family, the personal tragedies that caused him to lose his "incentive." (Incentive is one thing Dave has in abundance.) Jerry is full of surprises. He claims to have had a failed romance with actress Linda Evans. He lived in England, spent time on an ashram in Oregon, and went to the Cannes Film Festival. It's all baloney, of course, but it's what the family wants to hear. Jerry has a strange gift of giving others what they need. He's a little like Elijah the prophet, who took on disguises to reward the worthy. He helps Barbara relax. He gets Dave's gay son Max to open up to his parents. He gets anorexic Jenny to start eating. He gives the maid dignity. He shows Dave how to have fun, allowing him to vicariously lead a freer life. In the final scene, Jerry is appropriately dressed as Santa Claus, having dispensed his gifts to the needy rich family.

Jerry plays a part more commonly assigned to Jewish characters in films. More often, it is the Jew who is the catalyst for change, who enlightens, educates, or leads the gentile to greater compassion, ethical integrity, political awareness, or personal fulfillment. But unlike those Jewish redeemers, who serve as the moralizing force in the story, Jerry is far from altruistic. Something of a fraud, he's self-serving and hypocritical. Perhaps he's just what the Whitemans deserve. Maybe they are just what he needs.

The odd alliance formed between the Jewish Whitemans and the gentile Jerry reflects the complexity of modern life. Mazursky often explores the theme of freedom—having too much freedom or not enough freedom, the price of freedom, the illusion of freedom—and *Down and Out in Beverly Hills* wraps them all up in a shiny package. Although the film has darker undercurrents of discontent, its style is bright and its tone is light. This is a cheery, hip, and breezy comedy. Loosely based on Jean Renoir's *Boudu Saved From Drowning* (1932), the film depicts a deliriously multicultural America improbably thriving in the palm tree–lined paradise of Beverly Hills, the bastion of conspicuous consumption.

The Whitemans' Christmas party features an especially odd assortment of ethnic types: Dave's Chinese clients, the decorator Geraldo, the white-turbaned yoga instructor, the Jewish dog psychiatrist, Dave's parents Mel and Sadie (played by Dreyfuss's mother Geraldine), Dave's business manager Sidney Waxman (played by Mazursky), and his wife Pearl (Valerie Curtin). Orvis plays the piano. Son Max arrives with his gay punk pals. Only the Iranian neighbors have not been invited.

Dreyfuss, marvelously paired with Midler, is perfectly cast as Dave. He's a passionate, sweet man, although volatile and aggressive. A New York Jew transplanted into mellow California, he's trying to adjust. He has a great capacity for joy, but is also hostile. The first words we hear him say—the first line in the movie—are addressed to his yapping mutt: "Shut up, you putz." Dave resorts to Yiddish expressions such as *verkakte* and *schmuck* whenever he's upset. Dreyfuss captures Dave's smug self-satisfaction as well as his anxiety and insecurity. Despite his faults, Dave is a good guy, and Dreyfuss is expert at playing flawed good guys.

Midler has the more superficial role, and although she's not quite of the same acting caliber as Dreyfuss, she has all the right qualities for the part of the grownup princess. She's tastefully garish, a frustrated free spirit caught in the trappings of success. We suspect there's a funny and fun-loving person ready to burst out. In the film's climactic scene, as she chases Dave, who is chasing Jerry around the house, she clutches her flopping breasts in a hilarious last-ditch effort at decorum.

Although Mazursky was criticized for poking fun at modern Jewish materialism among the nouveau riche, he's not simply satirizing the lifestyle of the rich and shameless. He's underscoring a need for Jewish values, community, tradition, and, above all, family, a need that only intensifies with affluence and acceptance.

41

Holocaust

Republic Pictures Home Video (1978)
CAST: Meryl Streep, Michael Moriarty, Fritz Weaver, James Woods,
Joseph Bottoms, Tovah Feldshuh, David Warner
DIRECTED BY: Marvin Chomsky
475 minutes [Not rated]

We begin with the knowledge that the Holocaust is ultimately ineffable. The enormity of the horror beggars the imagination and defies understanding or explanation. At the same time, it must not be forgotten and cannot be ignored. How, then, do we communicate the inconceivable?

Television may seem an unlikely medium to tackle such a profoundly difficult and sensitive subject. Can the *Shoah* be served up as a mass entertainment that pauses every ten minutes to sell—of all things—soap, as *Holocaust* did? And yet, what better way to shed light on the cataclysmic event, illuminating it for the all-too-ignorant general public? How better to announce to the world that the Holocaust is not just some ancient aberration, of interest only to Jews, than through a prime-time miniseries?

No one could argue that *Holocaust* is the best film on the subject. Indeed, it has been rightly criticized on artistic, philosophical, and historical grounds. In terms of impact, however, it may be the most important film on the Holocaust ever made, at least prior to *Schindler's List,* which accounts for its inclusion in this ranking. *Holocaust* was seen by 120 million viewers—15 million in West Germany alone—and won eight Emmy Awards. The object of the most advance advertising of any television program in history, it sparked international debate in newspapers and magazines, on radio and TV talk shows, in churches and synagogues, on lecture tours, in classrooms, and, perhaps most importantly, in homes around the world.

It also paved the way for many more popular works on the Holocaust, including TV films such as *Playing for Time, Escape From Sobibor,* and *The Murderers Among Us: The Simon Wiesenthal Story.* It attracted readers to the subject, greatly boosting the Holocaust publishing industry. It even caused German citizens to denounce ex-Nazis. The public awareness it aroused led to the creation of the Carter Commission, which called for a national Holocaust memorial and

museum as well as an annual day of remembrance. It dramatically increased public support for Israel. The Holocaust became a household word following the release of this sweeping saga written by Gerald Green and directed by Marvin Chomsky. The catastrophic events in Europe from 1935 to 1945 unfolded before the American public in nine and a half hours—two hours shorter on video, which spares us the commercials that made the broadcast possible.

Holocaust focuses on a fictional family of successful Berlin Jews. The Weiss family's story neatly encapsulates various aspects of the Jewish experience during the Holocaust. Dr. Weiss (Fritz Weaver), a Polish Jew, and his proudly German–Jewish wife, Berta (Rosemary Harris), initially refuse to accept the inevitable. Dr. Weiss feels it is his duty to stay and help other Jews while his wife is sure that Germany is too civilized to make good on its threat against genteel citizens such as herself. Dr. Weiss is deported to the Warsaw ghetto, where he joins the Warsaw Jewish Council as well as the Resistance. He and his wife are reunited in Warsaw and sent to their death at Auschwitz.

Karl Weiss (James Woods), the eldest of their three children, marries a loyal and courageous gentile, Inga (Meryl Streep), whose family has little sympathy for Jews. Karl, an apolitical artist, is sent first to Buchenwald and then to the model camp of Theresien-stadt, where his secretly drawn antifascist artwork leads to his torture and eventual transfer to and death at Auschwitz. The Weiss's beloved daughter Anna is raped by Nazis. Deeply traumatized, she is committed to a hospital for treatment—which turns out to be immediate gassing. Anna is thus an early victim of Hitler's plan to rid the world of "undesirables," which began with the murder of mental patients, cripples, and other "imperfect" specimens.

Rudi Weiss (Joseph Bottoms) decides to take action before events overtake the family. He runs away, eluding the authorities, and eventually reaches Russia, where he joins the partisans. Along the way, he takes a wife, a Czech Zionist (Tovah Feldshuh). Arrested and sent to the death camp of Sobibor, he takes part in a daring escape, the largest prison camp break in Holocaust history. (The event was excellently documented in another TV drama, *Escape From Sobibor,* starring Alan Arkin.) Rudi alone survives. The film ends after the war with Rudi—without home, family, papers, or country—agreeing to smuggle a group of orphans into Palestine.

The emblematic fall of the Weiss family is juxtaposed with the rise of Erik Dorf, a fictitious character loosely based on Otto Ohlendorf, a Nazi bureaucrat. Dorf (Michael Moriarty), an unemployed lawyer, is initially reluctant to join the Nazi party. A weak and mild man, he is urged on by his ambitious wife (Deborah Norton). He becomes the chief counsel to Heydrich (David Warner), thereby joining the high Nazi command along with Himmler (Ian Holm) and Eichmann (Tom Bell). With a flair for semantics and legal maneuvering, Dorf invents the euphemistic language of the Final Solution: "special handling" (gassing), "relocation" (deportation to camps), "quarantine" (camps), and "autonomous Jewish territory" (ghetto) are among his creative catchphrases. A baby-faced, boot-licking killer, Dorf comes to represent the banality of evil and the methodical, cold, and calculating manner in which the Nazis conducted their program of Jewish genocide.

Although faulted for its dramatic shortcomings, *Holocaust* has been widely commended for the validity of its overall view. The *Holocaust* is presented as a specifically Jewish tragedy, which has not always been the case in films made before and after it. Although other victims are mentioned, Jews are the focus of the story. Heydrich emphasizes to Dorf early on the importance of Hitler's "racial issue," and as time goes on the annihilation of the Jews becomes the Nazis' highest priority. The film also expresses a strong pro-Zionist bias and warns of the danger of assimilation.

The drama has been criticized for merging fact and fiction, for casting non-Jews in central roles, as well as for getting minor details wrong. However, it covers a great deal of history, hitting many of the most significant events of the Holocaust, including the massacre of at least 33,000 Jews at Babi Yar, the engineering of Kristallnacht, and the Warsaw Uprising. The film is crystal clear in its depiction of the Nazi mechanism; its secrecy, orderliness, and reliance on blackmail are duly noted. Heydrich, who has secret files on everyone, admits that the Nazi high command is a rogues' gallery of criminals, thugs, and deviants. Anti-Semitism, Heydrich also says, "is the cement that binds us," adding that the ground has been well laid by centuries of Jewish oppression for the Nazis' dissemination of "politically useful lies." Hitler, we are told, is determined to go down in history for one thing: "wiping Jews from the face of the earth." *Holocaust* also implicates a host of bystanders. "Few governments will stick their neck out for the Jews," Heydrich correctly predicts. Rudi notes that the United States did not even fill its quota of Jews applying to emigrate from the Third Reich.

For all its thoroughness, *Holocaust* is a melodrama concocted for mass appeal. The success of *Roots* led to its creation in a time when Americans were becoming increasingly receptive to stories of ethnic pride. Herbert Brodkin, the producer of the telefilm *Judgment at Nuremberg* (which served as the basis for the 1961 feature film) and, later, the fact-based TV movie about neo-Nazism in America, *Skokie,* wanted to craft a drama that would make the Holocaust accessible to American audiences. The Weiss family, originally lower-class Poles more representative of the majority of Jews killed in the Holocaust, became a prosperous, educated, and assimilated German-Jewish family with whom Americans could more easily identify. Meryl Streep's righteous gentile showed how the Holocaust impacted non-Jews who chose not to abandon the persecuted minority.

Although screenwriter and novelist Gerald Green conducted exhaustive research, no Holocaust historian served as adviser on the epic drama. Hence, there are a number of quibbles with the script, such as Berta Weiss keeping her suitcase and treasured personal belongings in Auschwitz. Elie Weisel was among its harshest critics, but many respected Jewish authorities rose to its defense.

The Mauthausen concentration camp served as the set for various concentration camps in *Holocaust,* which was filmed in Germany and Austria. Brodkin wisely decided to avoid casting big-name stars in the film, instead relying on distinguished but lesser-known talents. The decision paid off. Moriarty won an Emmy for his performance, and the acting was universally praised. Many words have been used to describe and criticize *Holocaust,* which has been accused of trivializing, popularizing, Americanizing, and universalizing the *Shoah.* The miniseries may not express the personal devastation of the Holocaust as eloquently as we would like, but it does at least give a fair accounting of the events that took place in the not-so-distant past. If nothing else, it made the indifferent world sit up and take notice.

42

Dirty Dancing

Vestron Pictures (1987)
CAST: Jennifer Grey, Patrick Swayze, Jerry Orbach, Jack Weston
DIRECTED BY: Emile Ardolino
97 minutes [PG-13]

The time is 1963, the place Kellerman's Resort in the Catskills. Everyone calls Francis Houseman "Baby," and it has not yet occurred to her to mind. A sweetly nostalgic story of a girl with moral courage and abiding compassion, *Dirty Dancing* extols positive values that are linked to Baby's Jewish heritage. A cut above the typical teen movie, *Dirty Dancing* is a highly commercial, superficial, yet appealing coming-of-age drama buoyed by a bright performance by Jennifer Grey, the daughter of actor Joel Grey (*Cabaret*), and effective musical numbers.

Written by Eleanor Bergstein and directed by Emile Ardolino, *Dirty Dancing* is by no means uniformly flattering in the depiction of its successful, upwardly mobile Jewish characters. But it does convey respect for the warmth and mentoring of the traditional Jewish family and idolizes its independent Jewish heroine, whose strength of character reflects proudly on her upbringing. Baby is spending the summer between high school and college with her family. It is a time of transition for Baby as well as for the country. Kennedy is still alive, and so is idealism. Baby, poised on the verge of womanhood, still thinks her dad is the greatest guy in the world. Borscht belt resorts like Kellerman's are becoming passé. The fox-trot is giving way to more erotic, less inhibited dances. After-hours, the hired help at Kellerman's bump and grind to sexy Motown sounds.

Class and ethnic divisions still rule at the Jewish resort. Max Kellerman (Jack Weston) hires Jewish college students to wait tables and romance the guests' daughters, "even the dogs." The rest of the help, including the entertainment staff, are working-class gentiles who are expressly forbidden to mingle with the guests. Baby, who believes in equality and wants to change the world, is about to break the rules. She will help someone in need. She will engage in a summer romance with the dance instructor Johnny (Patrick Swayze), a boy from the proverbial wrong side of the tracks and a gentile to

SUMMER ROMANCE   In a reversal of the commonly depicted romance between a Jewish male and a gentile woman, *Dirty Dancing* is the story of a principled and strong-willed young Jewish woman (Jennifer Grey) who falls for—and inspires—her non-Jewish dance partner (Patrick Swayze).

boot. She will act on the principles she has been taught. Her father will not be pleased.

Although her background is never raised as an issue, Baby is clearly Jewish, and her values are directly attributed to her father, who has taught her to stand up for other people and to stick by her beliefs. She is contrasted sharply with her sister, a dim-witted Jewish–American princess who has absorbed only the materialistic values of her upbringing.

When Baby discovers that Penny, the hotel's star dancer, is pregnant and that the waiter who is responsible refuses to help her, she rushes to the rescue. She asks her father for the money Penny needs for an abortion, without telling him what it's for. Because the only time the doctor can perform the abortion is the night Penny and Johnny are scheduled to perform at a neighboring resort, Baby offers to fill in for her as Johnny's partner.

As Johnny gives her a crash course in dancing, an attraction develops. Johnny, handsome, loyal, and caring, has had none of the advantages Baby has enjoyed. Baby recognizes this inequity and does not judge Johnny for his lack of education and sophistication, instead viewing him with sympathy and admiring his personal qualities. Johnny is impressed that Baby acts on her convictions. In the end, he admits that she has taught him what kind of person he wants to be.

As in many films, the Jew is the moral exemplar who uplifts and edifies a gentile, serving as a humanizing influence by embodying culturally ingrained values. The story may not be terribly original, but Baby serves as a positive Jewish female role model for an age group that sorely needs such images. Another commercial drama aimed at a young crowd, *School Ties,* also offers a valiant and upstanding teenage Jewish hero.

Dirty Dancing is to be commended for not making Baby's father the villain. Jack Houseman, wonderfully played by Jewish actor Jerry Orbach, is a decent man, a dedicated doctor who has a close relationship with his daughter. There is a lovely scene in which Baby apologizes for letting her father down but tells him he has let her down too by only giving lip service to his liberal values and harboring prejudicial notions. As she walks away, Jake Houseman lets out a sob that suggests both his shame and his pride in the young woman who has just summoned her courage to challenge him.

A number of the other characters are more clichéd, particularly the smarmy sex fiend Robbie—whose purpose is to show that a Yale medical student can be a real putz—and Kellerman's equally snobbish nephew, a nebbish who thinks he's a *macher.* Baby's sister Lisa is also an unfortunate caricature of the bubble-headed bimbo and daddy's girl.

Coincidentally, 1987 saw the release of another film set in the Catskills featuring a principled young Jewish woman who engages in a summer romance with a non-Jew. *Sweet Lorraine,* which stars Trini Alvarado as a college student who wants to save her grandmother's resort, is low-key and charming. Steve Gomer's low-budget nostalgic comedy does not pack as much entertainment punch as *Dirty Dancing,* but the genuinely sweet film has less saccharine aftertaste.

43

The Front

Columbia Pictures (1976)
CAST: Woody Allen, Herschel Bernardi, Zero Mostel,
Michael Murphy, Danny Aiello
DIRECTED BY: Martin Ritt
95 minutes [PG]

The Front is the story of a schnook who becomes, first, a *macher* and, finally, a *mensch,* played by—who else?—Woody Allen. After directing and acting in five films, Woody Allen chose to relinquish the artistic control he so cherished and play a comic role in a serious film. The reason he agreed to be an actor for hire in *The Front* was that he felt the subject—the blacklisting of Hollywood artists for their political associations—was important and the story compelling.

He was right on both counts. *The Front* confronted a shameful chapter of American history, depicting the damage done to thousands of lives in the name of democracy while acknowledging the disproportionately large number of Jews whose careers were shattered by the House Un-American Activities Committee witch hunts. The decision proved a wise career movie for Allen as well, paving the way for audience acceptance of the more serious direction his career would take the following year with the release of *Annie Hall.*

Allen plays Howard Prince, a lowly, apolitical cashier and bookie who agrees to front for his old friend Al Miller (Michael Murphy), a blacklisted TV writer. Soon, Howard is putting his name on scripts by numerous blacklisted writers, becoming famous in the process. Although an imposter, Howard begins to bask in borrowed glory. At first, Howard enjoys his unearned success so much he sets aside his principles, even when his new girlfriend (Andrea Marcovicci) urges him to become actively engaged in the fight against this injustice. In the end, Howard realizes he has to take a stand regardless of the personal cost. Self-interest is pitted against social responsibility in this story of a classic underachiever who attains greatness by following the Jewish mandate to crusade for justice.

Although *The Way We Were* (1973) touched on the infamous HUAC Hollywood investigation of alleged Communist sympathizers, *The Front* was the first film to focus entirely on the blacklist. In 1991, Irwin Winkler's *Guilty by Suspicion* further examined the damage done, although without emphasizing the Jewish connection. *Citizen Cohn* (1992) also touches on the ravages of McCarthyism, focusing on the conservative Jewish opportunist who so gleefully hounded left-leaning Jews as McCarthy's strong right arm.

The Front originated with director Martin Ritt and his friend and collaborator, writer Walter Bernstein. Bernstein had been blacklisted in 1950 and did not work for ten years. Ritt was blacklisted in 1951 for his past Communist affiliation. A prolific TV director and actor at the time, Ritt spent the next six years teaching at the Actors' Studio in New York and occasionally acting and directing for the stage. Ritt made his film directing debut in 1957 for producer David Susskind, better known as the moderator of the long-running syndicated TV talk show *Open End* who broke the blacklist by hiring Ritt to direct *Edge of the City.*

Ritt and Bernstein began discussing ways to dramatize the disgraceful era while working together on *The Molly McGuires* in 1970. Ritt has said *The Front* was the film he was meant to make, and he took half his regular fee for the film, bringing many of his own experiences—as well those of his collaborators—into the project. Ritt hired two formerly blacklisted actors, Zero Mostel and Herschel Bernardi, to play leading roles, and cast once-blacklisted actors Lloyd Gough and Joshua Shelley in smaller parts.

Mostel plays popular comic actor Hecky Green, the stage name of Herschel Braunstein, who is the star of a show Howard "writes." Hecky is in hot water for marching in a few demonstrations years earlier. He is fired from the show but told he can redeem himself if he spies on this suspicious new writer, Howard Prince, who associates with blacklisted writers. Desperate to work, Hecky obliges and informs on Howard. But when Howard is called before the committee, Hecky is so ashamed at his betrayal of a friend, he commits suicide. It is Hecky's death that forces Howard to see how serious the situation has become. Hecky's suicide is loosely based on that of actor Philip Loeb, who costarred with Gertrude Berg in *The Goldbergs,* a show that was on television from 1949 to 1955 and featured a Jewish family. There are numerous autobiographical details in the script, for which Bernstein received an Oscar nomination. Hecky is humiliated at a Catskills resort, where he's given only half his promised and already insultingly low fee, an incident from Mostel's life.

Mostel, the son of a rabbi, had first run into censorship trouble after his first starring movie role in 1943 when he was fired by MGM for making leftist remarks in public. Mostel, who was not given another movie role for twenty-three years, was later blacklisted after testifying before HUAC. Although he denied having been a member of the Communist Party, Mostel

HOLLYWOOD ON TRIAL   Zero Mostel, himself a victim of the Hollywood witch-hunts, made his final screen appearance as a blacklisted actor in *The Front,* Hollywood's first full-fledged exposé of the shameful era.

was also banned from Broadway. Mostel made a meager income painting, working comedy clubs, and doing dates in England. In the 1960s, he was able to resume his stage career, earning Tony Awards for *Rhinoceros, A Funny Thing Happened on the Way to the Forum,* and *Fiddler on the Roof.* He returned to film in 1966 in the screen adaptation of *A Funny Thing Happened on the Way to the Forum,* although the part he created in *Fiddler on the Roof* was given to the Israeli actor Topol. *The Front* was Mostel's last film. He died of cardiac arrest a year after its release.

The Front makes it clear that the purpose of the McCarthy era investigations was not simply to acquire information but to frighten, intimidate, and make liberals debase themselves. As Howard's friend Al tells him, "They care about getting people to give names, proving that there's nothing they can't get people to do." *The Front* had the audacity to remind viewers of a dark, divisive time many Americans preferred to forget. It also did not ignore the subtext of anti-Semitism that marked the campaign against Hollywood's left-leaning community. In the film, almost all of the characters persecuted for their political beliefs are Jewish.

Despite the story's dark elements and its indictment of HUAC's methods and motives, *The Front* has many comic moments as well. Howard throws in quite a few Jewish jokes, some of which sound very much like they were written by Allen. Howard admits, for example, that the greatest sin in his family was to buy retail. He also comments that "Swimming isn't a sport. It's something you do so you shouldn't drown."

Ritt, who had remained angry that such a violation of First Amendment rights could take place in a country that prided itself on freedom of speech, did not want the film to be bitter or polemical, however. Instead, *The Front* takes a light, seriocomic approach to the subject—not preachy and not deadly serious, *The Front* attempted to reach, and therefore educate, a wide audience. Nevertheless, it was accused by some critics of being too slight, given its weighty subject matter. While noting its good intentions, a few reviewers felt the film, which ended a quarter-century silence on the subject, was not hard-hitting enough.

Ritt, however, often made entertaining, enjoyable movies that just happened to deal with important subjects, from racial prejudice to illiteracy, films that championed individualism and human dignity. Ritt, who died in 1990 without ever winning an Oscar, brought a sincere concern for social issues to numerous notable projects, including *Hud, The Great White Hope, Sounder, Norma Rae,* and *Nuts*. The son of Jewish immigrants who settled in New York's Lower East Side, Ritt has said that growing up as a Jew influenced the content of his films. Although he never made a film with an overtly Jewish subject, several featured strong Jewish characters, including *Nuts, Norma Rae,* and *The Front*. His films were filled with losers and loners, the underprivileged and the oppressed. Many of his heroes were women or working class or both.

At Ritt's memorial tribute by the Directors Guild of America, Bernstein noted that his lifelong friend had not been blacklisted for nothing. Ritt, he said, firmly believed in those things he was blacklisted for and continued to act upon them until his death. Throughout his long and distinguished career, Ritt made movies with the kind of themes that got him in trouble in the first place. That was his revenge on the forces that had tried to silence him.

44

Biloxi Blues

Universal Pictures (1988)
CAST: Matthew Broderick, Christopher Walken, Corey Parker
DIRECTED BY: Mike Nichols
105 minutes [PG-13]

Biloxi Blues, the second and best installment of Neil Simon's autobiographical film trilogy, was not only his most overtly Jewish film upon its release in 1988, but remains the most provocative examination of the Jewish personality offered by any original Simon screenplay.

Neil Simon began his career in 1961 with a comedy based on his own family, *Come Blow Your Horn,* later made into a movie with Frank Sinatra playing the writer as a young man. Simon returned to documenting his personal history twenty-five years later with *Brighton Beach Memoirs,* the first installment of a trilogy that finally earned him acclaim as a serious playwright. In the intervening quarter century, Simon had become America's most popular and prolific playwright, as well as a famously successful screenwriter, with Oscar nominations for *The Odd Couple, The Goodbye Girl, The Sunshine Boys,* and *California Suite.*

While many of his plays and screenplays contained implicitly Jewish characters, Simon rarely made an issue of their Jewish identity until he began to record his family's history. The sole exception was Elaine May's expressly Jewish, prickly 1972 comedy, *The Heartbreak Kid,* which is one of Simon's rare adaptations of work by another writer, Bruce Jay Friedman.

In the wryly funny but uncommonly insightful *Biloxi Blues,* Simon escapes the narrow confines of his family and home, where the first and third chapters of his early life story are set. *Biloxi Blues* casts its wisecracking Jewish hero into the larger world of the multi-ethnic and notoriously intolerant U.S. Army in the final days of World War II. Simon's alter ego, Eugene Morris Jerome, finds that boot camp in Mississippi is about as far from Brighton Beach as a sheltered young Jew can get. Eugene is not the only Jew in his platoon, however. He is not even the "most Jewish" of the raw recruits enduring the training regime at Fort Biloxi. That distinction falls to Arnold Epstein (Corey Parker), one of the most complex Jewish characters ever created by Simon.

While Eugene wears his Jewishness lightly—although not invisibly or with shame—Arnold wears his as a badge of honor. Eugene wants to get along, to be an American first and a Jew second. Arnold has no desire to fit in, and he flaunts his difference. Although he is not smug in his moral superiority, popularity is of no concern to him. He lives by his own code. "The Army has its logic, I have mine," he says, clearly defining himself as a Jew first and foremost. He is also an individual, which is the one thing the Army can't abide. No amount of training will turn him into an obedient, unquestioning soldier.

Eugene's reaction to Arnold, who stands up for his convictions regardless of the consequences, is revealing. Eugene respects Arnold, recognizing him as a young man of unwavering principle. He also resents him for setting such a rigorous and daunting example of Jewish values in action. Arnold, in effect, acts as Eugene's conscience, making him feel a little guilty about his own willingness to compromise and accommodate. Eugene is preoccupied with losing his virginity, falling in love, and honing his writing skills, all of which he does in the course of the drama. Arnold, to whom such concerns seem

THE ARTIST AS A YOUNG MAN   Matthew Broderick plays the young Neil Simon in *Biloxi Blues,* the second installment of the writer's autobiographical trilogy, which comprises the three most Jewish plays of his career.

trivial, wisely urges his fellow Jew to "take sides, to make a contribution to the fight, otherwise you'll never be a good writer."

Eugene says he admires Arnold's "constant and relentless pursuit of truth, logic, and reason," while admitting that his "obstinancy and unnecessary heroics drive me to distraction." As *New York* magazine critic David Denby observed, Arnold is "the Jew as moral exemplar and crank." Eugene realizes, "I wanted to be his friend because he didn't seem to need one." Indeed, Arnold is viewed as a solitary outsider who is not so much an attractive or even sympathetic character as he is a noble figure. He is a victim who "takes his punishment without complaint" and who is resigned to his role as the incorruptible defender of justice. Fittingly, we learn that Arnold Epstein will become the district attorney of Brooklyn, considered by the Mafia to be "the most feared man in New York."

Biloxi Blues achieves a level of reality that the other two films in the trilogy never quite attain. Quite possibly, the success can be attributed to director Mike Nichols, who had staged some of Simon's plays, beginning in 1963 with *Barefoot in the Park*, but had never directed one of his screenplays. Nichols (*The Graduate, Heartburn, Postcards From the Edge*) invests the material with greater emotional authority and subtlety than Gene Saks brought to *Brighton Beach Memoirs* and Paul Bogart was able to summon in the TV movie of *Broadway Bound*. Simon's work tends toward sentimentality and superficiality, and Nichols counteracts those qualities with his characteristically astringent tone.

In addition to being richer, deeper, and more sarcastic, *Biloxi Blues* is better cast. (For some reason, non-Jews are frequently cast in Simon's adaptations, from Anne Bancroft and Hume Cronyn in *Broadway Bound* to Irene Worth and Mercedes Ruehl in *Lost in Yonkers*.) Matthew Broderick, who starred in both *Brighton Beach Memoirs* and *Biloxi Blues* on Broadway, here reprises his acclaimed performance as Eugene, bringing a breath of innocence to the part of a smart aleck on the verge of manhood. Broderick manages to make the character amusing and appealing without being glib and ingratiating.

Corey Parker also makes a strong impression as Arnold, ably evoking the character's contradictions and refusing to make him more lovable than he needs to be. Parker, who went on to play Gene at a later age in *Broadway Bound,* is not afraid of his character's darker side. Christopher Walken is also first-rate as the demented drill sergeant of whom Eugene will later charitably observe, "Never underestimate the stimulation of eccentricity."

In *Biloxi Blues,* Simon also does not underestimate the stimulation of ethnicity, delving into the mind-sets of his two most vividly drawn Jewish characters.

45

The Diary of Anne Frank

20th Century–Fox (1959)
CAST: **Millie Perkins, Joseph Schildkraut, Shelley Winters, Lou Jacobi, Ed Wynn**
DIRECTED BY: **George Stevens**
150 minutes [Not rated]

The first Hollywood film to directly confront the Holocaust, which has since come to be considered the defining event of Jewish experience in the twentieth century, *The Diary of Anne Frank* handled its previously untouched subject with kid gloves. For many years regarded as the definitive Holocaust film, this gentle, refined, and incongruously hopeful movie that sought to universalize the *Shoah* is credited with cracking open a door that had been slammed shut for fifteen years.

Anne Frank, a German-Jewish girl, spent two years in hiding in Amsterdam before being discovered and sent to Auschwitz-Birkenau. She remains Hitler's best-known victim and has become a universally recognized symbol of the *Shoah*. She recorded her experiences in her diary and became the subject of an exhaustive and revealing Oscar-winning 1995 documentary, *Anne Frank Remembered,* which offers a wealth of information not contained in her diary or the 1959 film. One of 1.5 million children murdered in the Holocaust, Anne Frank died in Bergen-Belsen one month before the concentration camp was liberated by Allied forces. Her diary, recovered by her father after the war and published in Holland in 1947 and in America in 1952, as *The Diary of a Young Girl,* has sold 25 million copies and been translated into fifty-five languages.

The diary was first transformed into a poignant Pulitzer Prize– and Tony Award–winning Broadway play in 1956. Frances Goodrich and Albert Hackett, a non-Jewish husband-and-wife Hollywood writing team, then adapted their popular play for the screen. The play later served as the basis for a 1980 TV movie starring Melissa Gilbert. The groundbreaking 1959 screen version of *The Diary of Anne Frank* was directed by George Stevens, who felt a special affinity for the material, having covered the liberation of Dachau as a major at the head of the Army Signal Corps film unit. Joseph Schildkraut, who won an Oscar for his performance as Alfred Dreyfus in *The Life of Emile Zola,* reprised the role of Anne's father that he had played on the stage.

An Academy Award nominee for best picture and best director, the black-and-white movie won Oscars for cinematography, art direction, and best supporting actress (Shelly Winters). The reviews were mixed, with some critics expressing reservations about the performance by Millie Perkins, a non-Jewish newcomer cast in the title role after a nationwide search for a fresh face.

The now-dated film opens as Otto Frank returns to the hiding place above a spice factory where his family was sheltered by its Christian co-owners and Otto's secretary, Miep Gies. (Miep Gies, who recovered Anne's diary after her arrest but never read it, is interviewed extensively in *Anne Frank Remembered*.) As Otto finds Anne's diary and begins to read, the movie flashes back to the beginning of the story Anne recorded so memorably for posterity. Anne initially regards her hiding as an adventure. Forced to be quiet all day while workmen are in the building below, she reads *A Tale of Two Cities* in one sitting on the first day. Soon, however, tensions begin to develop between the two familes sharing the cramped quarters.

Otto Frank is a serious, respected, and gentle man. His wife (Gustie Huber) is similarly noble and dignified, as is Anne's kindly and mild older sister Margot (Diane Baker). The Van Daans (Shelley Winters and Lou Jacobi), however, are vulgar, volatile, and materialistic. Their son Peter (Richard Beymer, who went on to play the lead in *West Side Story*) is at first attracted to Margot but soon becomes romantically attached to Anne. Much of the film focuses on their romance and on the struggles between Anne and her mother. Although Anne displays typical adolescent angst, it is offset by her tender, romantic, idealistic nature. Tensions escalate further when Anne is forced to share a room with the fussy and cranky dentist Dussel, who joins the families. (Dussel is played by Jewish actor Ed Wynn, who was nominated for an Oscar for his performance.) For two years, the families live in fear, listening to the radio, squabbling over meager rations, and struggling to maintain their dignity and composure under pressure.

When the Nazis beat down the door to the factory, the resigned families brace themselves for their deportation. "For years we have lived in fear. Now we begin to live in hope," Otto Frank remarks. Because the audience knows that only Otto Frank will survive the *Shoah,* the statement rings false and hollow. The film ends, back in the attic after the war, with Anne's voiceover repeating her earlier proclamation that "people are really good at heart." To be sure, some of the movie's cheery optimism and naïveté can be attributed to the schoolgirl sensibility of its original author, who was but thirteen when she first began to record the experience of her desperate confinement. But this hopefulness, a product of Anne's youth, also offered a comforting vision of the Holocaust to audiences who were presumed unable to handle the starker reality. The screenplay emphasizes Anne's belief in the essential good-

ness of humankind, deleting her gloomier, harsher musings on the murderous rage that has led to her predicament. The timid screenplay also deletes the fact that Anne's sister was an ardent Zionist, turning her into a sweet, bland symbol of shining purity. This reinforces the notion of the Jew as passive victim, a saintlike figure whose stoical suffering is meant to assuage our guilt.

While Anne's sequestered situation gave her a narrow window on the world being ravaged, and thus does not convey the larger picture of the Holocaust, the filmmakers do attempt to show outside events with a number of dramatic devices, most notably by including a dream scene from the diary in which Anne imagines her best friend in the camps. When Dussel arrives, he fills in the details of the escalated persecution of the Jews, providing the viewer with additional information. The filmmakers also tested and rejected an optional ending that pictured Anne in the camps. Still, the movie avoids mention of annihilation, atrocities, or the deep-seated hatred of the Jews that fueled the Holocaust. Interestingly, novelist Meyer Levin, who wrote a dramatization of the diary that was eventually rejected by Otto Frank, claims that his harsher treatment was deemed too Jewish. In a letter to Levin, Otto Frank instructs him not to make "a Jewish play" out of the diary, which he saw as a personal document and a tribute to his daughter's triumphant spirit. Until his death in 1981, Levin maintained that Anne's message had been distorted by the play and film, which universalized the Holocaust experience and ignored the Jewish content and references to anti-Semitism that he felt were central to the diary. Levin's struggle to present a more authentic version of Anne's diary has been documented in two books, including *The Stolen Legacy of Anne Frank: Meyer Levin, Lillian Hellman, and the Staging of the "Diary"* by Ralph Melnick (Yale University Press, 1997).

In 1997, playwright Wendy Kesselman presented a newly adapted and more overtly Jewish version of *The Diary of Anne Frank* based on the 1995 "Definitive Edition" of the diary, which restored key passages deleted by Otto Frank and contains thirty percent more material than the original.

The 1959 screenplay made some disconcerting changes that further de-Semitized Anne's story. In the film Anne proclaims, "We are not the only people that've had to suffer. There have always been people that've had to—sometimes one race, sometimes another." The line, as Anne wrote it, actually reads: "We are not the only *Jews* who have had to suffer. Right down through the ages there have been Jews and they've had to suffer."

The adaptation has also been criticized for changing key elements of the story. Specifically, the disagreeable character of Mr. Dussel is initially baffled that he should be the victim of Jewish persecution, because he feels more Dutch than Jewish. Clearly, he represents the assimilated Jew who failed to perceive the danger of anti-Semitism. In an invented Hanukkah scene, Dussel does not know the prayers and songs. In reality, Dussel was a Hebrew scholar whose religion meant everything to him, according to his widow. Even more oddly, the filmmakers chose to name the character Dussel, which means "idiot." This was Anne's nasty nickname for Fritz Pfeffer, the dentist who actually shared the Frank's attic.

The Diary of Anne Frank is a sensitive but sentimental and woefully inadequate drama that marks Hollywood's first tentative steps on a journey that would eventually lead to fuller portrayals of the century's greatest horror.

46

Shine

Fine Line Features/Miramax (1996)
CAST: Geoffrey Rush, Armin Mueller-Stahl,
Lynn Redgrave, Noah Taylor, Nicholas Bell
DIRECTED BY: Scott Hicks
105 minutes [PG-13]

A masterfully rendered portrait of a tortured Jewish genius, *Shine* traces the tragic trajectory of a promising pianist who spent years in mental institutions before returning to the concert stage.

David Helfgott's talent comes naturally. His torture comes courtesy of his father, whose protective instincts were intensified to a pathological level by the loss of his family in the Holocaust. That, at least, is the theory put forward in Scott Hicks's sensitive and stylish independent feature that became the surprise hit of 1996. *Shine* wowed the Sundance Film Festival crowds and won the press prize and audience award at the Toronto Film Festival before nabbing five Oscar nominations, including best picture and best director.

This stunning Australian screen biography is based on the life of the child prodigy whose descent into madness is largely attributed to his totalitarian, brutal, control-freak father Peter, played by German actor Armin Mueller-Stahl, nominated for best supporting actor. Peter is a distant cousin of *The Pawnbroker*'s Sol Nazerman, another man damaged almost beyond recognition by the loss of his family in the Nazi death camps. Unlike earlier traumatized Holocaust survivors, however, Peter's pain has turned him into a destructive tyrant. Peter may, in fact, be the most unsympathetic survivor in screen history, rivaled only by the demonic father played by Ron Rifkin in *Substance of Fire*. David certainly stands as the screen's most extreme portrayal of the potential for damage in children of Holocaust survivors, emphasizing the long-term heritage of Jewish suffering during the *Shoah*.

Peter's own musical ambitions were dashed by his authoritarian father, and so, like many parents, he seeks the realization of his own dreams through his children. Unlike most parents, however, he is a paranoid individual who so fears any threat to his family that he will do anything to keep it intact. At first, when piano teacher Ben Rosen (Nicholas Bell), a gay Jewish man who becomes one of David's many surrogate fathers, offers to teach David, his father will not hear of it. "I teach him!" he says and slams the door.

Later, Peter's need for control is overcome by his desire to realize his dreams through David, and he begrudgingly entrusts Rosen with David's musical education. When young David becomes a national champion and is offered an opportunity to study in America, however, Peter refuses to let him go. Clearly, David will some day have to choose between his love for his father and his passion for music, a choice that will crush David, one of the screen's many sensitive Jews. Operating from a victim mentality, Peter pushes his devoted son mercilessly to succeed, telling him that winning is everything and steeping him in his "survival of the fittest" ethos, a lesson he learned from Hitler. He withholds his affection when his son fails and tells him no one

SINS OF THE FATHERS *Shine,* the story of a Jewish piano prodigy and his tyrannical father, stars Armin Mueller-Stahl as a Polish refugee traumatized by the loss of his family in the Nazi death camps who inflicts further pain on his brilliant, sensitive son.

will ever love him the way he does. Naturally, David is eager to please his father, which he will never be able to do without sacrificing his identity and autonomy. Like so many screen Jews before him, David is caught between filial duty and personal fulfillment.

As a teen, David (now played by Noah Taylor) is beginning to rebel against his tyrannical father, a character type that figured prominently in Jewish films of an earlier era, such as *The Jazz Singer.* Given a full scholarship to the Royal College of Music in London, David decides to go, even though his father forbids it and tells him he can never come back if he leaves—again like *The Jazz Singer.* In London, David's talent blossoms under the tutelage of his demanding but kindly instructor (John Gielgud). But David cannot fully free himself from his father's influence. He decides to perform the Rachmaninoff Concerto No. 3, the most challenging piano piece ever written, which his father has wanted him to perform ever since he was a boy and which Rosen deemed too difficult. Warned by his mentor that the profoundly emotional piece will "eat him alive" if he doesn't "tame it" and that no student "has been mad enough to attempt it," David throws himself into torturous preparation for his graduation concert. He does indeed master the Rach 3, but during the performance something snaps in the high-strung young man.

David returns to Australia, but his father, who has wept listening to a tape of the performance, refuses to see him. The adult David is now played by Geoffrey Rush, who won the best actor Oscar as well as a Golden Globe for his astounding performance. David undergoes shock therapy and spends the next decade in a mental hospital, forbidden to play the piano by doctors who have decided it is too dangerous to his fragile psyche. David's earlier nervousness has reached a manic level, and his speech consists of lengthy, jumbled, rapid-fire discourses that contain only the barest thread of logic. Unable to focus, to calm his chattering nerves, he spews out pieces of his painful past.

A woman volunteering at the hospital is amazed to discover the onetime national hero alone and forgotten. She takes him home and sets him up in a small apartment under supervision. One night, David gets lost in the rain and ends up at a cheerful pub. Soon he's playing piano there every night, building a following of new fans and making new friends. His condition improves slightly, and he takes a shine to the chipper, eccentric astrologer Gillian (Lynn Redgrave). Gillian offers David the unconditional love and acceptance he has never known and agrees to marry him. With her encouragement, the still badly rattled but marginally functional David returns to the concert stage. (In real life, Helfgott's concerts are more popular with audiences than with music critics.)

It is by no means a complete recovery, however, and hardly the triumph so many film critics declared it. In fact, one of the film's virtues is that it does not present David's story as the kind of uplifting miracle a Hollywood film might fashion. The critics, even so, are right about one thing: *Shine* is a smashing film featuring three tour de force performances by the actors who play David. Rush, in particular, is magnificent as a man forever balanced on the edge of lucidity. Director Hicks and his screenwriter, Jan Sardi, whose screenplay also received an Oscar nomination, show the brilliance that lies just below the surface of David's clouded mind. Some of David's cleverness is unintentional. At one point, he pulls out of his addled brain a curious but telling reference to his father's past. "Like Daddy's family before they were concentrated," he says. (Peter Helfgott emigrated from Poland before the war.) The horrors of the past clearly haunt Peter, a point made clear by his reaction to a piece of barbed wire separating his backyard from the neighbors, with whom his children are not allowed to play.

The film takes an avid interest in the amibiguities of David's Jewishness. His embittered father says, "Religion is nonsense." The cultured Ben Rosen takes a more cynical, opportunistic view. "It's also a goldmine if you know where to dig," he says, suggesting David could well use the money from a bar mitzvah, which he does.

Although Peter is a monster, the film makes us understand the suffering that has made him one. He simply cannot bear to lose the only thing he has left, his children. And he cannot protect them from the dangerous world if they leave his side. Ironically, it is his own possessive love that destroys his son, not the cruel world.

47

Daniel

Paramount Pictures (1983)
CAST: Timothy Hutton, Amanda Plummer, Mandy Patinkin,
Tovah Feldshuh, Lindsay Crouse, Ed Asner
DIRECTED BY: Sidney Lumet
130 minutes [R]

To millions, the execution of alleged atomic spies Julius and Ethel Rosenberg was a gross miscarriage of justice, at best a desperate act of cold war paranoia, at worst a reprehensible attempt to stifle the Left. For the individuals involved, however, it was a devastating personal tragedy. Two children were orphaned when the middle-class couple from the Bronx, second-generation Jewish immigrants, were sent to the electric chair for conspiracy to commit espionage in 1953.

In 1971, Jewish novelist E. L. Doctorow chronicled the Rosenberg family's legacy of pain in *The Book of Daniel,* which traces this shocking piece of contemporary Jewish history. The overtly political and implicitly Jewish novel is a fictionalized account of the infamous executions that imagines the emotional after-effects experienced by the Rosenberg children amid the political upheaval of the 1960s. Director Sidney Lumet's screen adaptation of the book, with a faithful screenplay penned by Doctorow, is more than a psychological drama about survivors of terrible trauma. *Daniel* is a political meditation on the connection between the Old Left and the New Left, as Doctorow has said. It is a story driven by moral outrage that deals with the high value placed on inherited social responsibility in the Jewish cultural tradition.

Like the book on which it is based, *Daniel* does not set out to definitively establish the innocence of the Rosenbergs, here called Paul and Rochelle Isaacson, although the film suggests their conviction was a matter of political expediency. Their persecution is presented as a nightmarish vision of Jewish victimization, senseless and brutal. There are many who feel that anti-Semitism played a part in the Rosenbergs' notorious case; their conviction certainly confirmed the notion of the Jew as traitor in the minds of many Americans. Those who believe the Rosenbergs were victims of a government frameup argue that they were chosen, in part, because it was easier to gain a conviction against

Jews. The film does not expressly support this accusation, but it does portray the Isaacsons as Jewish idealists ritualistically sacrificed for their beliefs.

History's scapegoats, the Isaacsons are clearly identified as Jews by the director, who includes many revealing details defining their Jewish backgrounds and milieu. Rochelle, who comes from a Yiddish-speaking home and retains a slight accent, reminds her mother of the sweatshops that killed her father. Paul, confronting mounted policeman during a labor strike, calls the cops "cossacks." Lumet clearly establishes the Jewish connection to political activism of the era. He does not, however, emphasize the Jewishness of Daniel, the son who struggles to come to terms with his parents' memory and to save his sister. (In reality, the Rosenbergs had two sons, Michael and Robert, whose lives Doctorow did not research.)

Cast in the title role after actively campaigning for the part, Timothy Hutton abandoned his clean-cut, wholesome image to convey the ubiquitous anger and alienation of the 1960s counterculture. His Daniel, a bedraggled and disaffected graduate student, can find no meaning in his life. Hutton gives a biting performance, using an icy detachment to chilling effect, especially in the scenes in which he looks directly into the camera and describes various forms of execution employed through the ages.

Daniel's unstable sister Susan (Amanda Plummer, who specializes in fragile psyches) has discovered a measure of purpose by joining the political protest movements of the 1960s. She urges her self-absorbed brother to honor their parents' memory by joining her and wants to turn their trust fund into a foundation supporting radical causes. Daniel is unable to shake off his apathetic cynicism, however, and remains isolated in his silent suffering, often lashing out at his uncomprehending wife (Ellen Barkin).

Activism proves a temporary distraction for Susan, who becomes overwhelmed by her childhood catastrophe and attempts suicide, landing in a mental hospital she will not leave alive. Rochelle's mother is also an hysterical and paranoid woman, suggesting Susan's insanity may be hereditary. But when Susan's and Daniel's foster mother insists that Susan is ill and can be made well again, Daniel disagrees. She's not sick, he says, looking into his own soul for the right word. She's "inconsolable," he concludes. Prompted by Susan's breakdown, Daniel begins his own journey of discovery, searching in vain for the truth, uncovering only contradictions and complications. Daniel is not looking for comfort, nor does he find any. But by confronting the past, he lights the way to his future. Daniel marches into the lion's den and emerges not unscathed but stronger, once again connected to the world of the living. He is ready to embrace his radical heritage. The film ends hopefully with Daniel, along with his wife and young child, joining a peaceful Vietnam War protest march.

THE LION'S DEN Timothy Hutton stars in *Daniel,* Sidney Lumet's screen adaptation of E. L. Doctorow's fictionalized novel speculating on the fate of the children of Julius and Ethel Rosenberg.

Daniel, like the novel, employs a radical structure that jumps back and forth in time. The film spends a good deal of time on Paul, played with burning intensity by Mandy Patinkin, and the passionate and maternal Rochelle, effectively portrayed by Lindsay Crouse. The film traces their courtship at City College in the 1930s and details their life of Communist commitment to improving the lot of the oppressed classes (referred to as "the common man" or the "proleteriat" and "the Negro"). The film does not question the Isaacsons' intentions or integrity. They may be naive or even misguided, but they are clearly depicted as being dedicated to building a better world.

Like the political filmmaker's other work, *Daniel* reflects Lumet's liberal persuasions, but this probing film is not simplistic propaganda. It does, for example, convey the danger of fanaticism. It also suggests that the children were pawns in a game they didn't understand. The victims of public institutions and agencies, they are also abandoned or inadvertently abused by the

Left. Susan's last words to Daniel convey their plight: "They're still fucking us, Daniel. You get the picture?"

The film suggests that although the charges against them were absurd, the Isaacsons were no "innocent babes in the woods" either in a scene in which the Jewish *New York Times* reporter (Lee Richardson) who covered the case talks frankly to Daniel. There is bitter irony in the fact that the judge who sentences them to death is also Jewish.

When Daniel visits the embittered widow of his parents' loyal lawyer, Jacob Ascher (excellently played by Jewish actor Ed Asner), he finds she blames the "difficult and stubborn" Isaacsons for her husband's early death. He also discovers that this dedicated and decent man, the children's only friend in a time of need, may have mishandled the case. Daniel then visits Linda Mindish, the daughter of the man who testified against his parents, their old friend and neighbor Selig Mindish (Joseph Leon). He finds that Linda (Tovah Feldshuh) has also struggled mightily to rebuild her life. Any answers Selig may have held are now lost in a haze of senility. Daniel concludes, "There's such a thing as too much hope."

Lumet (*The Pawnbroker*) was immediately attracted to the complex intertwining of personal and political drama when he read the novel in 1971. *The Book of Daniel* dealt with Lumet's favorite themes: social justice, guilt and responsibility, the importance of memory, and the primacy of family. The son of veteran Yiddish stage actor Baruch Lumet, with whom he enjoyed a close relationship, Lumet grew up in a politically committed household and felt a strong affinity for Doctorow's examination of family heritage and inherited social values, a theme he explored again in 1988's *Running on Empty.*

Doctorow wrote the screen adaptation two years later, and Lumet spent the next ten years trying to interest a studio in the project, finally scraping together a shoestring budget that required the actors to work for scale. Although the film had its share of critical admirers, *Daniel* was a box office disappointment. It was also criticized for fictionalizing history, generating far more controversy than the book had aroused.

Robert Meeropol, the younger Rosenberg son, admits that while Doctorow is entitled to his artistic creation, it is difficult to see one's life become the subject of conjecture and speculation. Meeropol, who took the name of the family that adopted him and his brother after their parents' execution, was disturbed by both the movie and the book, "which took an historical set of facts and built a story around them." The problem, for him, is that so many people assumed the fiction was fact. "The thing I like least about the book and movie," Meeropol said in an interview for this book, "is the movement of people who worked to save my parents is shown manipulating the children. In fact, even the most doctrinaire, old-style leftists were all remarkably sensitive to my needs and my brother's needs. They showed remarkable restraint and sensitivity."

Meeropol, who was three when his parents were arrested and six when they were executed—as Susan is in the book and film—said that in reality the trauma was worse for his older brother, who was more cognizant of the loss. Meeropol was not involved with the making of *Daniel,* except for an evening he spent with Ed Asner at the Russian Tea Room during the filming, at which time he expressed his strong reservations about the script. He especially disliked the depiction of his father as being "almost masochistic."

Meeropol also questioned the invention of Federal Bureau of Investigation informer Selig Mindish, who is conveniently senile by the time Daniel goes looking for answers. In fact, it was Ethel's brother David Greenglass who testified against the Rosenbergs to save his own life, and Meeropol has deliberately avoided any contact with him.

In one way, however, Doctorow's imagination served him well. The creation of a foundation to support radical causes was in fact an idea Meeropol and his brother discussed during the 1970s when they were engaged in lawsuits against the government that might have allowed them access to large sums of money. "We did want to take the devastation and make something good come of it," Meeropol explained. "We wanted to transform the tragedy into triumph. That's the theme I try to live by." In 1990, Meeropol created the Rosenberg Fund, a nonprofit organization that provides for the needs of children whose parents have been targeted for their progressive activity. Through donations, the Rosenberg Fund has awarded grants to more than 100 children and hopes to reach a $1 million endowment by the year 2000.

Although the Rosenbergs' son takes issues with how the book and film arrive at their conclusions, it is true that, like Daniel, he "came out with a positive attitude to my parents and with a commitment to creating a better world." That, of course, is the theme of *Daniel.* As Rochelle marches defiantly to her execution—unlike her husband, who faints dead away and has to be dragged to his death—she sees the rabbi assigned to accompany her. "I will not have him here," she says. "Let our deaths be Daniel's bar mitzvah."

It will, in fact, take Daniel many years to become a man and fulfill his Jewish mandate. First, as Lumet has said, he will have to dig himself out of his parents' grave.

48

Yentl

Metro-Goldwyn-Mayer/United Artists (1983)
Cast: Barbra Streisand, Mandy Patinkin, Amy Irving, Nehemiah Persoff
Directed by: Barbra Streisand
134 minutes [PG]

One can easily imagine Barbra Streisand's delight in discovering Isaac Bashevis Singer's *Yentl the Yeshiva Boy,* a story that was proudly Jewish and staunchly feminist. Streisand has always refused to downplay her Jewishness and has fought a long uphill—and very vocal—battle against sexism in the entertainment industry on her remarkable rise to superstardom.

Yentl, arguably the most thoroughly Jewish film of the 1980s and the best evocation of shtetl life since *Fiddler on the Roof,* was a daring, ambitious move for Streisand, who disproved industry opinion that the story was "too specifically Jewish" for general audiences. Streisand directed, produced, cowrote, and starred in *Yentl—*an unprecedented accomplishment for a woman in Hollywood. In fact, no man has ever produced, directed, scripted, starred in, and sung in a major Hollywood film. In her technically skilled directing debut, she continued to pioneer the trend toward overt ethnicity in film and to champion strong, principled female Jewish characters. *Yentl* stands as the most prestigious Hollywood production to favorably center on a female Jewish character. It is for these reasons *Yentl* is ranked among the greatest Jewish films. Opinion on its artistic merits has been sharply divided, however, which has typically been the case with Streisand's movies.

In the view of many, *Yentl* is a refreshingly original, brave, and moving drama, bold in its sexual politics and endearing in its nostalgia for Jewish history. Indeed, the movie is clearly the product of great love and determination and reflects the obvious emotional affinity Streisand felt for Singer's tale of terrible inner conflict.

Another camp holds that Streisand's well-intentioned efforts to turn the complicated folktale into a star vehicle for herself proved misguided and that her indulgent and bloated spectacle violates the spirit of the story, a mischievous and sophisticated yet brief and spare work detailing the contradictions of the human soul, written by Singer in a single afternoon in the 1950s. These complaints are well justified. But despite these legitimate reservations about the film's fidelity to the source material, there is no denying that this is a film that should be seen by anyone interested in the depiction of the Jewish experience on the screen.

Streisand was forty when she took on the role of a girl who disguises herself as a boy whose beard has not yet come in so that she can study Torah and Talmud. (In the 1936 Yiddish classic, *Yidl Mitn Fiddle,* Molly Picon, then thirty-seven, similarly disguises herself as a boy to play in a klezmer band and falls in love with a fellow fiddler.) Streisand was first shown the sexually ambiguous story while awaiting the release of *Funny Girl* in 1968 and immediately began to try to elicit interest in the property. She was told, however, that the story had no commercial promise. Undeterred, she acquired the rights—Singer had sold it to an impoverished producer, who sold it to Streisand—and vowed to someday make a movie out of it.

Streisand would eventually make good on her promise, but it would take long and arduous effort. First, director Ivan Passer backed out because he felt Streisand was too old and too famous to play the part, which Tovah Feldshuh had played on Broadway in an adaptation by Leah Napolin in 1975. Streisand then decided to direct the project herself. Ted Allan (Oscar-nominated for his Jewish coming-of-age drama *Lies My Father Told Me*) wrote the first of twenty scripts Streisand would commission, in addition to an unsolicited script by Singer. Allan's version was rejected, the writer felt, because it emphasized the anti-Semitism in Eastern Europe that caused so many Jews to leave, a fact that is conspicuously absent from the final film, a rosy fantasy in which the only problem for Jews appears to be that women were not allowed to read holy books. In the end, a script written by Streisand and reworked by British writer Jack Rosenthal (*Bar Mitzvah Boy*) was used.

Over the years, Streisand immersed herself in Jewish customs and laws and consulted with dozens of rabbis. During the course of her copious research, Streisand rediscovered her religious heritage and formed a deeper appreciation of her cultural roots. She spent a year studying Judaism with her son, Jason (by actor Elliott Gould), prior to his bar mitzvah in 1980. That same year, Orion Pictures placed the project in turnaround, frightened by the fiasco of *Heaven's Gate.* Streisand shot footage of herself in character and shopped the project around Hollywood. Although a bankable star, she was turned down by every studio before she found an ally at United Artists.

Yentl may be an audacious adaptation—light years from Paul Mazursky's marvelous adaptation of Singer's *Enemies, a Love Story*—but it is not without interest due to its subject. The movie opens in a Polish shtetl in 1904 (Singer's story is set in 1873) where Yentl defies social expectations for a young woman. She is not interested in marriage and burns everything she cooks. Her

widowed rabbi father (veteran character actor Nehemiah Persoff, known for his one-man show *Sholem Aleichem*) secretly teaches her, drawing the curtains because, he says, he's sure God will understand but the neighbors might not. Papa, a character Streisand modeled on her own father, who died when she was a baby, has a Camille-like cough, and, sure enough, Yentl is soon saying *kaddish* at his grave in open defiance of custom requiring a male to recite the sacred prayer for the dead.

That night, Yentl cuts her hair, dons men's clothing, and heads off in the night to follow her dream of being a Talmudic scholar. As Anshel, she/he joins a yeshiva and excels at his studies. The yeshiva "boy" is unable to contain her feminine feelings, however, and falls in love with the robust and brilliant Avigdor. (Mandy Patinkin, then largely known as a singer, was cast after Richard Gere and Michael Douglas turned the role down.) Avigdor, however, is smitten with the traditionally feminine and subservient Hadass (Oscar nominee Amy Irving). Anshel/Yentl, however, is appalled by the submissive creature, who is everything she resisted becoming. But as a man, she begins to see why the demure and docile Hadass is so appealing.

When Hadass's family calls off the match, Avigdor is heartbroken and begs Anshel to take his place as her groom so that he might at least continue to see Hadass. Anshel reluctantly agrees and marries Hadass, inventing excuses for not consummating the marriage. Instead, in an embellishment on the story, Yentl begins teaching her eager-to-please bride at night, thus making her a more liberated woman who can think for herself. In the end, Anshel bares her breasts and her soul, confessing the truth to Avigdor. Happily, he returns her affections. Sadly, however, he expects her to now be a "real woman" and assume the traditional female role. Yentl will not give up Talmud for her man, however. Avidgor returns to Hadass, and Yentl sets out for the New World, where she hopes to live as a woman and still pursue her religious education.

There is, of course, an irony in this ending, which was not the way Singer's tale ended. (Yentl moves on to another yeshiva in the story by Singer, who despised what he called the film's "kitsch ending.") In the movie, Yentl must move further away from Judaism to come closer to it; she must break free from its restrictive laws in order to embrace its wisdom. The movie ends optimistically on a ship bound for America, where Streisand sings mightily into the sea air in a scene closely resembling one in *Funny Girl*. This song, like the eleven that precede it, is a Broadway-style pop tune that has no musical connection to the movie's time, place, or ethnicity. In addition, the implication that Yentl will fare better in America does not make much sense, as Singer himself pointed out. What will she do there? Work in a sweatshop twelve hours a day?

Yentl opened to mostly mixed reviews, with a few devastating pans and a fair number of raves from influential critics such as Roger Ebert, who applauded its "special magic." It was a modest box office success, eventually grossing $60 million. The only Oscar it won was for Michel Legrand's musical score, with songs by Alan and Marilyn Bergman. Although Streisand won a Golden Globe for her direction, she was not nominated for a best director Oscar, setting off a storm of controversy. Streisand's shunning by the Academy led to charges that she was not nominated because of her sex, her religion, or her personality. Irving lost in the best supporting actress category to Linda Hunt, who ironically won for playing a man in *The Year of Living Dangerously.*

Singer, who was quite displeased with his own treatment as well as with the adaptation of his story, dismissed the movie as being without artistic merit or understanding for Yentl's "ideals, character, sacrifice and great passion for spiritual achievement." In an article for the *New York Times,* Singer wrote, "Miss Streisand was exceedingly kind to herself. The result is that Miss Streisand is always present, while poor Yentl is absent."

49

The Young Lions

20th Century–Fox (1958)
CAST: **Marlon Brando, Montgomery Clift, Dean Martin,**
Hope Lange, Maximilian Schell
DIRECTED BY: **Edward Dmytryk**
167 minutes [Not rated]

Noah Ackerman (Montgomery Clift) may appear timid as a mouse, but he proves the fiercest of the three young lions in this acclaimed drama. A rare postwar film that acknowledges the Holocaust as well as American anti-Semitism, *The Young Lions* vividly evokes the prejudice that ironically greeted Jews who joined the country's fight against Hitler. Noah, a Jewish soldier who serves in World War II, emerges victorious from his valorous battle with the enemy in Europe. On the home front, he successfully wages a personal war against anti-Semitism, thereby triumphing twice over the forces of Jewish oppression. In this biting epic, Noah goes to extreme measures to attain respect and acceptance, putting his life on the line in both battles.

Based on the 1948 first novel by bestselling Jewish-American author Irwin Shaw, *The Young Lions* examines various dimensions of heroism as exemplified by three soldiers. Marlon Brando is cast as Christian, an apolitical Austrian ski instructor who becomes a Nazi and lives to regret it. Christian represents heroism without honor. An example of misplaced loyalty, this disillusioned soldier is a reminder of what can happen when one follows orders instead of one's conscience. Dean Martin, in his first screen role, is typecast as Michael, a boozing, draft-dodging, selfish singer who initially shirks his duty but finally jumps into the fray. Michael represents reluctant heroism. When Michael finally commits himself—to a cause and to the woman he loves—he recovers his self-respect. True heroism is embodied by Noah, whose bravery and altruism inspire Michael to follow his example. Noah appears an unlikely hero. Slight of build, mild of manner, quiet, modest, gentle, and unassuming, Noah is the classic sensitive Jew. Noah redefines our image of heroism, here reshaped into a stammering, 135-pound Jewish intellectual who reads James Joyce and discovers hidden reservoirs of personal strength.

Clift was cast as Noah following the automobile accident that drastically altered his fabled good looks and left his ravaged, surgically reconstructed face partially immobilized. Clift capitalized on his newfound vulnerability and lack of vanity, playing Noah as a humble human being who just happens to be a shining symbol of decency and determination. Clift was attracted to Noah's persistence and said he related to his private suffering and his conviction that he was a drab, unappealing man, a loner who longed for approval yet needed to be accepted on his own terms. Noah remained Clift's favorite role.

Clift, whose father was openly anti-Semitic, was also battling internalized prejudice against his own homosexuality, making him acutely aware of Noah's struggle and his desire to prove himself. The *New York Times* declared his performance "strangely hollow and lackluster," describing him as being "in a glassy-eyed gaze," but most reviews were kinder. *Newsweek* called him "virtually flawless."

Although Noah represents an earnest attempt to create a positive Jewish character, which is the main reason for its inclusion in this ranking, *The Young Lions* aroused controversy due to its sympathetic depiction of the guilt-stricken Nazi, played with charm and warmth by Brando. Christian acts nobly as he performs his duties for the Fatherland, then is shocked and horrified when he stumbles on a death camp in the final days of the war. This insulting presentation of a decent, idealistic German soldier was indeed part of the cinema's troubling postwar practice of viewing Nazis charitably. This trend reached its nadir in *The Desert Fox* (1951), which turned German army field marshal Rommel into a four-star hero.

Brando, who has run into trouble in recent years for making remarks that have been interpreted as anti-Semitic, actively campaigned to make Christian more virtuous, a change that dismayed Shaw. When Brando suggested that Christian die Christ-like, rolling into a halo of barbed wire with his arms outstretched, Clift raised strenuous objections, and the crucifixion image was downplayed.

Adapted by Edward Anhalt (*The Man in the Glass Booth*), *The Young Lions* was directed by Edward Dmytryk, who tackled anti-Semitism on screen for the first time in Hollywood history in *Crossfire* (1947). Dmytryk, who was not Jewish, previously directed a number of films of interest to Jewish audiences, including *Hitler's Children* (1943), *The Juggler* (1953), and *The Caine Mutiny* (1954).

Noah's first encounter with anti-Semitism comes when he meets the father of Hope (Hope Lange), the girl he wants to marry. Hope comes from a small town in Vermont, and when she takes Noah home to meet her family, she is visibly nervous. Before Noah gets off the bus, she tells her father, "He's sweet, he's poor—and he's Jewish." The two men walk in the park, and Hope's

BATTLE ON THE HOME FRONT   Montgomery Clift, left, plays a valiant and virtuous Jewish soldier who fights anti-Semitism in the United States Army in the acclaimed screen adaptation of Irwin Shaw's *The Young Lions.*

father says he's never met a Jew before. "You're doing a terrible thing," he tells Noah, leading us to expect the worst. Instead, he delivers one of the film's best lines: "You're putting a man to the test of his principles." He then invites Noah home to turkey dinner.

In the army, Noah encounters much more virulent and violent anti-Semitism. Sergeant Rickett (Lee Van Cleef) sets the ball rolling by expressing outrage at the "dirty, filthy book" he finds in Noah's footlocker, *Ulysses,* and the dust on the windows. He stirs up anti-Semitism among the recruits, who taunt him and steal his money. Noah confronts the men, challenging the four biggest men in the unit to fistfights. He is badly beaten by the first three, but wins the last fight. After Michael brings the situation to the attention of the camp's colonel, Sergeant Rickett is punished, and the men embrace Noah, who has proved he's no weakling. Although his masochistic willingness to subject himself to physical abuse in order to gain respect will not sit well with all viewers, the film certainly intends us to applaud his bravery.

Later, when Noah's company liberates a Nazi death camp, a rabbi who has been imprisoned there asks Noah's commanding officer, Lt. Green (Arthur Franz) for permission to hold a religious service for the victims. Although a local official warns against it, permission is granted. Recognizing Noah's visible discomfort at the sight of the suffering of his people, Green tells him to take a walk outside the camp, further emphasizing Noah's hard-won acceptance as a Jew.

The Young Lions remains the only film to fully explore what it was like for a Jewish soldier to take part in the war to free the Jews of Europe.

50

Marjorie Morningstar

Republic Pictures (1958)
CAST: Gene Kelly, Natalie Wood, Claire Trevor, Ed Wynn
DIRECTED BY: Irving Rapper
123 minutes [Not rated]

Long before the derogatory term "Jewish–American princess" entered the American vocabulary, Marjorie Morningstar was unjustly saddled with the reputation. Until dethroned by Goldie Hawn in *Private Benjamin*, Marjorie remained the screen's best known JAP. It was a bum rap for Herman Wouk's heroine, who was meant to exemplify the very best of modern Jewish womanhood. The mistaken impression was due in part to shifting cultural values as well as to the ambivalence inherent in Wouk's writing.

Similarly, *Marjorie Morningstar* is an often misunderstood and underrated movie that, upon closer examination, extolls traditional Jewish values and is a forerunner of female-focused films of the 1960s and 1970s featuring Jewish heroines struggling with issues of autonomy, identity, and morality, including *Funny Girl, Hester Street, The Way We Were, Sheila Levine Is Dead and Living in New York,* and *Me, Natalie.* This being the 1950s, however, Marjorie's major dilemma is restricted to which mate she should choose.

Overtly Jewish in a time when few films contained specific Jewish references, *Marjorie Morningstar* was interpreted by many as a negative assessment of Jewish identity. Indeed, the film, like the book, spends a good deal of time criticizing Marjorie (Natalie Wood) and her mother (Claire Trevor). Gene Kelly, who plays the free-spirited, cynical song and dance man Noel Airman, calls nice Jewish girls like Marjorie Morgenstern "Shirleys." "It's a trade name for a respectable middle-class girl who likes to play at being worldly," he tells the stagestruck college girl, adding that she's a tease who will never sleep with him unless he marries her, which he has no intention of doing. "You're on a course charted by 5,000 years of Moses and the Ten Commandments. I'm a renegade," he continues, linking her values to her upbringing. When Marjorie's bourgeois mother cross-examines the bohemian Noel and expresses her disapproval of him as "a match," Marjorie disavows her matri-

THE WRONG MAN   The heroine of *Marjorie Morningstar*, played by Natalie Wood, left, shares a Passover seder with her beau (Gene Kelly), a self-described Jewish renegade who rejects traditional values, and her disapproving mother (Claire Trevor).

monial-minded mother's materialism. "You are your mother," he scoffs, noting she can always run home to daddy.

Marjorie is indeed pampered, privileged, and bound by convention. She is a 1950s dream girl, virtuous, idealistic, and loyal. Men fall in love with her left and right. Even Noel cannot resist her charms. Noel's accusation that she's just like her pragmatic, status-conscious mother proves unjust. Indeed, she tries to stay true to the values with which she was raised while struggling to become independent and pursue her own dreams. Unfortunately, the film takes a long time to reveal Marjorie in this favorable light.

Wouk, who grew up in the Bronx in an Orthodox family of immigrants, credited his grandfather, a rabbi, with having a lasting influence on his life. From his moral mentor, Wouk came to believe in traditional values, in the subjugation of personal desires for the greater societal good, and in submission to just authority. These tenets of faith were to be the themes of his popular novels, including his Pulitzer Prize–winning *The Caine Mutiny,* which was made into a famed film in 1955, starring Jose Ferrer as the Jewish lawyer who serves as the voice of truth and the story's true hero. Wouk's *Winds of War* was turned into a turgid fourteen-hour TV miniseries in 1983.

When Wouk sat down to write *Marjorie Morningstar* in the early 1950s, based on a play he had written in 1940, he intended to create a character drama based on his own experiences of Jewish culture. He hoped to depict the temptation of assimilation and success on second- and third-generation American Jews. In Wouk's 1955 bestseller, the characters' attitudes and behavior are intrinsically Jewish. Thankfully, in the film, their actions and personalities are similarly related to their heritage. Unlike many films of the 1950s, *Marjorie Morningstar* does not downplay the characters' Jewishness, except through the casting of well-known gentiles in the starring roles.

The part of Noel, in fact, was originally offered to Danny Kaye, who reportedly felt insecure about the character's Jewishness. Jack Warner then decided to underplay the Jewishness altogether by casting gentiles. "If it were made today," Gene Kelly wrote in his autobiography, "they'd probably star Barbra Streisand and Dustin Hoffman in it, which would be perfect casting. But in 1957, Hollywood's commitment to authenticity was nonexistent and, as a result, the picture suffered."

Director Irving Rapper and screenwriter Everett Freeman contemporize Wouk's novel a bit by changing the ending. Unlike the book's Marjorie, the film's heroine does not become a housewife. She does decide to give up on the permanently adolescent, irresponsible, unambitious Noel, but instead of settling down with a stodgy lawyer and giving up her dreams of stardom, she settles on Wally Wronken (Marty Milner), the successful Broadway writer who has been in love with her for years. Although he will surely dote on her and offers her security, the choice of Wally is not a complete capitulation to conformity. The filmmakers were perhaps wise to change the ending. As values were beginning to shift in the late 1950s, Wouk's ending might have been read as a complete copout. Marjorie's mature choice of Wally is not quite Wouk's endorsement of domesticity and conservatism, but rather a happy compromise.

In some ways a precursor to the films of the late 1960s and early 1970s that expressed great resentment for hidebound Jewish customs, vented hostility against the claustrophobic Jewish family, and rejected the materialism of the upwardly mobile Jewish generation, *Marjorie Morningstar* is awkwardly caught between two worldviews. It criticizes while it praises, leaving the audience uncertain of its intended effect, which is also a failing some literary critics ascribe to Wouk's writing.

Noel surprises us by turning out to be such a cad and a hypocrite. He disdains Marjorie's middle-class values, but when he falls in love with her, he transforms himself for a time into a model citizen. After appearing visibly uncomfortable at a Passover seder with her family, he tells her he was thinking about all those things he has been missing in life, "family—your kind of family—faith and tradition." His failure is that he cannot commit to those things. Today, we are more inclined to expect the renegade Noel to prove himself superior to those who disapprove of his unconventional lifestyle. Instead, in a sudden reversal of expectations (not unlike that in *The Caine Mutiny*), he is proven to be a shiftless, spineless poseur without talent, courage, or integrity. A lapsed Jew, Noel has changed his name from Ehrman—"honest man"—to Airman, a *luftmensch* with nothing to ground him.

Marjorie, on the other hand, stays firmly connected to her roots. Her positive attachment to her heritage is evidenced by her warm and loving relationship with Uncle Samson (Jewish actor Ed Wynn), an Old World spokesman for family and tradition. Understanding, wise, kind, and playful, Samson provides Marjorie with a link to her past and a moral grounding, quite possibly a reference to Wouk's beloved grandfather.

Although Natalie Wood's performance leaves a great deal to be desired, *Marjorie Morningstar* expressed a struggle between personal independence and cultural connection that continues to mark modern Jewish life.

Afterword

Why, you may be wondering, isn't the hugely popular *Sophie's Choice* or the critically acclaimed *The Garden of the Finzi-Continis* included in my ranking of the fifty greatest Jewish films of all time? And how could I have overlooked the Oscar-winning *The Shop on Main Street?* In all probability, you can think of at least one important, popular film that really should be in this book. I sympathize with your dismay at finding one of your favorite films slighted. There are, in fact, dozens of worthy movies that didn't make the final cut. I think you are entitled to an explanation of why some seemingly obvious choices were omitted.

First of all, I tried not to be too predictable in my picks. In addition to including what are widely considered indispensible milestones, I opted to honor a handful of lesser known and less obvious choices. In fact, I dearly wish I had the space to recommend a number of wonderful neglected films, such as *A Kid for Two Farthings, The Plot Against Harry, The Man in the Glass Booth, Leon the Pig Farmer, The Dunera Boys, The Quarrel,* and *The Two of Us.* But that would have meant bumping even more landmark movies than I already left out.

In order to create a healthy diversity of genres and subjects, movies with similar themes and subjects were sometimes merged. *The Frisco Kid* rode along with the better-known Jewish Western *Blazing Saddles.* Ernst Lubitsch's *To Be or Not to Be* found a home in another antifascist comedy of the period, Charles Chaplin's *The Great Dictator. Crossfire,* the first film to expose American anti-Semitism, has been incorporated into the review of *Gentleman's Agreement,* a more acclaimed treatment of the same subject released a few months later. Joan Miklin Silver's *Hester Street* was rolled into *Crossing Delancey,* the director's later feminist film refuting the assimilationist agenda that tends to dominate the movies.

In order to include works by a variety of film artists, I also condensed my list by eliminating films by already well represented filmmakers, even though they could easily merit inclusion. *The Way We Were,* I decided, was just one Barbra Streisand film too many. With three Woody Allen films already included, I had to forgo his growing-up-Jewish gem *Radio Days,* and his assimilation metaphor *Zelig.* Paul Mazursky's *Willie and Phil* and *Next Stop, Greenwich Village* easily deserve discussion, but I had to content myself with Mazursky's best film, *Enemies, a Love Story,* and the one most representative of his work, *Down and Out in Beverly Hills.*

Given the large number of worthy films about the Holocaust, I had to be especially careful not to get carried away with this weighty subject, arguably the defining event of the twentieth century. This book already contains ten films that deal directly with the Holocaust and another five that touch on the subject. Although critically acclaimed, *The Garden of the Finzi-Continis* was eliminated because on viewing it again I was bothered by its non-Jewish casting and the preponderance of negative Jewish images. If space allowed, I would have preferred to include *Escape From Sobibor, The Shop on Main Street, The Sorrow and the Pity,* or *Triumph of the Spirit,* which are briefly discussed elsewhere.

Sophie's Choice, one of the best-known films about the Holocaust, was left out because, despite its popularity, there is no way I could consider it "great." This objectionable story concerns a Polish gentile who survives the Holocaust only to be victimized by a crazy, demonic Jew, whose death serves to edify a gentile writer. Similarly, even more glaringly egregious films, such as the grossly anti-Semitic *Jud Suess,* made in Nazi Germany, may be historically important but do not belong in a ranking of great Jewish films. Conversely, *Grand Illusion* is widely considered a great movie and favorably features a Jewish character, but it is also highly sympathetic to the Germans, which makes it even more problematic than *The Young Lions,* which is included here.

Some important as well as excellent movies were left out because while their subjects, while of interest to Jewish viewers, contain only minor Jewish characters. *Judgment at Nuremberg,* for example, offered a groundbreaking discussion of the Holocaust in 1961, but focuses on non-Jews and downplays the Jews as primary targets of the genocide. *Mephisto* and *The Damned* are both fascinating looks at Nazi Germany, but do not focus on anti-Semitism or feature central Jewish characters.

The most glaring omission in this book is the absence of a Yiddish film. I cheated a little by including *Almonds and Raisins: A History of the Yiddish Cinema,* which allowed me to briefly discuss all the best Yiddish films instead of selecting one or two representative examples. Additionally, *The Dybbuk* is mentioned in the review of *The Golem, Tevye* is noted in *Fiddler on the Roof, The Cantor's Son* is discussed in *The Jazz Singer,* and *Yidl Mitn Fiddle* is referred to in *Yentl*. Similarly, Israeli films are dealt with in *Exodus,* although *Sallah* almost made it into the book as the most enjoyable Israeli film.

A number of the films considered and rejected were based on important literature. Despite the interest of the source material, however, the screen adaptations of *The Fixer, The Magician of Lublin, Joshua Then and Now,* and *Ship of Fools* were ultimately deemed too flawed to be included. The same is true of some fascinating historical dramas such as *Voyage of the Damned.*

Even though their subjects were enormously interesting, I simply didn't have room for some fascinating biographies of complex and controversial Jews, including *Lenny* and *Citizen Cohn.* Indeed, edgy material such as *The King of Comedy* sometimes gave way to more positive views of Jewish life and characters.

In an attempt to balance popular works with more provocative, original, or obscure films, I had to set aside some highly enjoyable commercial films, including *The Sunshine Boys, Mr. Saturday Night, Quiz Show, Unstrung Heroes, Miami Rhapsody,* and *My Favorite Year.* Because their Jewish content was more implicit than explicit, I also eliminated some recent films I really like, including *I.Q., Flirting With Disaster,* and *This Is My Life.*

A case could easily be made for any of these films, and a few more not mentioned, to be given an individual place of honor on these pages. My apologies to these worthy contenders and to you, their champions. Both you and they will have to wait for the next book.

Bibliography

Alter, Robert. *Defenses of the Imagination: Jewish Writers and Modern Historical Crisis.* Philadelphia: The Jewish Publication Society, 1977.

Anderegg, Michael A. *William Wyler.* Boston: Twayne Publishers, 1979.

Avisar, Ilvan. *Screening the Holocaust: Cinema's Images of the Unimaginable.* Bloomington, Ind.: Indiana University Press, 1988.

Baumgarten, Murray, and Barbara Gottfried. *Understanding Philip Roth.* Columbia, S.C.: University of South Carolina Press, 1990.

Behlmer, Rudi, ed. *Memo From Darryl F. Zanuck.* New York: Grove Press, 1993.

Bona, Damien, and Mason Wiley. *Inside Oscar: The Unofficial History of the Academy Awards.* New York: Ballantine Books, 1996.

Bosworth, Patricia. *Montgomery Clift: A Biography.* San Diego: Harcourt Brace Jovanovich, 1978.

Boxer, Tim. *Tim Boxer's Jewish Celebrity Anecdotes.* Middle Village, N.Y.: Jonathan David Publishers, 1996.

Boyer, Jay. *Sidney Lumet.* Boston: Twayne Publishers, 1993.

Brewer, Gay. *David Mamet and Film: Illusion/Disillusion in a Wounded Land.* Jefferson, Mo.: McFarland & Co., 1993.

Brode, Douglas. *Woody Allen: His Films and Career.* Secaucus, N.J.: Citadel Press, 1985.

Carnes, Mark, ed. *Past Imperfect: History According to the Movies.* New York: Henry Holt & Co., 1995.

Clarens, Carlos. *Crime Movies: An Illustrated History.* New York: W.W. Norton & Co., 1980.

Colombat, Andre Pierre. *The Holocaust in French Film.* Metuchen, N.J.: Scarecrow Press, 1993.

Cohen, Sarah Blacher, ed. *From Hester Street to Hollywood: The Jewish-American Stage and Screen.* Bloomington, Ind.: Indiana University Press, 1983.

Craniford, Ada. *Fiction and Fact in Mordecai Richler's Novels.* Lewiston, Me.: Edwin Mellen Press, 1992.

Crist, Judith. *Take 22: Moviemakers on Moviemaking.* New York: Viking Penguin, 1984.

Cunningham, Frank. *Sidney Lumet: Film and Literary Vision.* Limestone, Ky.: University Press of Kentucky, 1991.

Davidson, Arnold. *Mordecai Richler.* New York: Frederick Ungar Publishing, 1983.

Dick, Bernard. *Hellman in Hollywood.* Rutherford, N.J.: Fairleigh Dickinson University Press, 1982.

———. *The Star-Spangled Screen: The American World War II Film.* Limestone, Ky.: University Press of Kentucky, 1985.

Di Pietro, Robert, and Edward Ifkovic. *Ethnic Perspectives in American Literature.* New York: Modern Language Association of America, 1983.

Dmytryk, Edward. *It's a Hell of a Life but Not a Bad Living.* New York: Times Books, 1978.

———. *Odd Man Out: A Memoir of the Hollywood Ten.* Carbondale, Ill.: Southern Illinois University Press, 1996.

Donald, James, and Ali Rattansi. *Race, Culture and Difference.* Thousand Oaks, Calif.: Sage Publications, 1992.

Doneson, Judith. *The Holocaust in American Film.* Philadelphia: Jewish Publication Society, 1987.

Dresser, David, and Lester D. Friedman. *American Jewish Filmmakers: Traditions and Trends.* Urbana, Ill.: University of Illinois Press, 1993.

Eisner, Lotte. *Fritz Lang.* New York: Oxford University Press, 1977.

Erens, Patricia. *The Jew in American Cinema.* Bloomington, Ind.: Indiana University Press, 1984.

Essoe, Gabe, and Raymond Lee. *DeMille: The Man and His Pictures.* New York: A. S. Barnes and Company, 1970.

Farrell, Grace, ed. *Isaac Bashevis Singer: Conversations.* Jackson, Miss.: University Press of Mississippi, 1992.

Fowler, Douglas. *Understanding E. L. Doctorow.* Columbia, S.C.: University of South Carolina Press, 1992.

Fowles, Anthony, and Donald Zec. *Barbra: A Biography of Barbra Streisand.* New York: St. Martin's Press, 1981.

Fried, Albert. *The Rise and Fall of the Jewish Gangster in America.* New York: Columbia University Press, 1993.

Friedman, Lester D. *The Jewish Image in American Film.* Secaucus, N.J.: Citadel Press, 1987.

Fraser, George MacDonald. *The Hollywood History of the World.* New York: William Morrow, 1988.

Gabler, Neal. *An Empire of Their Own: How the Jews Invented Hollywood.* New York: Crown Publishers, 1988.

Gaydos, Steven, and Jerry Roberts. *Movie Talk From the Front Lines: Filmmakers Discuss Their Works With the Los Angeles Film Critics Association.* Jefferson, Mo.: McFarland & Co., 1995.

Girgus, Sam B. *The Films of Woody Allen.* New York: Cambridge University Press, 1993.

Griggs, John. *The Films of Gregory Peck*. Secaucus, N.J.: Citadel Press, 1984.

Halio, Jay L. *Philip Roth Revisited*. Boston: Twayne Publishers, 1992.

Herman, Jan. *A Talent for Trouble: The Life of Hollywood's Most Acclaimed Director, William Wyler*. New York: G. P. Putnam's Sons, 1995.

Heston, Charlton. *The Actor's Life*. New York: E. P. Dutton, 1976.

Hirsch, Foster. *Love, Sex, Death and the Meaning of Life: Woody Allen's Comedy*. New York: McGraw-Hill, 1981.

Hirschhorn, Clive. *Gene Kelly*. New York: St. Martin's Press, 1974.

Hoberman, J. *Bridge of Light: Yiddish Film Between Two Worlds*. New York: Museum of Modern Art and Schocken Books, 1991.

Holtzman, William. *Seesaw: A Dual Biography of Anne Bancroft and Mel Brooks*. New York: Doubleday & Co., 1979.

Ilson, Carol. *Harold Prince*. New York: Limelight Editions, 1989.

Insdorf, Annette. *Indelible Shadows: Film and the Holocaust*. New York: Random House, 1983.

Jackson, Carlton. *Picking Up the Tab: The Life and Movies of Martin Ritt*. Bowling Green, Ohio: Bowling Green State University Popular Press, 1994.

Jarvie, I. C. *Movies as Social Criticism*. Metuchen, N.J.: Scarecrow Press, 1978.

The Jewish Film Directory: A Guide to More Than 1,200 Films of Jewish Interest From 32 Countries Over 85 Years. Westport, Conn.: Greenwood Press, 1992.

Johnson, Robert. *Neil Simon*. Boston: Twayne Publishers, 1983.

Kael, Pauline. *5001 Nights at the Movies*. New York: Henry Holt and Company, 1991.

————. *For Keeps: Thirty Years at the Movies*. New York: Penguin Books, 1994.

Kane, Leslie. *David Mamet: A Casebook*. New York: Garland Publishing, 1992.

Katz, Ephraim. *The Film Encyclopedia*. New York: Harper Perennial, 1994.

Kazan, Elia. *Elia Kazan: A Life*. New York: Alfred A. Knopf, 1988.

Kellner, Douglas, and Michael Ryan. *Camera Politica: The Politics and Ideology of Contemporary Hollywood Film*. Bloomington, Ind.: Indiana University Press, 1988.

Kimbrell, James. *Barbra: An Actress Who Sings*. Brookline Village, Mass.: Branden Publishing Co., 1989.

Knopp, Josephine Zadovsky. *The Trial of Judaism in Contemporary Jewish Writing*. Chicago: The University of Illinois Press, 1975.

Kresh, Paul. *Isaac Bashevis Singer: The Magician of West 86th Street*. New York: The Dial Press, 1979.

Lax, Eric. *Woody Allen: A Biography*. New York: Alfred A. Knopf, 1991.

Lecker, Robert. *Mordecai Richler*. Boston: Twayne Publishers, 1983.

Lenburg, Jeff. *Dustin Hoffman: Hollywood's Anti-Hero*. New York: St. Martin's Press, 1983.

Loshitzky, Yosefa, ed. *Spielberg's Holocaust*. Bloomington, Ind.: Indiana University Press, 1997.

Lyman, Darryl. *Great Jews of Stage and Screen*. Middle Village, N.Y.: Jonathan David Publishers, 1987.

Maland, Charles. *Chaplin and American Culture*. Princeton, N.J.: Princeton University Press, 1989.

Maltin, Leonard. *The Great Movie Comedians: From Charlie Chaplin to Woody Allen*. New York: Harmony Books, 1982.

———. *Leonard Maltin's 1997 Movie & Video Guide*. New York: Signet Books, 1997.

May, Lary. *Screening Out the Past*. Chicago: University of Chicago Press, 1980.

Mazzeno, Laurence. *Herman Wouk*. Boston: Twayne Publishers, 1984.

McBride, Joseph. *Steven Spielberg: A Biography*. New York: Simon and Schuster, 1997.

McCarty, John. *Hollywood Gangland: The Movies' Love Affair with the Mob*. New York: St. Martin's Press, 1993.

Miller, Gabriel. *Screening the Novel*. New York: Frederick Ungar Publishing, 1980.

Miller, Randall, and Allen Woll. *Ethnic and Racial Images in American Film and Television*. New York: Garland Publishing, 1987.

Morris, Christopher. *Models of Misrepresentation: On the Fiction of E. L. Doctorow*. Jackson, Miss.: University Press of Mississippi, 1991.

Mosley, Leonard. *Zanuck: The Rise and Fall of Hollywood's Last Tycoon*. Boston: Little, Brown and Company, 1984.

Navasky, Victor. *Naming Names*. New York: Viking Press, 1980.

Norman, Barry. *The Story of Hollywood*. New York: New American Library, 1987.

O'Brien, Tom. *The Screening of America: Movies and Values from "Rocky" to "Rain Man."* New York: Continuum Publishing, 1990.

Paul, William. *Ernst Lubitsch's American Comedy*. New York: Columbia University Press, 1983.

Picon, Molly, with Jean Grillo. *Molly!: An Autobiography*. New York: Simon and Schuster, 1980.

Pinsker, Sanford. *The Comedy That 'Hoits': An Essay on the Fiction of Philip Roth*. Columbia, Mo.: University of Missouri Press, 1975.

———, ed. *Critical Essays on Philip Roth*. Boston: G. K. Hall & Co., 1982.

———. *The Schlemiel as Metaphor*. Carbondale, Ill.: Southern Illinois University Press, 1991.

Reimer, Robert C., and Carol J. *Nazi-Retro Film: How German Narrative Cinema Remembers the Past*. New York: Twayne Publishers, 1992.

Riese, Randall. *Her Name Is Barbra*. Secaucus, N.J.: Birch Lane Press, 1993.

Rodgers, Bernard F., Jr. *Philip Roth*. Boston: Twayne Publishers, 1978.

Schumach, Murray. *The Face on the Cutting Room Floor: The Story of Movie and Television Censorship*. New York: William Morrow and Company, 1964.

Sennett, Ted. *Warner Brothers Presents*. Memphis: Castle Books, 1971.

Shindler, Colin. *Hollywood Goes to War*. Boston: Routledge & Kegan Paul, 1979.

Siegel, Barbara, and Scott Siegel. *American Film Comedy*. Englewood Cliffs, N.J.: Prentice-Hall, 1994.

Sklar, Robert. *City Boys: Cagney, Bogart and Garfield*. Princeton, N.J.: Princeton University Press, 1992.

Spada, James. *Streisand: The Woman and the Legend*. New York: Doubleday & Co., 1981.

Spignesi, Stephen. *The Woody Allen Companion*. Kansas City, Mo.: Andrews and McMeel, 1992.

Taylor, John Russell. *Strangers in Paradise: The Hollywood Emigrés, 1933–1950*. New York: Holt, Rinehart and Winston, 1983.

Taylor, Philip. *Steven Spielberg: The Man, His Movies and Their Meaning*. New York: Continuum Press, 1992.

Taylor, William. *Sydney Pollack*. Boston: Twayne Publishers, 1981.

Thomas, Tony. *The Films of Gene Kelly*. Secaucus, N.J.: Citadel Press, 1974.

Thomson, David. *A Biographical Dictionary of Film*. New York: Alfred A. Knopf, 1994.

———. *Warren Beatty and Desert Eyes*. New York: Doubleday & Co., 1987.

VideoHound's Golden Movie Retriever. Detroit, Mich.: Visible Ink, 1997.

Vincendeau, Ginette, ed. *Encyclopedia of European Cinema*. New York: Facts On File, 1995.

Wernblad, Annette. *Brooklyn Is Not Expanding: The Comic Universe of Woody Allen*. Rutherford, N.J.: Fairleigh Dickinson University Press, 1992.

Wright, William. *Lillian Hellman: The Image, the Woman*. New York: Simon and Schuster, 1986.

Yacowar, Maurice. *Loser Take All: The Comic Art of Woody Allen*. New York: Frederick Ungar Publishing, 1979.

Yudkin, Leon Israel. *Jewish Writing and Identity in the Twentieth Century*. New York: St. Martin's Press, 1982.

Zinnemann, Fred. *Fred Zinnemann: A Life in the Movies*. New York: Charles Scribner's Sons, 1992.

Index

Abraham, E. Murray, 132, 134
Adler, Luther, 105, 107
Aiello, Danny, 163
Ajar, Emile, 119
Alda, Alan, 102–103
Aleichem, Sholem, 9, 64
All the President's Men, 132
Allan, Ted, 184
Allen, Jay Presson, 98–99
Allen, Woody, 28–33, 102–104, 108, 132, 135–37,
    163, 165
All That Jazz, 98
*Almonds and Raisins: A History of the Yiddish
    Cinema,* 62–64
Altman, Robert, 132
Anhalt, Edward, 188
Angry Harvest, 111, 131
Anne Frank Remembered, 170–71
Annie Hall, 28–32, 163
Ansky, S., 57, 63
Anspach, Susan, 132, 134
Anti-Semitism, 14–15, 37–41, 39, 42, 49, 68, 71,
    80–82, 84, 99, 101, 107, 113–16, 120, 124,
    141–42, 144, 149, 158, 165, 172–73, 178, 184,
    187, 189
Apprenticeship of Duddy Kravitz, The, 72–75
Ardolino, Emile, 160
Arkin, Alan, 75, 138, 158
Arnstein, Nicky, 34–36
Asner, Ed, 178, 181–82
Assante, Armand, 95
Assimilation, 4, 24–25, 31, 39, 52–53, 63, 65,
    72–75, 92, 154, 158, 173, 192
Assisi Underground, The, 6
Au Revoir, Les Enfants, 59–61
Avlarado, Trini, 162
Awakenings, 15
Aykroyd, Dan, 121–22

Bancroft, Anne, 147, 169
Barbash, Uri, 45

Barefoot in the Park, 169
Barkin, Ellen, 179
Bar Mitzvah Boy, 184
Baron, Sandy, 135
Barton Fink, 138
Baxter, Anne, 46
Beatty, Warren, 94–95, 97
Bedelia, Bonnie, 132–33
Bell, Nicholas, 174
Bell, Tom, 158
Ben-Ami, Jacob, 63
Ben-Hur, 46–51
Bening, Annette, 94, 97
Benjamin, Richard, 90, 137
Benny Goodman Story, The, 138
Benson, Robby, 3–4, 6
Benny, Jack, 71
Berenson, Marisa, 98–99
Beresford, Bruce, 121, 124
Berg, Gertrude, 148, 164
Bergman, Alan and Marilyn, 186
Berle, Milton, 138
Berlin, Jeannie, 31
Berlin, Irving, 23
Bernardi, Herschel, 9, 64, 163–64
Bernstein, Walter, 164, 166
Berri, Claude, 59, 61, 120
Besserer, Eugenie, 21–22
Betrayed, 82
Beymer, Richard, 171
Big Fix, The, 4, 132–34
Bikel, Theodore, 9
Billy Bathgate, 95
Biloxi Blues, 167–69
Blacklisting, 163
Blazing Saddles, 76–79, 132
Blume in Love, 152, 154
Body and Soul, 40, 83–86
Boese, Carl, 55
Bogart, Humphrey, 132
Bologna, Joseph, 138

Bonnie and Clyde, 88
Book of Daniel, The, 178, 181
Bottoms, Joseph, 156, 158
Boxing as metaphor, 83–86
Boyd, Stephen, 46, 49
Boys From Brazil, The, 143–45
Bozyk, Reizl, 52, 54
Brando, Marlon, 187–88
Brice, Fanny, 33–36
Brickman, Marshall, 28
Brighton Beach Memoirs, 108, 147, 167, 169
Broadway Bound, 138, 147, 169
Broadway Danny Rose, 135–38
Broderick, Matthew, 167, 169
Brodkin, Herbert, 159
Brooks, Mel, 33, 71, 76–79, 137
Bruce, Lenny, 145
Brynner, Yul, 46, 48
Bugsy, 16, 94–97
Burns, George, 137

Cabaret, 98–101, 160
Cabinet of Dr. Caligari, The, 55
Caesar, Sid, 137–38
Cahan, Abraham, 54
Caine Mutiny, The, 126, 188, 191, 193
California Suite, 167
Cantor, Eddie, 26
Cantor's Son, The, 24, 63
Carmen Jones, 45
Casino, 95
Cast a Giant Shadow, 45
Cat Ballou, 78
Cayrol, Jean, 19
Cemetery Club, The, 121
Champ, The, 86
Chan, Charlie, 22
Chaney, Lon, 150
Chaplin, Charles, 68–71
Chariots of Fire, 80–82
Chayefsky, Paddy, 141
Chosen, The, 3–6, 89, 134
Citizen Cohn, 164
Clift, Montgomery, 187–88
Close, Glenn, 125, 127
Cobb, Lee J., 42, 44
Coen, Ethan, 138
Coen, Joel, 138
Cohen, Mickey, 96
Come Back, Little Sheba, 107
Come Blow Your Horn, 167
Compulsion, 34
Coogan, Jackie, 150
Cooper, Gary, 94
Coppola, Francis Ford, 95
Corbett, Monica, 135
Costello, Frank, 95
Crane, Norma, 10
Crimes and Misdemeanors, 29, 102–104

Cronyn, Hume, 169
Crosland, Alan, 21–24
Cross, Ben, 80, 82
Crossfire, 37, 40, 42, 188
Crossing Delancey, 52–54, 114
Crouse, Lindsay, 178, 180
Crystal, Billy, 137
Curtin, Valerie, 155

Damned, The, 101
Daniel, 89, 178–82
Dauphin, Claude, 118, 120
David, 61, 131
Davis, Bette, 126
Day of Atonement, The, 25
Delpy, Julie, 129–30
DeLuise, Dom, 79
De Mille, Cecil B., 46–49
Denby, David, 137, 169
De Niro, Robert, 95, 117
Derek, John, 46, 48
Der Golem: Wie Er in die Welt Kam, 55–56
Dershowitz, Alan, 125–28
Desert Fox, The, 188
Deutsch, Ernst, 55
Diamond, Neil, 27
Diary of Anne Frank, The, 48, 170–73
Dickens, Charles, 149
Dirty Dancing, 126, 160–62
Disappearance of the Jews, 116
Dmytryk, Edward, 37, 39, 187–88
Doctorow, E. L., 95, 178–79, 181–82
Douglas, Kirk, 43, 45
Douglas, Michael, 185
Down and Out in Beverly Hills, 152–55
Dreyfuss, Richard, 33, 72, 74, 132, 134, 151–52, 155
Driving Miss Daisy, 121–24
Dunera Boys, The, 130–31
Duvivier, Julien, 57
Dybbuk, The, 57, 63

Ebb, Fred, 99
Eddie Cantor Story, The, 34
Edge of the City, 164
Eldad, Ilan, 57
Elliott, Denholm, 73
Elstein, David, 62
Enemies, a Love Story, 65–67, 152, 184
Enter Laughing, 138, 147
Escape From Sobibor, 156, 158
Ethnicity, 34, 149, 151, 183
Europa Europa, 129–31
Evans, Robert, 92
Every Time We Say Goodbye, 119
Exodus, 24, 42–45

Fagin, 149–51
Falk, Peter, 133

Farrow, Mia, 102, 135–36
Feher, Gabor, 112
Fejito, Raphael, 59–60
Feldshuh, Tovah, 156, 158, 178, 181, 184
Ferrer, Jose, 126, 192
Fiddler on the Roof, 7–11, 64, 165, 183
Fiennes, Ralph, 12, 16
Final Solution, 12, 17, 71, 158
Fine, Morton, 88
Fitzgerald, Geraldine, 87
Fixer, The, 82
Fleischer, Richard, 27
Flirting With Disaster, 147
Fonda, Jane, 139, 142
Force of Evil, 85
Forsyth, Frederick, 144
Forte, Nick Apollo, 135–36
Fosse, Bob, 34, 98–99, 137, 145
Four Daughters, 84
Frank, Anne, 170
Frank, Otto, 172–73
Frankenstein, 55
Franz, Arthur, 189
Freeman, Everett, 192
Freeman, Morgan, 121–23
Freund, Karl, 56
Frey, Leonard, 10
Friedkin, David, 88
Friedman, Bruce Jay, 31, 167
Frisco Kid, The, 79, 132
From Here to Eternity, 140
Front, The, 163–66
Fuchs, Leo, 64
Funny Girl, 9, 24, 33–36, 48, 98, 138, 184, 186, 190
Funny Lady, 35
Funny Thing Happened on the Way to the Forum, A, 165

Gale, Jackie, 135
Galeen, Henrik, 55
Gambler, The, 95
Garbo Talks, 89, 147
Gardiner, Reginald, 70
Garfield, John, 37, 39–40, 83–86
Gere, Richard, 124, 185
Gentleman's Agreement, 37–41, 84
German
    expressionism, 55, 57, 88
    Holocaust films, 61, 131, 170, 172
Gielgud, John, 80–81, 176
Gies, Miep, 171
Gilbert, Melissa, 170
Glaser, Michael, 10
Gleason, Joanna, 102
Glengarry Glen Ross, 116
Goddard, Paulette, 68, 70
Godfather, Part II, The, 95, 132
Golan, Menahem, 95

Goldbergs, The, 164
Goldblum, Jeff, 126
Goldman, William, 132, 144
Goldstein, Allan, 108–109
Golem, The, 55–58
Gomer, Steve, 162
Goodbye Columbus, 90–93, 147
Goodbye Girl, The, 167
Goodbye to Berlin, 99
Good Earth, The, 105
Goodrich, Frances, 170
Gordon, Edwin, 4
Gordon, Ruth, 92
Gough, Lloyd, 164
Gould, Elliott, 33, 35, 94, 96, 132–33, 184
Goz, Harry, 9
Graduate, The, 90, 169
Grant, Cary, 94
Grass, Gunter, 101
Great Dictator, The, 68–71
Green, Gerald, 107, 157, 159
Green, Joseph, 64
Greenberg, Harry, 97
Greenglass, David, 182
Greenwich Village, 114, 147, 152
Grey, Jennifer, 126, 160
Grey, Joel, 98–99, 160
Grieco, Richard, 95
Griem, Helmut, 98–99
Griffith, D. W., 26
Griffith, Melanie, 5
Guilty by Suspicion, 164
Guinness, Alec, 146, 148, 150

Hackett, Albert, 170
Hallie, Philip, 20
Hannah and Her Sisters, 29
Harareet, Haya, 46, 49
Hardwick, Cedrick, 48
Harlow, Jean, 94
Harnick, Sheldon, 9
Harris, Rosalind, 10
Harris, Rosemary, 157
Hart, Moss, 39–40
Havers, Nigel, 80–81
Hawkins, Jack, 46
Haworth, Jill, 44
Hayes, Helen, 64
Heartbreak Kid, The, 31, 167
Hearts of the West, 138
Heckert, Eileen, 92
Helfgott, David, 174, 176–77
Hellman, Lillian, 139–42
Hello, Dolly!, 9
Hepburn, Katharine, 34
Hester Street, 52, 54, 190
Heston, Charlton, 46–47
Heydrich, 158–59
Hicks, Scott, 174, 177

Hilberg, Raul, 19
Hill 24 Doesn't Answer Anymore, 45
Hill, Virginia, 95, 97
Hiller, Arthur, 89, 144
Hirchbein, Peretz, 63
Hitler's Children, 188
Hoberman, J., 64
Hobson, Laura Z., 38
Hoffa, 117
Hoffman, Dustin, 33, 95, 137, 143
Hofschneider, Marco, 129–30
Holland, Agnieszka, 111, 129, 131
Hollywood Ten, 39
Holm, Celeste, 37, 39
Holm, Ian, 82, 158
Holocaust, 4, 14, 18–19, 39–40, 187
    dramas, 59, 61
    films, 12, 15, 17, 20, 42, 87–89, 111, 130
    ignored by Hollywood, 37, 46
Holocaust, 14, 107, 156–59
Homicide, 114–17
Honeymoon in Vegas, 77
*Hotel Terminus: The Life and Times of Klaus
    Barbie,* 20
Houdini, 34, 138
House I Live In, The, 148
House of Games, 117
House of Rothschild, The, 39
House Un-American Activities Committee, 39, 50,
    85, 163–65
Huber, Gustie, 171
Hud, 166
Hudson, Hugh, 80
Hughes, Howard, 94
Hunt, Linda, 186
Hustler, The, 85
Huston, Angelica, 65–67, 102
Hutton, Timothy, 178–79

I Am a Camera, 99
I Am a Fugitive From a Chain Gang, 107
I Love You, Alice B. Toklas, 147
I Love You, Rosa, 120
In-Laws, The, 77
Irons, Jeremy, 125, 127–28
Irving, Amy, 52, 54, 183, 185–86
I Sent a Letter to My Love, 119
Isherwood, Christopher, 99
Israel
    founding of, 4–6, 42–45

Jacobi, Lou, 17–71
Jaffe, Sam, 40
Jarrett, Jerry, 9
Jazz Singer, The, 21–27, 62, 176
Jennings, Dean, 95
Jessel, George, 25–26
Jesus Christ Superstar, 10

Jewish
    children as subject of Holocaust films, 59, 111
    comedy, 137
    cultural differences with gentiles, 28–29, 31
    family films, 108
    family life, 109
    females in film, 183
    gangster films, 94–95
    identity crisis, 90, 114
    immigrant experience, 72
    mothers, 146–48
    mysticism, 55, 57
    negative stereotype, 58, 149
    pre-Holocaust Eastern European life, 57–58
    resistance, 44, 142
    survival, 7–8
    victims of Holocaust, 144
Jewish Godfather, The, 95
Jewison, Norman, 10
Jews
    and blacks, 121–24
    as saviors, 106–107, 113, 125–26, 152, 162
Jolson, Al, 21–22, 24–27, 33, 62, 99
Jolson Sings Again, 26
Jolson Story, The, 26, 138
Jones, Quincy, 88
Joshua Then and Now, 75, 114
Juarez, 105
Judgment at Nuremberg, 6
Juggler, The, 188
Julia, 6, 139–42
Just Tell Me What You Want, 89

Kael, Pauline, 8, 142
Kagan, Jeremy Paul, 3–4, 132–33
Kahn, Madeline, 76, 79
Kane, Carol, 52
Kanin, Garson, 34
Karel, Russ, 62
Karlin, Rita, 133
Karski, Jan, 19
Kavner, Julie, 147
Kazan, Elia, 37, 39–40, 128
Kazan, Nicholas, 128
Keaton, Diane, 28, 30, 108
Keeler, Ruby, 25
Keitel, Harvey, 94, 96
Kelly, Gene, 190, 192
Keneally, Thomas, 14
Kennedy, Leon Isaac, 86
Kerchbron, Jean, 57
Kid for Two Farthings, A, 150
King, Alan, 65–66, 141–42
King David, 51, 121
King of Comedy, The, 138
Kingsley, Ben, 12–13, 15–16, 94, 96, 145
Klugman, Jack, 90, 92
Korman, Harvey, 76–77
Kotcheff, Ted, 72, 75

Krabbe, Jeroen, 52, 54
Krige, Alice, 80

Lacombe, Lucien, 61
Lamarr, Hedy, 48
Lanctot, Micheline, 72–73
Landau, Martin, 102–103
Lang, Fritz, 55, 57
Lange, Hope, 187–88
Lansky, Meyer, 16, 94–96
Lanzmann, Claude, 17–19
Last Angry Man, The, 105–107
Lawford, Peter, 42, 44
Lean, David, 150
Lederer, Otto, 25
Lee, Canada, 83–84
Legrand, Michel, 186
Leibman, Ron, 125
Lennart, Isabel, 34
Lenny, 98, 137, 145
Leon, Joseph, 181
Leon the Pig Farmer, 114
Leone, Sergio, 95
Lepke, 34, 132
Lerner, Michael, 138
LeRoy, Mervyn, 146, 148
Lester, Mark, 149, 151
Levin, Ira, 144
Levin, Meyer, 172
Levinson, Barry, 95
Lies My Father Told Me, 184
Life of Emile Zola, The, 105, 107, 170
Lion King, The, 127
Lipson, Paul, 9
Little, Cleavon, 76–77
Loeb, Philip, 164
Loew, Judah ben Bazalel, 56
Lombard, Carole, 71
Long Goodbye, The, 132
Lost in Yonkers, 169
Lubitsch, Ernst, 71
Luciano, Charles "Lucky," 94–95
Lumet, Sidney, 5, 34, 87–89, 178–82
LuPone, Patti, 121–22

MacDowell, Roddy, 57
MacGraw, Ali, 90–91, 93
Macy, William H., 114–15, 117
Madame Rosa, 67, 118–20
Magician of Lublin, The, 138
Majority of One, 121, 146–48
Malamud, Bernard, 82
Malina, Judith, 65–66
Malle, Louis, 59–61
Mamele, 64
Mamet, David, 114–17
Manesse, Gaspard, 59–60
Man for All Seasons, A, 140

Man in the Glass Booth, The, 6, 144, 188
Mankowitz, Wolf, 150
Mann, Daniel, 105, 107
Mantegna, Joe, 114, 117
Marathon Man, 132, 143–45
Marjorie Morningstar, 147, 190–93
Marrying Man, The, 95
Martin, Dean, 187
Martin, Nan, 90, 93
Marty, 141
Masada, 51
Mason, Jackie, 77
Matthau, Walter, 137
Mature, Victor, 48
Max and Helen, 145
May, Elaine, 31, 167
Mayer, Louis B., 48
Mazursky, Paul, 65, 67, 152, 154–55, 184
McAvoy, May, 21, 23
McCarthyism, 37, 40, 50, 145, 165
McGuire, Dorothy, 37–38
Medford, Kay, 33, 36
Medved, Michael, 15
Meeropol, Robert, 181–82
Memory of Justice, The, 20
Me, Natalie, 190
Mengele, Dr. Josef, 143–45
Midler, Bette, 34, 122, 152–53, 155
Midnight Cowboy, 87–88, 145
Miles, Sylvia, 52–53
Miller, Barry, 3–4, 6
Milner, Marty, 192
Mineo, Sal, 45
Minnelli, Liza, 98–99
Mirror Has Two Faces, The, 36
Miss Rose White, 6
Mitchum, Robert, 37
Mizrahi, Moshe, 118–19
Mobsters, 95
Modern Times, 69
Molly McGuires, The, 164
Moody, Ron, 149, 151
Moriarty, Michael, 156, 158, 159
Mostel, Zero, 9, 76, 163–65
Mr. Skeffington, 126
Mueller-Stahl, Armin, 174
Muhich, Donald F., 154
Muni, Paul, 105, 107
Murderers Among Us: The Simon Wiesenthal Story,
    The, 15–16, 96, 145, 156
Murder Incorporated, 137
Murnau, F. W., 55
Murphy, Michael, 163
Musicals, 8–9, 98, 149
My Favorite Year, 137
My Mother, My Father, and Me, 141

Napolin, Leah, 194
Nasty Girl, The, 131

Nazis, 99–101, 143–44, 171
  neo-, in America, 159
Neeson, Liam, 12, 15
Network, 89, 141
Newman, Paul, 42, 44
New York Stories, 30, 36, 147
Next Stop, 114, 147, 152
Nichols, Mike, 167, 169
Night and Fog, 19–20
Nolte, Nick, 152
Norma Rae, 126, 166
Norton, Deborah, 158
No Way to Treat a Lady, 92, 132, 147
Nuts, 36, 139, 166

Oakie, Jack, 68, 70
Odd Couple, The, 167
Odessa File, The, 6, 144–45
Odets, Clifford, 84
Oedipus Wrecks, 30, 36, 147
Oland, Warner, 21–22
Old Neighborhood, The, 116
Olin, Lena, 65–67
Oliver!, 9, 149–51
Oliver Twist, 150
Olivier, Laurence, 27, 143, 145
Once Upon a Time in America, 95
Opatoshu, David, 42, 44
Open End, 164
Operation Eichmann, 45
Ophuls, Marcel, 20
Orbach, Jerry, 102, 160, 162
Ordinary People, 125, 139
Outside Chance of Maximilian Glick, The, 108–110
Oysher, Moishe, 24, 63

Palestine Liberation Organization (PLO), 141–42
Palmer, Lilli, 83
Parker, Corey, 167, 169
Parks, Larry, 26
Passer, Ivan, 184
Patinkin, Mandy, 180, 183, 185
Pawnbroker, The, 6, 67, 87–89, 116, 174, 181
Peck, Gregory, 37–39, 84, 143
Peerce, Larry, 90, 92
Pena, Elizabeth, 152
Pentimento, a Book of Portraits, 139
Perel, Solomon, 129–30
Perkins, Millie, 170–71
Persoff, Nehemiah, 183, 185
Philips, Wendy, 95
Pichel, Irving, 150
Picon, Molly, 10, 64, 184
Pidgeon, Walter, 33, 35
Pinsker, Sanford, 135
Playing for Time, 107, 142, 156
Play It Again, Sam, 132
Plummer, Amanda, 178–79
Poelzig, Hans, 56

Pollack, Nancy, 105–106
Pollack, Sydney, 36
Polonsky, Abraham, 83–86
Porter, Katherine Anne, 101
Portnoy's Complaint, 90, 147
Postcards From the Edge, 169
Postman Always Rings Twice, The, 116
Potok, Chaim, 3–6
Prejudice
  inter-Jewish, 109
Preminger, Otto, 42–43, 45
Private Benjamin, 190
Private Izzy Murphy, 26
Producers, The, 76, 79
Pryor, Richard, 77, 79
Purple Heart, The, 39

Quaid, Randy, 72, 74
Quarrel, The, 3, 67, 109
Questel, Mae, 33, 36
Quiz Show, 82, 138

Radio Days, 108
Raft, George, 94
Rahmes, Ving, 114–15
Raiders of the Lost Ark, 14
Rain Man, 95
Ramer, Henry, 72–73
Raphaelson, Samson, 25
Rapper, Irving, 190, 192
Redford, Robert, 36, 138
Redgrave, Vanessa, 139, 141–42, 174, 176
Reed, Carol, 149–50
Reed, Oliver, 151
Reiner, Carl, 138
Reinhardt, Max, 55
Renoir, Jean, 155
Resnais, Alain, 19
Return of Bobby Fischer, The, 15
Revere, Anne, 37, 41, 83–84
Reversal of Fortune, 107, 125–28
Revolt of Job, The, 111–13, 120
Richards, Evan, 153
Richardson, Lee, 181
Richardson, Ralph, 42, 44
Richler, Mordecai, 72, 75
Riegert, Peter, 52–54
Ritt, Martin, 163–66
Robards, Jason, 139, 142
Robbins, Jerome, 9, 34
Robinson, Edward G., 46, 48
Rocky, 86
Roots, 159
Rosenberg Fund, 182
Rosenberg, Ethel and Julius, 178
Rosenblum, Ralph, 92
Rosenthal, Allen, 74
Rosenthal, Jack, 184
Rosenthal, Lefty, 95

Rose Tattoo, The, 107
Ross, Herbert, 34
Rossen, Robert, 83, 85
Roth, Philip, 90, 92
Rubinek, Saul, 108–109
Rubinowitz, Solomon, 9
Ruehl, Mercedes, 169
Running on Empty, 181
Rush, Geoffrey, 174, 176–77
Russell, Rosalind, 146, 148

Saint, Eva Marie, 42–43
Saks, Gene, 169
Sallah, 45
Salmonova, Lyda, 55, 58
Samson and Delilah, 48–49
Sanchez, Jaimie, 87, 89
Sandler, Susan, 52, 54
Sargent, Alvin, 139
Sauvage, Pierre, 20
Scenes From a Mall, 152
Schary, Dore, 42
Scheider, Roy, 145
Schnell, Maximilian, 3–4, 6, 139, 142, 144, 187
Schindler's List, 12–16, 28, 96, 130, 156
Schindler, Oskar, 12–16
Schlesinger, John, 145
Schlondorff, Volker, 101
School Ties, 82, 162
Schroeder, Barbet, 125, 127
Schulman, Arnold, 92
Schultz, Dutch, 95
Schwartz, Maurice, 9, 64
Scooler, Zvee, 64, 73
Scorsese, Martin, 95, 117, 138
Scott, Adrian, 37, 39
Scott, George C., 151
Search, The, 140
Sefer Yezirah, 56
Segal, George, 92, 132
Seven Beauties, 130
Seven Faces, 105
Seventh Cross, 140
Sharif, Omar, 33, 35–36
Shaw, Irwin, 187
Shaw, Robert, 144
Sheila Levine Is Dead and Living in New York, 190
Shelley, Joshua, 164
Shine, 174–77
Ship of Fools, 101
Shoah, 17–20, 26, 156
Shop on Main Street, The, 111
Shylock, 149
Siegel, Benjamin, 94–97
Signoret, Simone, 118–19
Silver, Joan Micklin, 52, 54
Silver, Ron, 65, 125, 128
Simon, Neil, 31, 108, 137–38, 167, 169
Simon, Paul, 28

Simon, Roger, 65, 134
Sinatra, Frank, 167
Singer, Isaac Bashevis, 57, 65, 67, 138, 183–84, 186
Six Day War, 35
Small, Neva, 11
Smith, Will, 126
Somebody Up There Likes Me, 86, 126
Sorrow and the Pity, The, 20
Spartacus, 43
Speed-the-Plow, 116
Spielberg, Steven, 12, 14–15
Spigelgass, Leonard, 146
Stardust Memories, 30
Star Is Born, A, 36
Stark, Ray, 34
Steiger, Rod, 3–4, 6, 87, 89
Stein, Joseph, 9
Stein, Margaret Sophie, 65, 67
Steinberg, Norman, 77
Steinruck, Albert, 55, 58
Stereotypes, 22, 58
    Jewish American princess, 161, 190
    ethnic, 78
    negative, 92, 150
Stern, Isaac, 10
Stern, Itzhak, 13, 15–16
Stevens, George, 170
Stolen Legacy of Anne Frank: Meyer Levin, Lilian Hellman, and the Staging of the "Diary," The, 173
Story of Louis Pasteur, The, 105, 107
Stranger Among Us, A, 5, 89
Strasberg, Lee, 95
Streep, Meryl, 107, 156–57, 159
Streisand, Barbra, 33–36, 183–86
Sunshine Boys, The, 137, 167
Susskind, David, 164
Swayze, Patrick, 160
Sweet Lorraine, 162
Szabo, Istvan, 101

Tandy, Jessica, 121–23
Taylor, Noah, 174, 176
Tell Them Willie Boy Is Here, 84
Temessy, Hedl, 111
Ten Commandments, The, 46–51
Testament of Dr. Mabuse, The, 57
Tevye, 7, 9–11
Tevye and his Daughters, 9
They Were Ten, 45
Things Change, 117
This Is My Life, 147
Thomas, Danny, 27
Tin Drum, The, 101
Toback, James, 95
To Be or Not to Be, 71
Topol, Chaim, 7–8, 45
Trevor, Claire, 190

Triumph of the Spirit, 86, 130
Trumbo, Dalton, 43
Turturro, John, 138
Twelve Chairs, The, 79
Two of Us, The, 59, 120

Uhry, Alfred, 121–22
Ulmer, Edgar, 63
Uncle Moses, 63
Unger, Alan, 77
Unmarried Woman, An, 152
Unsettled Land, 45
Unstrung Heroes, 108, 114
Untouchables, The, 116–17
Uris, Leon, 42
Used People, 121, 147

Valiant, The, 107
Verdict, The, 89, 116
Vichy France, 20, 59
Visconti, Luchino, 101
Virginia Hill Story, The, 96
Vision as metaphor, 5, 104
von Bulow, Claus, 125–28
von Bulow, Sunny, 127–28

Wajda, Andrej, 131
Wagner, 70
Walken, Christopher, 31, 167, 169
Wandering Star, 9
Warden, Jack, 72
Warner Bros., 25–27, 122
Warner, David, 156, 158
Warner, Jack, 26, 84, 192
Warwick, Robert, 40
Waterston, Sam, 102
Wayne, David, 105–106
Way We Were, The, 36, 114, 163, 190
Weapons of the Spirit, 20
Weaver, Fritz, 156–57
Wegener, Paul, 55–57
Weisel, Elie, 159
Welles, Orson, 62

*We Only Kill Each Other: The Life and Bad Times
    of Bugsy Siegel,* 95
Wepper, Fritz, 98–99
Wertmuller, Lina, 130
West Side Story, 9, 171
What Makes Sammy Run?, 74
Where's Poppa?, 92, 147
Who Shall Live and Who Shall Die?, 19
Wiene, Robert, 55
Wiesenthal, Simon, 143, 145
Wilder, Gene, 76–77, 79
Williams, John, 10
Willie and Phil, 114, 152
Winds of War, 192
Winkler, Irwin, 164
Winters, Shelley, 170–71
Wiseman, Joseph, 72
Witness, 5
Wizard of Oz, The, 148
Wood, Natalie, 190
Woods, James, 75, 156–57
Wouk, Herman, 190–93
Wyler, William, 33–35, 46, 48–49
Wynn, Ed, 170–71, 190, 193

Year of Living Dangerously, The, 186
Yentl, 9, 36, 183–86
Yentl the Yeshiva Boy, 183
Yiddish films, 62–64
Yidl Mitn Fiddle, 64
York, Michael, 98
Youb, Samy Ben, 118
Young Frankenstein, 79
Young Lions, The, 6, 39, 187–89

Zametkin, Michael, 38
Zanuck, Darryl, 22–24, 26, 39–40, 122
Zanuck, Richard, 122
Zieff, Howard, 138
Ziegfeld, Florenz, 35
Ziegfeld Follies, 35
Zinnemann, Fred, 139–40, 142
Zylberman, Noam, 108